BUILD
MORE STUFF WITH
WOOD

12 New Projects for Beginning and Intermediate Woodworkers

The Taunton Press

The Taunton Press
Inspiration for hands-on living®

The Taunton Press, Inc.
63 South Main Street
Newtown, CT 06470-2344
Email: tp@taunton.com

Editor: Peter Chapman
Jacket/Cover Design: Stacy Wakefield Forte
Interior Design: Stacy Wakefield Forte
Layout: Stacy Wakefield Forte
Photographer: Asa Christiana
Illustrator: Dan Thornton

The following names/manufacturers appearing in *Build More Stuff with Wood* are trademarks: 3M®, Amazon.com®, Bluetooth®, Briwax®, Corian®, DMT® DuoSharp®, eBay®, Grizzly®, Home Depot®, Infinity Cutting Tools™, Irwin®, Lee Valley®, Lie-Nielsen®, Lowe's®, Minwax®, Norton®, Polycrylic®, Powertec®, Quick-Grip®, Rockler®, SealCoat®, Stanley®, Titebond III®, Veritas®, Watco®, WD-40®, Woodcraft®, WoodRiver®, X-Acto®, Zinsser®

Library of Congress Control Number: 2022916491

Printed in the United States of America
10 9 8 7 6 5 4 3 2 1

About Your Safety: Working wood is inherently dangerous. Using hand or power tools improperly or ignoring safety practices can lead to permanent injury or even death. Don't try to perform operations you learn about here (or elsewhere) unless you're certain they are safe for you. If something about an operation doesn't feel right, don't do it. Look for another way. We want you to enjoy the craft, so please keep safety foremost in your mind whenever you're in the shop.

dedication

To my strong, independent daughters, Lucy and Jane

ACKNOWLEDGMENTS

Thanks to Peter Chapman, Executive Editor at The Taunton Press, for greenlighting these books and supporting me through the process. He is the finest editor I've worked with, and I've known a few. He's also a great teammate on the soccer field, where we spent many weekends and evenings together.

I wouldn't be where I am without the inestimable *Fine Woodworking* magazine (and website), where I worked for 15 enriching years, developing many of the ideas and projects featured in these books. There is no better resource for the craft, and I designed these books as an on-ramp to *Fine Woodworking*'s super-highway of advice and inspiration.

At *Fine Woodworking*, I worked longer and more closely with Mike Pekovich than anyone else, in or outside the office. He's an extremely insightful woodworker and content creator, and I've learned a lot from him about both of those crafts. When I was promoted to chief editor—Mike's boss on paper—we effectively co-managed the magazine, leaning as much as ever on each other's insights and opinions. When I moved West to pursue a freelance career, we swapped positions again, picking right up where we left off. I wish that all of you find teammates as talented and generous as Peter Chapman and Mike Pekovich.

I'm grateful also to Doug Drake, who collaborated on the side table in Chapter 5 and facilitates the classes I teach at the Guild of Oregon Woodworkers, and my friend Chris Gardner, who has volunteered his time, shop, and backyard for quite a few of my photo and video shoots.

As always, my deepest appreciation is for my family, who have loved and supported me in too many ways to count.

TABLE OF CONTENTS

foreword

IT CAN BE TOUGH getting a foothold in the craft of woodworking. When starting out, the problem isn't that there's not enough information on the subject, but too much. Worse, the information available often lacks context. When learning to cut a dovetail, for example, you might find 50 ways to go about it but still be left scratching your head when deciding which method to choose.

I'm very familiar with this problem because I'm responsible for adding to it. I've spent the last 25 years at *Fine Woodworking* magazine, currently as the editor and creative director, doing my best to help craft woodworking content of the highest quality. During that time, I've helped create thousands of articles on the topic, and while much of it is devoted to a fundamental understanding of the craft, I must admit that it doesn't offer the most effective gateway into woodworking.

Writing about woodworking basics is tough. When starting in on my first book, *The Why and How of Woodworking*, my original intent was to cover everything one would need to know in order to succeed at this craft. I quickly realized, however, that if I started at the beginning, I'd never come close to covering the topics that I was most passionate about. So, I leap-frogged over a lot of information that would be important to a novice and got right into the stuff I love most. When writing a follow-up book, *Foundations of Woodworking*, my intent once more was to back up and cover the absolute basics, and even then, important topics such as choosing a tablesaw or making a push stick failed to make the cut. It seems that no matter how much you try to explain, there's always more to know. Fortunately for us all, Asa has taken on that challenge admirably.

It's said that to explain something simply, you must first understand it deeply. Teaching the basics isn't easy. In fact, I'd say that is probably the most difficult aspect of the craft to explain. It takes an author with a tremendous amount of experience and knowledge, and just as important, one that is a good teacher as well. Asa checks all these boxes and combines it with irresistible enthusiasm.

For as long as I've known Asa, his passion has been directed toward helping people who are just starting out. It's said that to explain something simply, you must first understand it deeply. Teaching the basics isn't easy. In fact, I'd say that is probably the most difficult

aspect of the craft to explain. It takes an author with a tremendous amount of experience and knowledge, and just as important, one that is a good teacher as well. Asa checks all these boxes and combines it with irresistible enthusiasm.

I met Asa when he first came to work as an editor at *Fine Woodworking* magazine. Through the years he developed an expertise for combining words and photos and illustration to convey content in a clear and engaging manner that very few can match. Traditionally, an author is just that. They are expected to provide a manuscript in which others are tasked with surrounding with photos and drawings. Asa is able to bring a holistic view to the content of his books, effectively wielding all of the resources at his disposal to create books that are insightful and engaging.

Asa's first book, *Build Stuff with Wood*, addressed a reader just stepping into the craft. It offered a handful of fun projects easily made from tools and lumber available at a local home center. This book continues that journey, adding a few more tools accompanied by more ambitious projects. Along the way, Asa leads you with wit and patience, making this book an invaluable companion. For the beginner, the projects offer an excellent entryway into the craft. For intermediates, the stylish, straightforward projects are a nice respite from complex furniture that takes weeks or months to complete. For experienced woodworkers like me, these books offer the perfect answer to a common question: When someone asks me, "How do I get started?" I simply point them to Asa's books and tell them to get going.

—*Michael Pekovich*

introduction:
the journey continues

I GREW UP IN A WORLD with four channels of television and no smart phones, a bygone era when kids attended shop classes, built model rockets and tree forts, and wandered the outdoors with minimal supervision. Since the Internet and video games arrived, however, there have been at least two generations who've seldom had the chance to be bored or build things with their hands.

Being unfamiliar with tools not only makes it tough to build a skateboard ramp or fit out a camper van, but it also makes it difficult to fix things when they break, leaving you at the mercy of others when your sink springs a leak or the toilet won't flush. You lose satisfaction too. "Building stuff" is fundamental to human nature and, I would offer, to human happiness. As we spend more and more time staring at screens, we become less connected to the world around us—and each other.

It's not all bad news, however. You don't have to spend long on YouTube or Pinterest to see an equal and opposite pull in the other direction toward tactile materials and tangible accomplishments. And that's

what this book and the other books in this series are all about.

I can't think of a more powerful, practical way to satisfy that ancient urge to make things than woodworking. Wood is widely available in an incredible array of colors and qualities, and you can cut and shape it with relatively affordable tools, creating a world of beautiful, useful items.

In a past life on another coast, I worked as an editor at *Fine Woodworking* magazine, where I saw a wide variety of paths people take into this craft, and the pros and cons of each. This is my take on the easiest path for most people.

One common mistake is diving in too deep and too fast and getting stuck. Sometimes the first projects that inspire you are also out of your reach, though you might not realize it yet. You see a charming workbench, for example—a complex, classic design with traditional joints—and end up buried under a pile of half-finished workpieces, feeling demoralized.

WE STARTED WITH FIVE BASIC POWER TOOLS...

All of the projects in *Build Stuff with Wood*, the first book in this series, were made with just a few handheld power tools, proving almost anyone can start woodworking, regardless of budget or background.

CIRCULAR SAW WORKS WONDERS. A shopmade cutting guide like this one helps an inexpensive circular saw cut plywood and other sheet goods as cleanly and accurately as a tablesaw.

THE ALMIGHTY CHOPSAW. A basic miter saw, or "chopsaw," will cut solid lumber quickly and accurately to length. I used it on almost every project in Book 1, and it stars again in this book.

JIGSAW IS A CURVE MASTER. I cut every curve in Book 1 and 2 with this excellent Milwaukee jigsaw. Add premium blades, designed for wood, and it will make surprisingly smooth cuts.

AN IMPACT DRIVER IS A BETTER CORDLESS DRILL. This type of cordless drill works only with hex-shanked bits, but it makes it much easier to drive screws, and it drills just fine too.

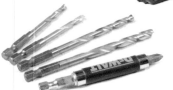

SMALL ROUTER ROUNDS OUT THE LIST. A router is indispensable for profiling edges in a wide variety of ways, as well as a host of other tasks. This compact, 1-hp router from DeWalt is part of an affordable combo kit that includes two handy bases, equipping it for 90% of the routing tasks you'll face.

If you start with projects that are more fun than "fine," at least at first, you'll have more success and be more likely to fall in love with this amazing craft. And if you start with simpler, less-expensive tools, you'll be able to give this hobby a serious try without emptying your bank account.

HOW BOOK 2 IS DIFFERENT FROM BOOK 1

In the first book, *Build Stuff with Wood,* I assumed zero tools, skills, and experience, taking readers through a variety of doable projects using nothing more than a handful of handheld power tools, all relatively affordable at any stage of life, and all easy to pack up and take with you if you're young and mobile. So no big machines like tablesaws, bandsaws, and planers, at least not at first. Working with small, handheld power tools doesn't mean you can't build amazing stuff, however.

In this book, the second in the series, I'm assuming you either read Book 1 or don't need it. So I'm adding a few larger tools, namely a basic tablesaw, a benchtop drill press, and a handy benchtop sanding machine. These tools open up a new world of projects and possibilities. You'll learn how to choose the right models for you and how to use them safely and skillfully. And you'll still get a lifetime of use out of the tools you acquired for Book 1.

In Book 3, I plan on adding the bandsaw, jointer, and planer to the mix—three larger machines that let you take full control of your material and do just about anything with wood.

In keeping with my overall approach, I'm going with affordable versions of these stationary power tools. The tablesaw is a portable contractor's version, easy to roll into position and stow in a corner. I had

one very much like it for the first 10 years of my woodworking hobby, before I sold it to another aspiring woodworker. The drill press and sander are benchtop models, which can do everything floor models can while saving you considerable cash and floor space.

If these purchases are out of your grasp at the moment, you'll still be able to build many of the projects in this book using the handheld power tools from Book 1.

We'll also be raising our hand-tool game in Book 2. In *Build Stuff with Wood,* our hand-tool collection consisted of nothing more than a simple handsaw, available for $25 at any home center, and a variety of utility items like a tape measure and a combination square, also cheap and widely available. In Book 2 we add a block plane and a basic chisel set, which will improve your woodworking in countless ways. I waited until now to introduce them, because hand tools don't work if you can't sharpen them and getting a truly sharp edge can be a tricky process. So

> I'm adding a few larger tools, namely a basic tablesaw a benchtop drill press, and a handy benchtop sanding machine. These tools open up a new world of projects and possibilities.

I'm including a simple shopmade sharpening station that will keep your chisels and plane blades razor sharp for decades to come.

It's also high time you had a real workbench, and that's the first project in this book. Believe it or not, you can make this bench in a day, using construction

lumber and the same basic tools featured in Book 1. However, as I'll be saying ad nauseam, being a beginner doesn't mean you have to compromise. This bench is sturdy enough for a lifetime of woodworking. I still use the one I built 25 years ago, though I eventually added a hardwood top and fancier vises.

Since I covered a lot of shop setup tips in Book 1, like how to create a warm, well-lit workplace with ample storage, I won't be including as much of that in Book 2. But improving your workspace is an ongoing process, so I'll give additional tips on work support stands, dust collection, and more.

GET READY FOR A LIFETIME OF FULFILLMENT

The skills and concepts in these books are time-tested and fundamental. What you do with them is up to you.

For Nick Offerman, who wrote the foreword to Book 1, the woodworking skills he picked up building scenery for a theater company in Chicago helped to support him between acting auditions in L.A., where he built yoga huts for show-biz moguls and worked the overnight shift at Disneyland fixing rollercoasters.

...AND BUILT A PILE OF AWESOME PROJECTS

This is just a small sample of the cool projects in Book 1, which proved you don't need tons of tools to build durable, useful, stylish projects.

EASY GARDEN BENCH. You can build this bench with off-the-shelf deck lumber, a cordless drill, and any kind of saw. I adapted this design from a similar bench made by my friend Mark Edmundson for the first *Build Stuff* book.

DOUBLE THE VOLUME AND DOUBLE THE FUN. This passive speaker, sized to suit any smart phone, is another fun project from Book 1.

TRANSFORMING TABLES. This simple bookcase is made from three tables that can also stand vertically as individual pieces.

QUICK PLUG FOR ANOTHER BOOK BY YOURS TRULY. Between *Build Stuff with Wood* and this sequel, I wrote *Handmade* (Taunton Press, 2018), which is packed with projects in all sorts of materials, including wood, leather, concrete, metal and more. This is a bottle caddy made from upcycled pallet wood.

LET THERE BE LIGHT. I made this hanging light by gluing strips of cherry veneer onto a simple plywood frame.

THIS BOOK ADDS FIVE MORE VERSATILE TOOLS...

While you'll continue to use the hand-held power tools in Book 1 for decades to come, it's time to add a few stationary machines, as well as a few essential hand tools.

DRILL PRESS IS ACCURATE AND CONTROLLED. While your cordless drill or impact driver will always have its place, there's no beating a drill press for serious woodworking. It keeps the drill dead-square to the work, and lets you dial in depth, speed, and hole location. I'll be using my trusty old drill press, but here's a good new one from Grizzly (model G7943).

A PORTABLE TABLESAW. The tablesaw is a woodworking workhorse, ripping solid lumber to narrower widths, crosscutting it to accurate length, cutting up large sheet goods, machining accurate joints, and much more. I'll show you how to do all of that with a compact, portable, affordable model from Bosch.

YOUR FIRST HANDPLANE. A low-angle block plane will remove saw marks with a single stroke—leaving a flat, crisp surface—and also put nice little chamfers and roundovers on sharp edges, leaving them friendly to the hand and eye.

BEST BENCHTOP SANDER FOR THE MONEY. A stationary sander lets you rest workpieces on its table, giving you amazing control. This unique, affordable benchtop model from Ridgid combines a drum sander and belt sander, letting you sand inside and outside curves as well as flat items too.

WOODWORKING CHISELS ARE ANOTHER WORKHORSE. You can use a basic set like this to pare all sorts of joints for a perfect fit, as well as other tasks too numerous and varied to list here.

For others, their first few projects are enough to convince them to make woodworking a lifelong career.

For most of you, however, woodworking will simply be a fulfilling hobby. I say "simply" and "hobby," but the amateur journey is incredibly rich and the payoff profound. Without the pressure to make money, you can build whatever you like. My house in Portland, Ore., is the third we've owned (and hopefully the last), and the third I've been able to make truly our own, adding fences, gates, furniture, rolling shoji screens, pocket doors, window trim, hardwood floors, built-in cabinets, and a Murphy bed, all designed and built to suit our taste and needs.

In the process of making three houses unique and personal, I've also saved tens of thousands of dollars on renovations. But the payoff goes way beyond money. It's hard to describe the peace and fulfillment I feel in my warm, well-lit workshop. Making things, building skills, getting out of your head and into your hands—these things bring a deep sense of satisfaction that transcends words.

I feel satisfied again when each project is done and installed, becoming a permanent part of our lives. It might be nothing more than the two small frames I made from white-oak scraps to hold pictures of my daughters on a family trip to England, capturing a time we all treasure. Then there are the thousands of family dinners we've had on the walnut dining table I made from a massive, natural-edge slab. Or the big platform bed we still use, with echoes of my kids running around its edges.

Each project is a gift that never stops giving, to us and everyone who visits, offering a glimpse of the handmade world accessible to all of us. What I also know is that this craft doesn't have to be scary or

Making things, building a sense of mastery, getting out of your head and into your hands—these things bring a deep sense of satisfaction that transcends words.

complicated if you relax, take it one project at a time, be courageous enough to make mistakes, and let your skills build naturally.

So let's continue this journey. As the Buddhists say: Start where you are.

...AND 12 EXCITING NEW PROJECTS

The new tools and techniques open up a world of new possibilities. The projects in this book are just the beginning.

FINE FURNITURE. I'll show you how to use a $20 doweling jig to make a houseful of tables, including this side table with a floating top (left) and the handsome base for this slab-topped coffee table (above).

BEAUTIFUL BOXES. Once you learn to make tight miter joints on the tablesaw, you'll be able to use them for a host of projects, including this small tea box (above left) and Bluetooth speaker (above).

A REAL WORKBENCH. We'll build this workhorse workbench, with an optional storage cabinet, using basic materials, tools, and skills.

CLASSIC BENCH WITH HAND TOOLS. One you have your saw and chisel basics down, you'll be ready to build this Shaker bench (right) with traditional mortise-and-tenon joinery (above).

build a great
workbench
with basic tools

IN BOOK 1 WE GOT BY with a very simple workstation: basically, a surplus kitchen cabinet on wheels. If you built that project, hold onto it. It will serve you well as a base for your miter saw or some other benchtop power tool, with handy storage below. The top is also at a nice height—a bit taller than a normal workbench—for working with a handheld router.

READY FOR ACTION. This solid, versatile workbench can be built with nothing more than a cordless drill, a circular saw, and a small router, but it's capable enough for many happy years of woodworking.

A SERIOUS WOODWORKING VISE. This cast-iron type is easy to bolt onto any workbench. It features a quick-action screw and a pop-up bench dog.

For Book 2, it's time you had a real workbench, large enough to handle any project, solid enough to stand up to mallet blows and chisel chops, and heavy enough to stay put when you push a handplane across it.

A woodworking bench is not only a work surface, it's also a work holder. So we are adding a real woodworking vise, one that will team up with a row of "dog holes" to hold work in a wide variety of helpful ways. I'm going with a very effective vise, but also one that is very easy to attach to your bench: a cast-iron, quick-action model that attaches with lag bolts. Bolt it on, add some wood jaws to protect your workpieces, and you're ready to roll.

I designed the workbench in this chapter for a video series called "Start Woodworking," hosted by yours truly and my good friend Matt Berger, which lived on FineWoodworking.com for many years. Since then, I've taught this project a number of times in a class I call "Build a Bench in a Day," at the Guild of Oregon Woodworkers, my local woodworking club.

That class always fills up quickly, for one big reason: While most workbench designs are too challenging for beginners to tackle, this one isn't. I've seen countless beginning and even intermediate woodworkers attempt to build a big, impressive workbench only to get bogged down in a pile of expensive hardwood and tricky joints.

The bench featured in this chapter fits the mission of these books: It's easy enough to be your first real workbench, and good enough to be your last. It can be made from relatively inexpensive construction materials using just a few small power tools, all covered in Book 1: a circular saw, a cordless drill, and a small router, plus some basic hand tools like a tape measure and a hacksaw.

This was the first workbench I built, and the base has survived for 25 years. I eventually replaced the plywood top with a traditional hardwood one with additional vises, but it's likely to be a decade or more before you'll need to do the same.

LONG BOLTS ARE THE SECRET TO A STRONG BASE

What makes this bench so easy to build are long threaded rods (called "all-thread") that pass through the base, from end to end and front to back, holding the legs and rails together without the need for fancy joinery. With a nut and washer on each end, the long

YOUR WORKBENCH DOUBLES AS A TABLESAW OUTFEED TABLE

As you'll learn in the next chapter, every tablesaw needs some additional support on the back end to catch large or long workpieces as they travel past the saw table. In a small shop like mine, it makes a lot of sense to size your workbench so it can double as an outfeed table.

For the vast majority of tablesaws, this works great. All you have to do is size your bench so it ends up just a hair (say ⅛ in.) lower than the top of your tablesaw (see the photos on p. 19). If your saw has a mobile base

and/or your workbench is on wheels, like ours, be sure to take those into consideration.

Unfortunately, for the tablesaw we are using in this book, a portable Bosch 4100, its folding, mobile stand raises the saw up too high to be paired with a workbench. So I'll be using a separate work-support stand for outfeed support. Another option would be to make a long box that sits atop your workbench to line up with the Bosch's high table.

For almost all other saws, however, matching your workbench to the height of the tablesaw will place the benchtop at a comfortable working height.

ADD A TOOL CABINET. Flip ahead to Chapter 3 to build a handsome storage cabinet that slides into the base of your new bench.

bolts pass through the legs and then into slots in the rails that hide them from view. Not only do the bolts create a very solid base, they can also be tightened up over time, as the construction lumber continues to dry and shrink a bit.

To keep the bolts from colliding where they cross inside the legs, they are offset from each other slightly, as shown in the drawing on p. 25. In my original bench, I simply left the nuts and washers visible in their counterbores, and you can do that too if you like the industrial look. But this time I covered them with slick little black plastic caps available on Amazon.com for just a few bucks.

The wood parts of the base are construction lumber—fir or pine 2x4s and 4x4s you can buy anywhere. Look for premium-grade, kiln-dried 2x4s to get the best appearance and minimize warping. You can cut these parts to length with a miter saw, a circular saw (with multiple cuts on the thick 4x4s), or any handsaw.

If you have a thickness planer, a woodworking machine that planes fresh surfaces on boards, you can use that to take a whisker off your lumber and clean up its faces, but you can also use a sanding block or power sander to do the same thing.

It's easiest to drill the deep holes and shallow counterbores (slightly larger holes that hold the nuts and washers) on a drill press, to be sure they pass squarely through the legs, but you can do it with a handheld drill if you are careful to keep it square. As for the slots in the rails, you've got options there too. The fastest way to cut them is on a tablesaw, using a dado set (a stacked set of blades we'll cover in the next chapter), but you can also do it with a router.

The $3/8$-in.-dia. all-thread bolts come in 6-ft. lengths at the home center, so you'll need to cut those to create 2-ft.- and 4-ft.-long bolts that match the width and length of the base. I sized the base and top of this workbench to make the most efficient use of the materials, but those 6-ft.-long bolts also mean you can make the base that long too, and wider than the one shown here, if you have room for it in your workshop.

The bottom rails will support a nice storage shelf, as you can see in the photo on p. 33. Or you can build the tool cabinet in Chapter 3, which takes advantage of that dead space under the bench to add a ton of helpful storage.

Down at the bottom of the legs, I bolted on casters from Rockler.com, which drop to make the

GREAT WAYS TO HOLD WORK

You'll need to hold workpieces in a variety of ways, and this workbench has you covered.

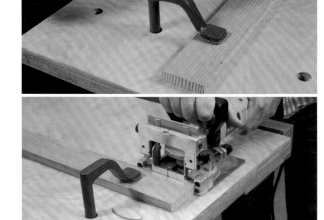

BETWEEN BENCH DOGS. These handy devices drop into the 3/4-in. holes on your workbench, teaming up with the pop-up dog on your vise to hold work without getting in the way of a sander or router, for example, like traditional clamps would.

HOLDFAST IS QUICK AND VERSATILE. This traditional work-holder is fantastic for quick operations on a pile of workpieces. You just give the top a whack (above top) to get it to grab, finish your task (above middle), and then whack the back to release it (above bottom).

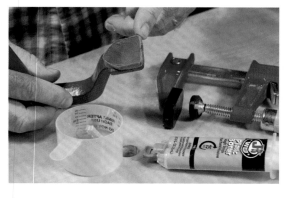

MAKE IT FRIENDLY. Use quick-set epoxy to attach a piece of leather to the end of your cast-iron holdfast, and it won't leave a mark on your work.

CLAMP LONG WORKPIECES ON EDGE. Add a ³⁄₄-in. dowel to the far end of the workbench, located level with the bottom of your vise jaws, and you'll be able to clamp long workpieces on edge for a variety of operations.

SIZE IT TO BE YOUR TABLESAW OUTFEED TABLE. Measure the height of your tablesaw, make the workbench about ¹⁄₈ in. shorter overall, and it will serve as a great outfeed table for supporting long workpieces. The casters make the bench easy to roll into place for the job.

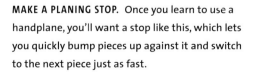

MAKE A PLANING STOP. Once you learn to use a handplane, you'll want a stop like this, which lets you quickly bump pieces up against it and switch to the next piece just as fast.

MAKE IT MOBILE. Bolt-on workbench wheels from Rockler let you raise the bench to roll it around a small workspace and drop it onto its legs to make it stable and solid.

bench mobile and lift just as easily to set the bench down solidly. In a small shop like mine, it's incredibly helpful to mobilize all the big tables and machines.

The top rails have an additional slot hidden inside their top edge, for attaching the top as shown on p. 31.

SOLID TOP AND A REAL WOODWORKING VISE

All you really need for a workbench top is a strong, flat surface, with a woodworking vise attached. The easiest way to make a top like that is by gluing together two layers of $^3/_4$-in.-thick plywood or MDF (medium-density fiberboard). I used MDF for the top of the rolling workstation in Book 1. For the workbench I'm going with Baltic-birch plywood, which is made of thin plies of wood in alternating stripes of dark and light, making the edges really nice looking.

Plywood is usually sold in large 4x8 sheets, and you'll need a full one for the two layers of this workbench top. This can be tough to handle and transport, especially if you don't have a van or pickup truck, but you'll find home centers and other lumber retailers quite willing to make some big cuts in your full sheets to help you get them home. You'll just need to know where those cuts need to be. So bring your plans along to the store.

I'll be making the tool cabinet in Chapter 3 out of the same Baltic-birch ply, which will tie in nicely with the top. I finished all of the birch plywood with Minwax Tung Oil Finish, which adds a bit of warm color that pairs nicely with the color of the workbench base. (See Chapter 9 for much more on finishing.)

It might sound intimidating to glue two big pieces of plywood together since you need even pressure in all areas for a strong, gap-free result, but I have a slick trick for that. You simply use $1^1/_4$-in. drywall screws as clamps, driving them down through one piece and partway into the second, and then flipping over the top so you don't see them. After the glue sets, you can pull out the screws and save them for another project.

The vise is a classic cast-iron model that simply bolts onto the underside of the benchtop. A woodworking vise holds work in a variety of ways. It can obviously clamp a workpiece with its edge facing upward. But it also includes a small metal "dog" that you can slide up out of the adjustable jaw, where it will work in tandem with a dog inserted in the benchtop to hold workpieces flat on the bench.

What's cool about holding work between bench dogs is that the dogs don't stick up past the top surface of the workpiece, meaning they won't get in the way of a router or a sander, for example. To allow round bench dogs to be inserted in the top, as well as a number of other cool work-holders, you simply drill a row of $^3/_4$-in.-dia. holes in the benchtop, in line with the sliding dog in the vise.

For a full tour of your new workbench, and a few more of the ways it can hold work and help you make great projects, see the photos at on pp. 18–19. And read on, because we'll be relying on our solid, versatile bench throughout this book. So let's get started building it!

solid bench for woodworkers of all levels

All you'll need are a few pieces of construction lumber, a sheet of nice plywood, and some simple hardware to build this workbench, along with a good woodworking vise.

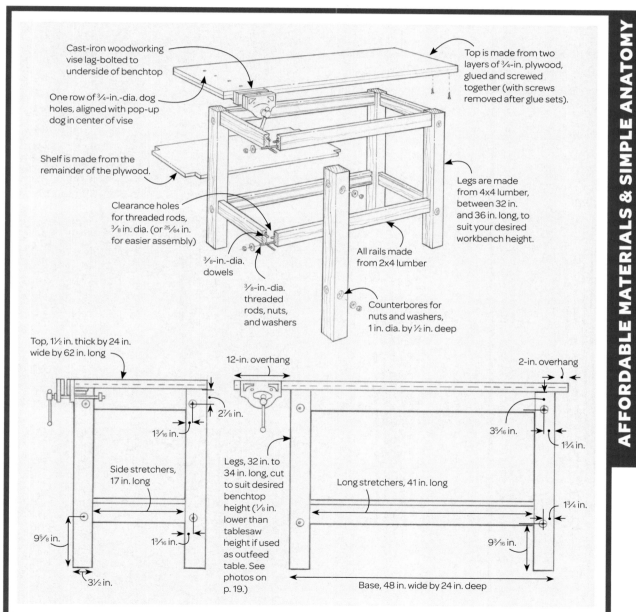

Cast-iron woodworking vise lag-bolted to underside of benchtop

Top is made from two layers of ¾-in. plywood, glued and screwed together (with screws removed after glue sets).

One row of ¾-in.-dia. dog holes, aligned with pop-up dog in center of vise

Shelf is made from the remainder of the plywood.

Legs are made from 4x4 lumber, between 32 in. and 36 in. long, to suit your desired workbench height.

Clearance holes for threaded rods, ⅜ in. dia. (or ²⁵⁄₆₄ in. for easier assembly)

All rails made from 2x4 lumber

⅜-in.-dia. dowels

⅜-in.-dia. threaded rods, nuts, and washers

Counterbores for nuts and washers, 1 in. dia. by ½ in. deep

AFFORDABLE MATERIALS & SIMPLE ANATOMY

Top, 1½ in. thick by 24 in. wide by 62 in. long

12-in. overhang

2-in. overhang

2⅞ in.

1³⁄₁₆ in.

3⁵⁄₁₆ in.

1¾ in.

Side stretchers, 17 in. long

Legs, 32 in. to 34 in. long, cut to suit desired benchtop height (⅛ in. lower than tablesaw height if used as outfeed table. See photos on p. 19.)

Long stretchers, 41 in. long

1¾ in.

9⅝ in.

1³⁄₁₆ in.

9³⁄₁₆ in.

3½ in.

Base, 48 in. wide by 24 in. deep

PREP THE PARTS FOR THE BASE

We're using construction lumber here, so spend extra time at the lumberyard or home center to pick nice-looking pieces, and try to find kiln-dried material, which won't shrink as much.

1 CUT TO LENGTH. Use a miter saw to cut a clean end on each part, and then place that end against a stop, screwed onto your miter-saw fence, to ensure that corresponding parts come out the same length. You can also use a handsaw or circular saw to cut the parts to length, working to a pencil line.

2 PLANE OR SAND THE PIECES. Use a sanding block to clean up the faces of your workbench parts, or better yet, run them through a planer if you have access to one, taking off just a whisker.

3 LABEL THE LEGS. Flip the legs around to decide which faces look the best and arrange those so they'll face forward in the finished workbench. Record the proper array by drawing a square on the ends. I used the double lines to indicate the longer rails at the front and back of the bench.

MATERIALS & SUPPLIES

BASE
- (4) 8-ft.-long 2x4s, kiln-dried
- (2) 8-ft.-long 4x4s, kiln-dried (if possible)
- (4) 6-ft. lengths of ⅜-in. threaded rod (a.k.a. "all-thread")
- (16) ⁵⁄₁₆-in. washers
- (16) ⅜-in. nuts
- (16) ⅜-in.-dia. dowels (between 2 and 3 in. long)

TOP
- (1) 4x8 sheet of ¾-in. Baltic-birch plywood (or other nice plywood, or MDF)
- (1) bottle of wood glue (Titebond III)
- (1) box of 1¼-in.-long drywall screws, coarse thread
- (16) S-clip-type tabletop fasteners

VISE
- Rockler 9-in. Quick Release Workbench Vise, or similar model
- 4¼-in.-dia. by 2½-in.-long lag bolts and washers

WOOD FINISH
- Base: Watco Danish Oil, natural tint
- Top: Minwax Tung Oil Finish

DRILL THE LEGS

You'll be drilling the larger, shallower counterbores first, to contain the nuts and washers, and then deep holes in the center of those counterbores. So your layout marks go on the outside faces of the legs. (See the drawing on p. 25 for the positions of these holes.)

1 LAY OUT EACH HOLE. Use a tape measure and combination square to lay out criss-cross marks at each hole location.

2 DRILLING TRICK. To keep a drill from wandering in wood grain, use an awl to dimple the center of your marks.

3 COUNTERBORES ARE FIRST. Use a 1-in. Forstner bit to drill a 1/2-in.-deep hole at each location. A Forstner bit leaves a nice flat bottom for the nuts and washers to sit against.

4 DRILL THE BOLT HOLES ALL THE WAY THROUGH. Set up your combo square as a visual guide to help you keep these holes square to the leg, and place a piece of scrap underneath to avoid drilling into your worktable.

5 A DRILL PRESS IS EVEN BETTER. If you have one of these, it will keep the holes perfectly square to the legs, making the parts easier to align.

SLOT THE RAILS

The rails get ³⁄₈-in.-by-³⁄₈-in. slots in a variety of locations (see the drawing on p. 25). I'll show you how to cut these with a small router, and then a quicker way if you have a tablesaw.

1 CLAMP DOWN THE RAILS. To ensure the clamps won't get in the way of the router, hold the parts at both ends with handscrews (traditional wooden clamps), and then clamp the handscrews to your work surface.

2 SET UP YOUR ROUTER. Attach your router's edge guide and make it easier to use by adding long wood strips as shown. Any straight ³⁄₈-in. router bit will work, or even a ¹⁄₄-in. bit with a couple of passes. My bit had curved edges, but the normal square kind works perfectly also.

3 ROUT THE SLOTS IN ONE SHOT. If you have a ³⁄₈-in. bit, you can set it to the full ³⁄₈-in. depth and rout the slot in a single pass.

4 FASTER WITH A TABLESAW. If you've read ahead and own a tablesaw, you can set up a ³⁄₈-in.-wide dado stack and cut these slots more quickly and easily.

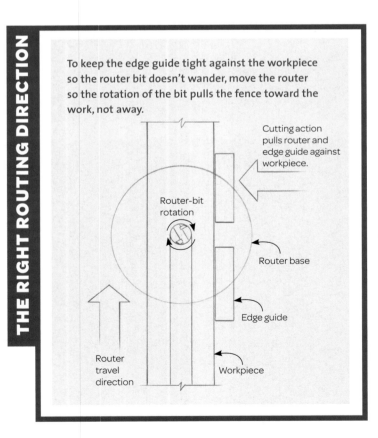

THE RIGHT ROUTING DIRECTION

To keep the edge guide tight against the workpiece so the router bit doesn't wander, move the router so the rotation of the bit pulls the fence toward the work, not away.

Cutting action pulls router and edge guide against workpiece.

Router-bit rotation

Router base

Edge guide

Router travel direction

Workpiece

PREP THE RODS

The threaded rods will likely come in 6-ft. lengths, which will break down perfectly into the 2-ft.- and 4-ft.-long sizes you need for this project.

1 SIMPLE SAW FOR METAL. A hacksaw, armed with a standard blade, will make short work of these cuts.

2 BEVEL THE ENDS. File a small chamfer on the fresh-cut ends, using a flat mill file and rolling the rods as you form the bevel to keep it even and smooth. This will help the nuts go on smoothly.

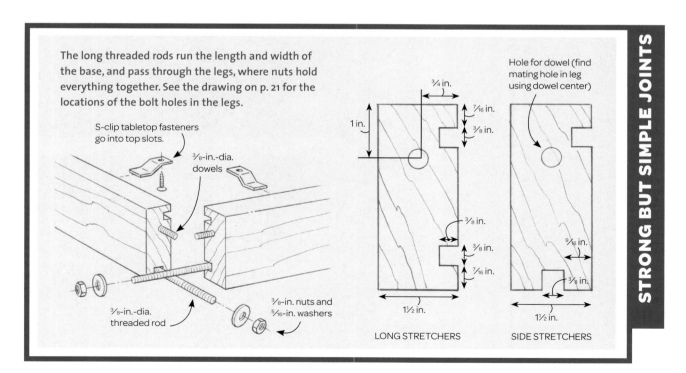

The long threaded rods run the length and width of the base, and pass through the legs, where nuts hold everything together. See the drawing on p. 21 for the locations of the bolt holes in the legs.

S-clip tabletop fasteners go into top slots.

³⁄₈-in.-dia. dowels

³⁄₈-in.-dia. threaded rod

³⁄₈-in. nuts and ⁵⁄₁₆-in. washers

Hole for dowel (find mating hole in leg using dowel center)

¾ in.
1 in.
⁷⁄₁₆ in.
³⁄₈ in.
³⁄₈ in.
³⁄₈ in.
⁷⁄₁₆ in.
1½ in.

LONG STRETCHERS

⁹⁄₁₆ in.
³⁄₈ in.
1½ in.

SIDE STRETCHERS

STRONG BUT SIMPLE JOINTS

ADD A DOWEL TO EACH JOINT

The threaded rods will help keep the parts in place as you assemble the base, but a small dowel makes the job easier and ensures that the rails remain stable.

1 DRILL THE RAILS. Drill a ³⁄₈-in. hole into the ends of each rail, anywhere near the top edge. Use a tape flag to make sure each hole is at least 1 in. deep and do your best to keep the drill level. (It helps to drop to one knee and sight along the drill bit and workpiece.)

2 THE MAGIC DOWEL CENTER. This handy little gizmo lets you transfer the location of a dowel hole from one part to another. Place a ³⁄₈-in. dowel center in each end of each rail you are working with.

3 TRANSFER THE DOWEL LOCATIONS TO THE LEGS. Starting with the ends of the bench, place dowel centers in the ends of the rails, insert the threaded rods in the legs, position the parts on the rods, and then squeeze the legs together to mark the dowel locations.

4 DRILL AT THE DOWEL HOLES IN THE LEGS. Take apart the legs and rails, look for the little dimples made by the dowel centers, and drill there. (The nearby hole is the one that holds the threaded rod).

ASSEMBLE THE BASE

Assemble the short ends of the base first, and then add the longer rails and rods to complete it.

1 DOWELS AND RODS. Tap a dowel into each leg, slide the rods into place, and then tap the parts together.

2 WASHERS AND NUTS FINISH THE JOB. Add washers and nuts to the ends of the threaded rods and lock the parts together tightly with a socket wrench. Assemble both ends of the bench.

3 NOW THE LONG RAILS AND RODS. Start by using the long rails to locate the mating dowel holes in the legs, just as before, then drill for the dowels and attach the last four rails to complete your sturdy workbench base.

FINISHING TOUCHES

Flip-up casters and a simple oil finish are optional but recommended for looks and performance.

1 WORKBENCH CASTERS FROM ROCKLER. These sturdy wheel sets bolt onto any wooden workbench. Start by bolting on the brackets according to the instructions, and then attach the wheels.

2 ANY OIL FINISH WILL DO. I used Watco Danish Oil, in the natural (untinted) color, for the base, and Minwax Tung Oil Finish on the benchtop, which adds a bit of warmth to the blonder birch wood. Just brush on these finishes liberally and wipe off the excess. Be careful not to leave the oil-soaked rags wadded up afterward, as they can heat up and burst into flames that way. Lay them out flat to dry before discarding them.

3 CAP THE HOLES. You can leave these holes open and the bolts showing, but I capped mine off with inexpensive plastic plugs from Amazon.com. You might need to trim a little more off the ends of the threaded rods to get the caps to seat fully.

BUILD THE TOP

The workbench top is made from two layers of any plywood or MDF. I recommend Baltic-birch plywood, which has nicer edges than other types. You'll need to start with a 4x8 sheet, which can be tough to transport, but most retailers will be quite happy to make a cut or two at the store. You'll just need to tell them where.

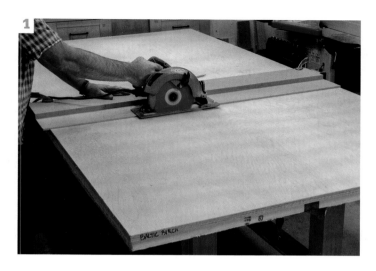

1 HOW TO BREAK DOWN A BIG SHEET. Whether you do it at the store or at home, you'll need to cut your full sheet into smaller pieces that are safe to handle on a small tablesaw. The easiest way to do that is to lay the sheet on a piece of rigid-foam insulation and use a circular saw. A shopmade cutting guide keeps the cuts straight and splinter-free.

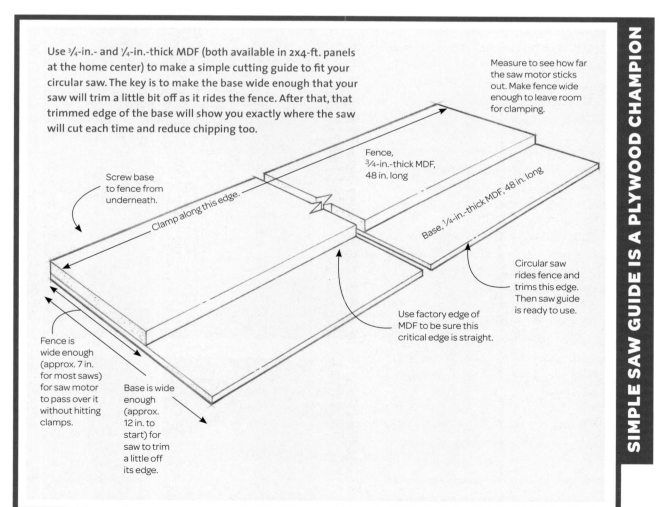

Use ¾-in.- and ¼-in.-thick MDF (both available in 2x4-ft. panels at the home center) to make a simple cutting guide to fit your circular saw. The key is to make the base wide enough that your saw will trim a little bit off as it rides the fence. After that, that trimmed edge of the base will show you exactly where the saw will cut each time and reduce chipping too.

Measure to see how far the saw motor sticks out. Make fence wide enough to leave room for clamping.

Fence, ¾-in.-thick MDF, 48 in. long

Screw base to fence from underneath.

Clamp along this edge.

Base, ¼-in.-thick MDF, 48 in. long

Circular saw rides fence and trims this edge. Then saw guide is ready to use.

Use factory edge of MDF to be sure this critical edge is straight.

Fence is wide enough (approx. 7 in. for most saws) for saw motor to pass over it without hitting clamps.

Base is wide enough (approx. 12 in. to start) for saw to trim a little off its edge.

SIMPLE SAW GUIDE IS A PLYWOOD CHAMPION

2 RIP TWO EQUAL PIECES. After cutting off one end of your full sheet, cut the large, remaining piece down the middle to get the two layers of your workbench top. The fastest, cleanest way to do this is on the tablesaw, using a work-support stand to catch the parts. But you can also do it with your circular saw and cutting guide.

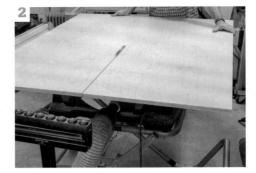

3 DRILL THROUGH THE BOTTOM LAYER. We'll be clamping these two pieces together with 1¼-in. drywall screws, so drill clearance holes for those now, just larger than the screws, and countersink the holes slightly so the screw heads end up just a hair below the surface. Make sure the outer holes are close to the edges and lay them out in a grid roughly 6 in. to 8 in. apart.

4 TWO COUNTERSINKING OPTIONS. I used the combo drill at right, but you can also drill first and then use a separate countersink, like the one at left. After drilling, sand the chips off the back side of the holes, so they don't keep the layers apart.

5 SPREAD AN EVEN LAYER OF GLUE. I used Titebond III, which gives you more working time (before it starts curing) than other glues. Use a brush or small piece of wood to spread it evenly, right out to the edges.

6 DRYWALL SCREWS ACT AS CLAMPS. Drive each screw until it seats firmly, but not so far that it pokes out of the top side of the benchtop. Let the benchtop dry overnight, and then remove the screws.

7 TRIM THE EDGES. No matter how careful you are, the edges will be slightly misaligned, so use a flush-trim router bit to trim one flush with the other. Then use a sanding block to put a light bevel on all of the sharp corners.

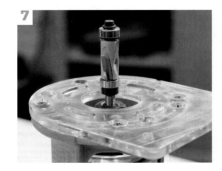

8 HANDY ROUTER BIT. Any flush-trim bit will do, but I used this "Mini-Mega" bit (#06-128) from Infinity, which has bearings at the top and bottom. That feature lets it ride against either layer of the plywood, meaning you won't have to flip the top or switch bits.

BOLT ON THE VISE AND ATTACH THE TOP

The cast-iron, quick-action vise bolts on easily, but the top of the vise jaws need to end up just a whisker below the top of the workbench. So you'll need to add a plywood spacer under the top first.

1 GLUE ON A PAD. Try various layers until the vise jaws end up just short of the top surface. A piece of the 3/4-in. plywood and an additional piece of 1/4-in. MDF worked perfectly for this vise. Glue the pieces to each other and the underside of the benchtop all at once.

2 MARK AND DRILL THE BOLT HOLES. Lay the vise bracket on the pad to mark the holes for the lag bolts. Use a 3/16-in. bit to drill pilot holes for the 1/4-in. lag bolts, attaching a tape flag to make sure the drill stops short of the other side (top side) of the benchtop.

3 LAG BOLTS ARE QUICK AND SOLID. Give the spacer pad a few hours to dry firmly, and then remove the clamps and use a socket wrench to drive the lag bolts and attach the vise.

4 ATTACH THE TOP. The additional slots in the top rails are for attaching the benchtop, using S-type tabletop fasteners as shown.

FINISH UP YOUR NEW BENCH

Add wood jaws to the vise to keep it from marring workpieces, drill dog holes to help hold work in other ways, apply a simple oil finish to the top, and your new workbench is complete.

1 MARK THE WOOD JAWS. The vise has threaded holes for attaching wood jaws with standard bolts. After cutting some of your ¾-in. plywood to make the jaws, insert ¼-in. dowel centers in the threaded holes and clamp the wood jaws in the vise to mark the bolt holes.

2 DRILL THE WOOD JAWS. You'll need shallow counterbores for the nuts and washers, and then through-holes for the bolts. A drill press will help, but you can drill these holds with a handheld drill also.

3 JAWS BOLT ON EASILY. With the holes drilled accurately, the jaws attach with standard machine bolts and washers.

4 DRILL DOG HOLES. Draw a light pencil line across the bench, on the vise's center line, and space ¾-in.-dia. dog holes 4 in. or 5 in. apart. A Forstner bit, held in a cordless drill, offers an easy way to drill these holes.

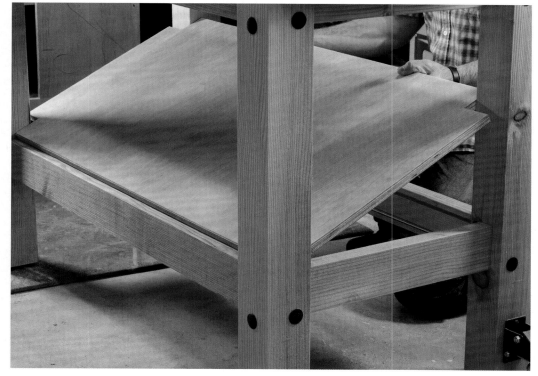

LOWER SHELF IS AN EASY OPTION. In Chapter 3 we'll be building a great tool cabinet sized to fit into the base of this workbench, but until you have time for that, you can add storage space with a simple shelf. Measure the distances from rail to rail, lay out and cut notches for the legs, and then drop in your shelf. A jigsaw will do a great job on the notches, but other saws will work too.

2

get the most from your tablesaw

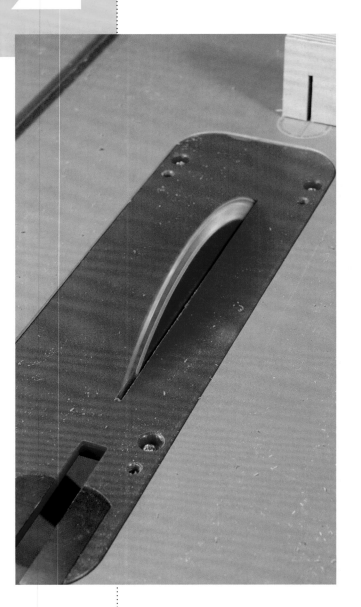

WHILE WE'VE GOTTEN by so far with a handful of handheld power tools, it's time to add your first real woodworking machine, the mighty tablesaw. You won't find another tool that adds as much speed and accuracy to your work. The tablesaw is also one of the most dangerous tools. But I'll show you how a well-adjusted machine, used properly, doesn't have to be scary at all. A healthy respect is always important, however. So please take my safety advice to heart.

The first tablesaw most people buy is a smaller, portable model, which won't eat up too much of your budget or floorspace. Not all of these jobsite-style saws are created equal, so I'm featuring a Bosch saw that packs serious performance into a $600 package. That said, if your budget allows, feel free to step up to a larger, more powerful model. Buying a used machine is a good way to get a lot more for less. Just don't feel like you have to spend thousands of bucks to add a tablesaw to your workshop.

TABLESAW IS A WORKSHOP WORKHORSE

The following is just a small taste of what a tablesaw can do for you. Flip through the rest of this book to see more of the indispensable angles, notches, and other joints a tablesaw can cut, and the wide range of projects they make possible.

BEST TOOL FOR RIPPING. The fence on a tablesaw stays parallel to the blade, letting you trim boards narrower in width, leaving behind a very smooth edge in the process.

ACCURATE CROSSCUTS. Using the miter gauge that comes with every saw, you can cut workpieces to accurate length also.

A WORLD OF JOINERY. In the next chapter, I arm the tablesaw with a small stack of dado blades to make this drawer joint. In later chapters we'll make miter joints, finger joints, and more.

TABLESAW CUTS PARTS TO SIZE AND JOINS THEM TOGETHER TOO

The main reason most people buy a tablesaw is to size (or "dimension") materials accurately. Generally speaking, there is no better tool for the job.

The first step is "ripping" a board or piece of plywood to a precise width. You do that against the rip fence, which slides side to side, staying parallel to the blade as it does, ensuring that the edge you cut is parallel to the one riding the fence.

After that, you can use the tablesaw to crosscut those pieces to accurate length, using the miter gauge included with your saw (or a better aftermarket model). In a later chapter we'll also be building a shop-made crosscut sled to suit your saw, for even more accurate crosscuts, on pieces that are too long or wide for the miter gauge.

> **The main reason most people buy a tablesaw is to size (or "dimension") materials accurately. Generally speaking, there is no better tool for the job.**

As I've pointed out earlier, the humble circular saw and miter saw can also make some of these cuts; they just can't do it as quickly or easily as the tablesaw. But rip cuts and crosscuts are just the beginning of what this machine can do. After using the tablesaw to cut workpieces to accurate overall size, you can also use it to join those parts together. These joinery cuts range from simple miters, bevels, dadoes, and rabbets to the precise, interlocking fingers of box joints and dovetails.

Many of these joinery cuts are made possible with a unique stack of blades, called a dado set or stack dado, which can cut wide notches all at once. We'll cover the dado set and a range of useful tablesaw joints in later chapters, along with a variety of fun, useful projects you can make with each one. In this chapter, I'll cover the basic cuts and safety practices. Those are critical, so let's learn to walk before we run.

CHOOSING THE RIGHT TABLESAW FOR YOU

Tablesaws come in a variety of sizes, with widely varying price tags. What you get for the big bucks are much more mass, which adds up to less vibration and smoother cuts; a much larger table; a more robust, accurate rip fence; and a more powerful motor, which will slice through the biggest, toughest timbers without hesitating. All that said, you can get most of the benefits of a tablesaw in a much more compact affordable unit, like the Bosch 4100 I'll be using throughout this book.

One way to get more for your money is to buy used. I recommend this especially for larger tablesaws, which tend to stay put in workshops and are generally harder to beat up and damage. Buying a used portable model, on the other hand, could be asking for problems, as these models are not quite as robust and often get beat up by contractors, who carry them from job to job in the back of a pickup truck. Whether you buy new or used, I highly recommend that you buy a tablesaw built in the last 10 years or so, which means they will have a new safety device I consider to be critical on any tablesaw.

the splitter is the most important component

My No. 1 piece of tablesaw advice is to use the splitter whenever possible. It sits just behind the blade, riding in the slot the blade makes—called the "kerf"—where

CHOOSING A TABLESAW

Tablesaws vary widely in price, power, and size, but a compact, affordable model can be a very effective tool.

BEST VALUE IN A SMALL SAW. My favorite portable tablesaw is the Bosch 4100, which I'll use throughout this book. It has plenty of power, updated safety equipment, and an extending rip fence that lets you cut material up to 30 in. wide. The "gravity-rise" stand folds up to let you store the saw in a small space. All that for a street price of $600.

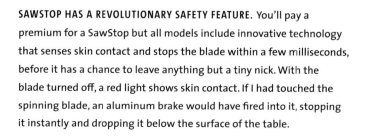

BIG CABINET SAWS ARE SERIOUS PERFORMERS. What you get with a full-size tablesaw like the SawStop Professional Cabinet Saw is much more power and cutting capacity, smoother cuts, a more accurate rip fence, smoother controls, and the ability to add a router table. But saws like these cost 5 to 6 times more than a portable saw and take up a lot more floor space.

SAWSTOP HAS A REVOLUTIONARY SAFETY FEATURE. You'll pay a premium for a SawStop but all models include innovative technology that senses skin contact and stops the blade within a few milliseconds, before it has a chance to leave anything but a tiny nick. With the blade turned off, a red light shows skin contact. If I had touched the spinning blade, an aluminum brake would have fired into it, stopping it instantly and dropping it below the surface of the table.

it prevents the board from pivoting and contacting the back end of the blade, which happens to be spinning toward you at 120 mph.

We'll cover kickback in the upcoming section on ripping, but let's just say that when a board gets snagged on the back of the blade, very bad things happen. The problem in the past, at least in the United States, was that blade splitters were so poorly designed that they were usually discarded by frustrated users. That made kickback a frighteningly regular occurrence, leading to many of the tablesaw horror stories you've probably heard.

With almost any type of splitter in place, however, kickback is nearly impossible, and today's much-improved splitters can eliminate it entirely. Starting in 2008, the Underwriters Laboratories (UL) began requiring that a new type of splitter—called a "riving knife"—be built into new tablesaw designs, with existing designs required to add them by 2014.

Modeled after far-superior European splitters, the riving knife has been a game-changer for tablesaw safety in North America. While the old-school splitters sat tall and rigid behind the blade, often with a troublesome plastic blade cover attached to them, a riving knife sits just below the top of the teeth, moving up and down with the blade as you change its height and angling sideways as well when you change the blade angle. In short, this means that the riving knife can stay on the saw in almost any situation—keeping you safe from kickback—whether you are cutting all the way through a board, cutting just a shallow slot, or making a bevel cut of some kind. And when you do need to remove the riving knife temporarily, when using a dado set, for example, it pops on and off the saw in seconds.

If you're buying a used saw, your best option is to look for one manufactured in the past 10 years or so, so you get this great new type of splitter. If you have an older tablesaw, however, all is not lost. There are aftermarket splitters you can add to any saw, which are much more convenient to use than the original

safety gear. And there are also easy ways to add a shopmade splitter to your tablesaw's throat plate. Dig around the Internet, and you'll find those.

sawstop takes safety to another level

Right around the time riving knives became mandatory in U.S. tablesaws, a brand-new company electrified the woodworking world with an innovative tablesaw technology that stops the blade instantly upon skin contact.

In a widely viewed test, SawStop proved the technology by rolling a hot dog into the spinning blade, showing that it received only the slightest nick before the electronics activated the brake, which not only rams a sacrificial aluminum cartridge into the teeth but also pulls the blade down into the saw cabinet and out of sight—all in a matter of a few micro-seconds.

After its first large tablesaw was a massive hit with woodworkers, SawStop began rolling out a full line of saws in all sizes. In just a decade, these innovative machines have become the top choice of woodworking schools and community workshops, as well as many hobbyists and pros.

Being a humble journalist and woodworker, it took me a while to discard my old reliable tablesaw and splash out the cash for a SawStop, but I'm happy I did. I've used a number of SawStop models at this point, and I can tell you they are excellent tablesaws that work as advertised, bringing a woodworker additional peace of mind, knowing that no matter what happens on the saw, you'll be safe.

But these new tablesaws are not cheap, as the technology can double the price of a smaller saw and add roughly $1,000 to the price of a larger one. Also, the technology works by sensing electrical conductivity, so contact with wet wood and metal can also set it off. I've seen that happen when a user tried to cut pressure-treated wood and also when the

EVERY TABLESAW NEEDS A TUNE-UP

Even the best tablesaw needs a few adjustments and upgrades to work safely and do its best work.

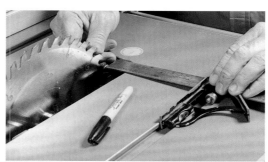

REPLACE THE BLADE WHEN YOU CAN. Tablesaw manufacturers always save a few bucks on the blade. To get better results, replace it with a premium combination blade like this 10-in. "Super General" from Infinity Tools. It's a "thin-kerf" model, which is great for smaller saws, letting them cut through tougher, thicker boards with less power.

ALIGN THE BLADE AND MITER SLOTS. To check their alignment, raise the blade as high as it will go, mark a tooth on your saw, and use a combination square as shown at top to measure the distance between the miter slot and that tooth. Lock the square when its blade just touches the tooth. Then rotate that same tooth to the back and see if the blade on your square just touches it lightly. If it doesn't, your saw is out of alignment. Adjustments vary depending on the saw, so read the manual to find out how to align the table with the blade.

DIAL CALIPERS ARE A SECRET WEAPON. Digital or analog dial calipers are surprisingly affordable and will add precision to your work in countless ways. I used mine to measure the splitter (riving knife) on the Bosch saw to make sure I bought a blade that was just slightly thicker.

LINE UP THE RIP FENCE LAST. Now that you know your miter slots are lined up with the blade, line up the fence with a miter slot, and it will also be parallel to the blade. All rip fences have a way to adjust their angle slightly.

metal fence of a miter gauge contacted the blade. And whenever the blade brake is activated, the blade is embedded in it and effectively ruined, so you lose not only a new blade but also a replaceable brake cartridge, which can cost you $150 to $200 altogether.

Also, since kickback is responsible for the majority of hand-to-blade contact, you can eliminate the majority of tablesaw danger by simply using the splitter or riving knife and avoid most of the rest by following the smart safety practices I'll outline in this chapter. I worked safely without a SawStop for many years. That said, when I finally invested in one myself, I felt instantly safer. So the choice is up to you.

TABLESAW TUNE-UP

One of the inconvenient truths of woodworking is that most major tools need at least minor adjustment to do their best work. One place saw manufacturers cut costs is on the sawblade, which is the disposable part of the machine. So the first way to improve performance is to replace the stock blade with a better model from a company that specializes in blades.

start by aligning the blade and fence

While better tablesaws are adjusted carefully at the factory, even those can be bumped out of whack during shipping, and a misaligned saw can force workpieces into the side or back of the blade, leading to jamming and even kickback. The good news is that alignment is easy to check and easy to correct. The first step is to make sure the blade is parallel to the miter slots on the table. You can check this with nothing more than your combination square, as shown in the top right photos on p. 39.

Depending on the type of saw you have, adjusting the alignment of the table and blade will be done in one of two ways. I won't go into those adjustments in this book, but they are covered well in your machine's

manual. And manuals for older saws are available online. Pro tip: Always read the manual!

Once you have the miter slots aligned with the blade, the next step is to align the rip fence with the miter slots, meaning it will also be perfectly parallel to the blade. All rip fences are easily adjustable, so this part of a tablesaw tune-up is quick and easy.

While you're tinkering with the rip fence, touch it lightly against the blade, lock it there, and set the adjustable pointer to zero. A rip fence rides on a rail with fractional measurements on it. Get the fence's pointer set accurately and you'll be able to set up accurate rip cuts in seconds, with no need to locate your measuring tape and check the distance to the blade.

Tablesaws also include a miter gauge, which slides in the miter slots and has a fence that keeps a workpiece square to the blade. So the next check is to make sure the fence on that miter gauge is actually square. I'll show you how to do that shortly, in the crosscutting discussion.

a few other key upgrades

Speaking of the miter gauge, that's another accessory that falls short on most tablesaws, which is why so many woodworkers end up replacing their original miter gauges with an aftermarket model. The key to a good miter gauge is the ability to quickly and positively return the fence to a perfect 90 degrees after you set it to some other angle.

You'll be able to limp along with the stock miter gauge for a while before you spring for a spendy one, but one thing you'll need to replace right away, before making your first rip cut, is the poorly designed push stick that came with your saw. I'll show you a shopmade push stick that does a much better job controlling workpieces and won't cost you any more than a scrap of plywood and a few minutes of work (see p. 41).

a safe, secure push stick

Your tablesaw will come with a traditional-style push stick. It's better than nothing for that machine, but only barely. If you have a bandsaw, carry this "tablesaw" push stick over there and leave it. It will work great on that machine.

On the tablesaw, however, the little bird's-mouth opening on the end of a long stick will do a poor job of controlling workpieces. There just isn't enough of the stick touching the work. There are a number of good push-stick designs, but all of them include a long contact area that rides the top of a board, helping you steer it much better.

The push stick in this book checks all the boxes and is easy to make with simple tools. Draw the pattern on p. 42 onto a piece of 3/4-in.-thick plywood or MDF, cut it out using the tablesaw and jigsaw (or bandsaw), and sand the hand-grip area for comfort.

The push stick will get chewed up when you make very narrow cuts (see the photo at right below), and that's just as it should be. Just make another when the first one is too beat up to do its job anymore.

TRADE YOUR OLD PUSH STICK FOR A BETTER ONE

The push stick that comes with your saw is not the best tool for safely controlling boards. A shopmade push stick will do a much better job, keeping you safer.

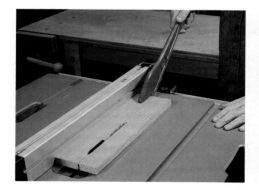

THE PROBLEM. Tablesaws come with a push stick like this. Its small mouth contacts only the very back edge of a board, making it very hard to keep the workpiece on track as it moves through the blade.

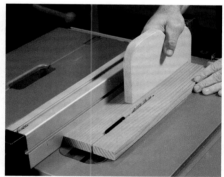

EASY SOLUTION. Make a push stick that contacts much more of the board, making it easy to steer safely.

DESIGNED TO BE ABUSED. On very narrow cuts like this, your push stick will ride right through the blade to control both parts of the workpiece. When your shopmade push stick gets too chewed up, you just make another one.

PLYWOOD PUSH STICK MADE EASY

There are lots of designs for good push sticks. All of the best will have a long contact surface on the bottom, with a small hook on the end, and be tall enough to keep your hand out of harm's way.

1 LAY OUT THE SHAPE AND CUT TO OVERALL SIZE. Trim your material to the right overall width, lay out the shape in pencil, and then cut it to overall length.

2 CUT OUT THE PERIMETER. Use a jigsaw and/or bandsaw— depending on what you have access to—to cut out the shape of your push stick. The bandsaw makes it easier, but the jigsaw works just fine too.

3 SOFTEN THE HAND-GRIP AREA FOR COMFORT. I used my benchtop sander to smooth the areas where my hand goes and soften the sharp edges. You can also sand by hand or even use a router to round the edges.

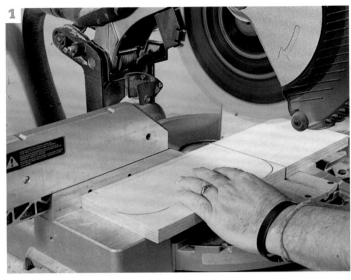

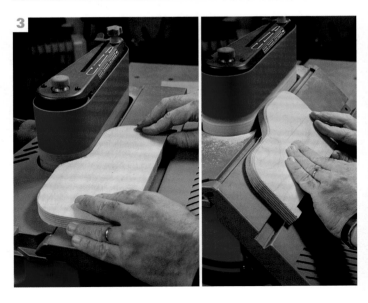

TABLESAW PUSH STICK

This simple shape can be cut out of any piece of ³/₄-in.- or ¹/₂-in.-thick piece of plywood or MDF. Don't be too fussy about the precise dimensions and curves, and make more than one at a time, as push sticks are designed to get chewed up by the blade on narrow cuts.

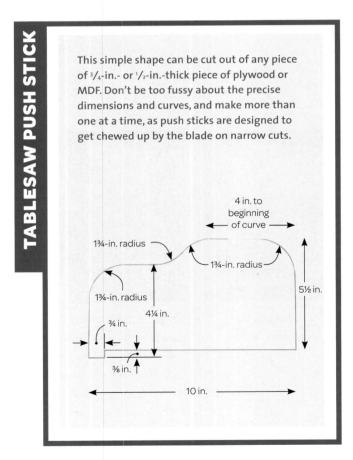

4 in. to beginning of curve

1¾-in. radius

1¾-in. radius

1¾-in. radius

5½ in.

4¼ in.

¾ in.

⅜ in.

10 in.

SAFE, ACCURATE RIP CUTS ARE JOB ONE

The most common cut you'll make on your tablesaw is a rip cut, which happens when you slide a board along the rip fence to cut it narrower in width. The tablesaw rips lumber more easily and accurately than any other tool, letting you turn off-the-shelf lumber into custom workpieces of all sizes. This ability is a big reason why I'm including the tablesaw in this book, as it opens up a new world of project possibilities. While learning how to rip boards safely, you'll learn how to avoid the tablesaw's main dangers and work without worries.

what kickback is, and how to prevent it

There are two main hazards on the tablesaw. Both are very real—and very avoidable. The first is kickback. The front edge of the sawblade, the part closest to the user, is your friend. Spinning downward toward the table, it keeps the workpiece under control as it cuts. And that's the only part of the blade you want to cut wood. The back part of the blade, which is spinning upward, toward you, is the enemy. While that part of the blade will rub the sides of a cut very slightly, you do not want it to make significant contact.

If your rip fence is parallel to the blade, and *if* you've got the splitter/riving knife in place, and *if* your workpiece is relatively flat and straight, and *if* you're controlling it well with your hands and/or a push stick, the board will stay on track and sail right past the back of the blade with no trouble.

However, if any of those things are not true— especially if the splitter isn't in place—the wood can pivot or get jammed sideways onto the back of the blade. And if it makes significant contact with those teeth, it can wrench forcefully sideways and spring back at you at upward of 150 mph, with catastrophic results. If your hand is near the blade when kickback happens, it can be pulled into the blade before you have a chance to react.

Not to worry, though. The splitter/riving knife is there to prevent all of this from happening. Acting as a physical barrier to kickback, it prevents the board from touching the back of the blade. But it has to be in place to work its magic.

Even with the splitter in place, there's still the slightest chance of kickback before the board reaches it. So you don't want the board wandering off track and pushing sideways against the blade. That can happen for two main reasons. One is a poorly adjusted rip fence, which is not parallel with the blade. The other is a twisted, cupped, or warped board, which won't stay flat and stable as you push it. To rip a wonky board like that, you're much better off using your bandsaw, or if you don't have one of those yet, a jigsaw. These have narrow, flexible blades that won't cause kickback.

> Acting as a physical barrier to kickback, [the splitter/riving knife] prevents the board from touching the back of the blade. But it has to be in place to work its magic.

blade contact is the other danger

You don't have to know anything about tablesaws to realize that the spinning blade is dangerous in itself. Like kickback, hand-to-blade contact is also preventable. While almost all tablesaw splitters and riving knives include some sort of cover intended to block your hands from contacting the blade, those types of blade guards tend to be more trouble than they are worth, getting in the way so often that they inevitably get tossed.

HOW TO PREVENT KICKBACK

Rule number one of safe tablesaw use is to use a splitter to prevent dangerous kickback. All modern saws include a riving knife, which is a very convenient and effective type of splitter. If you have an older saw, it will have an old-school splitter that will accomplish the same task. You can also make a simple splitter that fits into a shopmade throat plate.

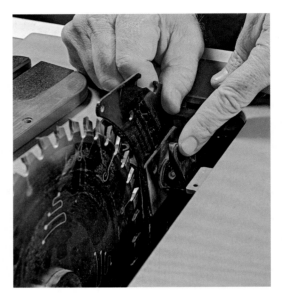

BEST TYPE OF SPLITTER. Modern saws like the Bosch and SawStop come with a riving knife that can be adjusted just below the level of the top of the blade. It then moves up and down with the blade, and angles sideways with it too, so it can stay on the saw almost always.

HOW KICKBACK HAPPENS. Without a splitter in place, a board is free to twist sideways onto the back of the blade, which can send it toward you at 150 mph or more.

HOW THE SPLITTER WORKS ITS MAGIC. The splitter sits in the slot created by the blade, acting as a physical barrier to the board twisting off track and contacting the back of the blade.

SLOT CUTS TOO. While old-school splitters stand up tall and don't move with the blade, getting in the way of any cut that doesn't go all the way through a board, riving knives sit just below the top of the blade, moving with it as you adjust the blade height, allowing cuts that don't go all the way through a workpiece.

Luckily, the new riving knives include a low-profile option that dispenses with the blade cover but still leaves the splitter in place to do its job. That does leave the blade exposed, but there are easy ways to keep your hands clear of it. The first is to avoid any sort of sleeves or jewelry that might dangle toward the blade and pull your hands after it. The second is to use push sticks and push pads.

A push stick and/or push pad is a must anytime that your hands need to come within 2 in. or 3 in. of the blade to control the workpiece. This happens most frequently on rip cuts narrower than 4 in. or so. As you'll see on p. 46, it's easy to leave a push stick within easy reach, so you can grab it when you need it.

outfeed support is a must

Every machine has an infeed side and an outfeed side. On the tablesaw, your hands can control the workpiece safely as it approaches the blade but not when it exits the cut, especially if the workpiece is long and extends far past the back of the table.

Once a piece has been pushed past the blade, especially during a rip cut, it ends up dangling off the back side of the tablesaw. Let it go, and it will drop to the floor and suffer damage. Press it down at the front end to keep it from dropping, and you'll be pressing down hard right near the blade, which is a bad idea.

With proper outfeed support, however, you can simply focus on making a good rip cut and keeping your hands safe, knowing the workpiece will slide nicely off the back of the saw. The best form of outfeed support is a table of some kind. On stationary tablesaws, people often attach a light plywood table permanently to the back edge. Others make their workbench just a hair shorter than the saw, as I recommended in the previous chapter, so it can double as an outfeed table when needed (see the sidebar on p. 16).

If a table or workbench isn't an option, a work-support stand will do. These adjustable stands will provide additional support for a variety of machines, from a bandsaw to a miter saw, drill press, or tablesaw. I like the type of stand that has large round bearings on top, so workpieces can slide freely in any direction.

rip-cut choreography

I've been teaching safe tablesaw use for a couple of decades now, and I always advocate the same process for rip cuts. Whenever possible, I recommend using your hands to control workpieces. Hands provide direct feedback and unmatched control. And for rip cuts wider than 4 in. or so, hands are all you need. For rip cuts narrower than that, you'll be using a push stick to keep your fingers safe.

You can start almost all rip cuts with your hands only, but you'll need to have the push stick within reach. The rip fence is generally placed to the right of the blade, which makes your right hand the push hand. It sits farther back on the board, grabbing the back end of the board when possible. Your left hand is the steadying hand, keeping the board flat against the table and rip fence. Check the photos on pp. 46–47 for the rest of the process, which includes a safe way to steady the board mid-cut and reach for the push stick when necessary.

two rip-cut no-nos

To make a safe rip cut, you need the longest edge riding the rip fence. That means you shouldn't place a significantly shorter edge—such as the end of the board—against the rip fence. You won't have enough control over the workpiece, and it will be way too easy to twist it as you slide it, which will lead to kickback.

Once your rip cut is complete, there's one more important safety tip: Do not reach over the top of the blade to retrieve the workpiece or the piece you cut off it (called an "offcut"). That's asking for trouble. Walk around to the back of the saw to grab those pieces.

SAFE RIPPING 101

Rip cuts are in line with the grain, used to trim material to any desired width by sliding it along the rip fence. Here's how to safely rip any sort of material. The main goals are to keep the work against the rip fence throughout the cut, and your hands out of harm's way.

IF YOU DON'T HAVE A STRAIGHT EDGE, MAKE ONE. To prevent kickback on the tablesaw, you need your material to have at least one straight edge to run along the rip fence. If both edges of a board are curved or bumpy, draw a straight line and cut along it with a jigsaw or bandsaw.

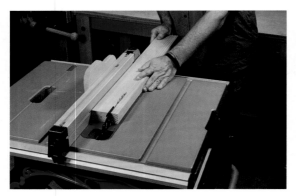

START WITH YOUR HANDS. With your push stick placed within easy reach, a typical cut starts with you controlling the workpiece with hands only. The rip fence generally goes to your right, making your right hand the push hand and your left the guide. That guide hand stays planted on the table—a safe distance from the blade—throughout the cut, keeping the work firmly against the rip fence.

REACH FOR THE PUSH STICK. Once the back edge of the board is on the table, stop pushing for a moment, steadying the board with your left hand while you reach for the push stick. You don't have to shut off the saw to do this.

FINISH THE CUT WITH THE PUSH STICK. Place the push stick in the middle of the back edge—not against the fence—and use it to finish the cut safely. Your left hand can come away once the board passes it.

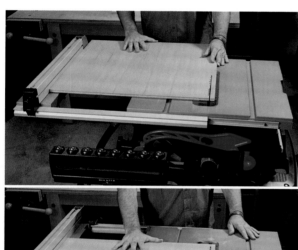

WIDE RIP CUTS. For rip cuts wider than 54 in. or so, you can control the work with your hands only. They have the same jobs as before: One guides as long as possible, and one pushes through.

ADD OUTFEED SUPPORT. If you don't have support in place for long pieces as they exit the back of the tablesaw, you'll have to press down hard on the front end to prevent them from tipping backward, which will be a dangerous distraction. An adjustable stand like this, with round bearings or a roller on top, is a great solution.

CROSSCUTTING WITH YOUR MITER GAUGE

A good rip cut creates a workpiece with two perfectly parallel edges. At that point you can cut it accurately to length. These cuts across the grain are called crosscuts, and there are a few ways to do them on the tablesaw.

The most basic approach is using a miter gauge—either the one that came with your saw or an aftermarket model. The miter gauge has some limitations, but it's lightweight and simple to use, making it great for small crosscuts. For larger workpieces and the highest possible accuracy, you'll want to use a crosscut sled, and I'll show you how to make a simple, solid one later in the book (see Chapter 4). The miter gauge is guided by a "miter bar" that rides in one of the tablesaw's "miter slots." A short fence is included to guide the workpiece.

four reasons to add an auxiliary fence

The first thing your basic miter gauge needs is a longer fence. You can make one from any piece of straight, $3/4$-in.-thick plywood or MDF. The miter-gauge fence should have little slots or holes for screwing on that auxiliary fence; if it doesn't, you can drill them with a standard twist drill.

The fence offers four awesome benefits. First, it offers much better support for the workpiece as it slides across the table, keeping it perfectly square to the blade. Second, if you attach it so the blade cuts into it, the little slot cut by the blade will show where every other cut will land, so you can simply line up your pencil mark with that slot. Third, crosscuts tend to leave some chipping at the back edge, and the little zero-clearance blade slot in the auxiliary fence will prevent that as well. Last, the auxiliary fence lets you clamp a work stop at the far end. A stop is a handy little block of wood that catches the ends of boards

so you can cut a series of matching parts to the exact same length.

set your miter gauge square to the blade

The last step before using your tricked-out miter gauge is to set its fence perfectly square to the blade. Adjustments vary based on the type of gauge you have, but the squaring process is the same.

Start by placing a reliable square against both the blade and the auxiliary fence you screwed onto the gauge's fence. Make sure the square isn't hitting the teeth of the blade but is resting up against the flat plate area. Look for a gap between the square and the blade and adjust the fence until it's gone. That will get you very close, but to be absolutely sure, make a cut on a straight piece of wood and check that corner with your square.

Once you know the fence is set accurately, lock it firmly in that position, and if it includes a little stop at 90 degrees, adjust that so you can always bring the fence quickly back to that square position.

crosscut basics

To cut a board to accurate length, start by trimming one end cleanly, so you know it's square. Hold the piece firmly against the miter-gauge fence as you push it through the spinning blade and leave the little offcut alone until the blade stops spinning. If you have multiple pieces to cut, trim a clean end on all of those too.

Now you're ready to set up a stop block to cut the other end of each piece to perfect length. Using the little slot you've cut in your auxiliary fence, measure over to where you want the stop block to be and make a pencil mark there. Then clamp a stop block at that mark. To cut all of your pieces to accurate length, with no measuring involved, just place their fresh-cut ends against the stop block and crosscut away!

when the miter gauge comes up short

For a few reasons, the miter gauge is not the best tool for crosscutting very wide, heavy, or long workpieces. For one, it gets wobbly and unsafe as soon as you pull the fence off the front of the saw table. Second, the miter gauge essentially drags workpieces across the table, which works fine for small parts but not so great when that little gauge is trying to keep a long, heavy workpiece square to the blade.

So if your workpiece is too big and heavy to be safely supported by the miter gauge, find another way to crosscut it. One is simply to use your circular saw and cutting guide. Another is to make a crosscut sled for your tablesaw, as we'll do in Chapter 4.

Well, those are the tablesaw basics. I know it's a lot to take in all at once, but it's all pretty critical. So if anything still seems fuzzy, give this chapter one more read. You'll be relying on these techniques and principles for the rest of your woodworking life, so they are well worth the investment.

SAFE WAY TO CROSSCUT SHORT PIECES

When you need to cut off a series of identical short pieces, there is an unsafe way to do it and a much better way.

DON'T USE THE RIP FENCE AS A CROSSCUT STOP. Once the short piece is cut free, it will be trapped between the blade and rip fence, where it can twist and spring toward you.

CLAMP A STOP BLOCK TO THE FENCE. Clamp a block well ahead of the blade and bump your workpiece against it before cutting. Then, when the small piece is cut free, it will have room to twist or move without causing problems.

UPGRADE YOUR MITER GAUGE FOR SMOOTH CROSSCUTS

Your tablesaw comes with a miter gauge for crosscutting parts to length, but it needs some help.

1 **FENCE IS TOO SHORT.** The short fence on a standard miter gauge does not adequately control large boards, leading to poor cuts.

2 **ADD AN AUXILIARY FENCE.** Rip a straight piece of ¾-in.-thick plywood and screw it onto your miter-gauge fence. Most miter gauges have holes or slots for this, but you can drill holes in them if they don't.

3 **SQUARE IT UP.** Place a square against the fence and blade, making sure the square doesn't touch the teeth. Adjust the miter gauge so there is no gap between the square and the blade and then lock down the 90-degree stop on the miter gauge, so it is easy to return the fence to 90 degrees if you move it.

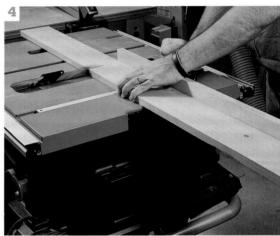

4 **MUCH BETTER SUPPORT.** The long fence makes it easy to keep boards stable and square to the blade.

5 **EASY CUT ALIGNMENT.** The slot the blade cuts in the auxiliary fence shows you exactly where the blade will cut, making it easy to line up a pencil mark and cut right to the line.

6 **EASY TO ADD A STOP BLOCK.** If you make the fence a little longer than your workpieces, you can add a stop block for repeat cuts. Just hook your tape into the blade slot in the fence and make your mark on the fence. Before clamping on the block, use a square to draw a line at your mark, so the stop block goes on square too.

7 **STOP-BLOCK BASICS.** To use a stop block effectively, first make a clean, square crosscut on one end of your workpiece. That end goes against the block to cut the opposite end to accurate length.

8 **EVEN BETTER CROSSCUTS.** Aftermarket miter gauges have longer fences and a more precise way to set them at common angles. Later in this book we'll build a crosscut sled, which will provide an even more versatile and accurate means for crosscutting, as well as a variety of joinery cuts.

TABLESAW UPGRADE: ZERO-CLEARANCE THROAT PLATE

As you read through this book, you'll start to understand why zero-clearance cut support is a big deal in woodworking. Many sawing and drilling operations exert heavy pressure on workpieces. That pressure isn't a problem where the bit or blade enters the cut, but it can cause extreme chipping (called "blowout") where it exits at the bottom or back of the workpiece.

The simple cure for this problem is zero-clearance cut support. This is what we created when we attached that extra fence to our miter gauge, and it's the same thing you'll see me doing on the drill press, when I place a piece of plywood or MDF under the workpiece I'm drilling.

Another place on your tablesaw that could use zero-clearance support is the throat plate, which fills the big opening around the blade, called the throat. Your standard throat plate will have an extra-large slot in it, designed to allow the blade to be tilted sideways for bevel cuts. This throat plate will do its basic job, preventing boards from diving into the big opening in the table, but it doesn't support the bottom edge of cuts. That's OK for rip cuts, which are in line with the grain and don't tend to splinter,

MAKE CLEANER CROSSCUTS

The standard throat plate for a tablesaw has an extra-wide slot, which is fine for rip cuts, but not so great for crosscuts, which are prone to chipping along the bottom edge.

1 THE PROBLEM. The wide slot in a standard throat plate does not support the bottom edge of the cut, allowing chipout like this.

2 THE SOLUTION. You can make or buy a blank throat plate for most table saws. This one is made for our Bosch saw and screws down securely. It also has small screws that will bring it perfectly level with the saw table. After installing it, bring the spinning blade up through it to create a tight, "zero-clearance" blade slot.

3 THE PROOF. The zero-clearance blade slot prevents chipping at the bottom edge of the cut, making your work much cleaner.

but not for crosscuts, which tend to chip out on the bottom edge. Also, when you trim just a sliver off any board, the thin offcut tends to dive down into that extra-large slot, where it can jam and cause problems.

This is why most woodworkers either buy or make a blank throat plate for their saws, and then bring the spinning blade up through it to create a zero-clearance blade opening. This tight blade slot eliminates chipout and lets you work more safely.

On our Bosch portable saw, it's tricky to make your own throat plates, because the thickness of the stock throat plate doesn't match the thickness of commonly available plywood. But Bosch

sells blank throat plates for this purpose; they are very inexpensive on Amazon, so I'm using a few of those.

Since we're buying our blank plates, I won't go into the process of making them. If you do make your own, however, the only tricky step is finding a safe way to hold it down when you bring the spinning blade up through it. Watch a few tutorials on YouTube for easy ways to do it. By the way, this step isn't a problem with Bosch's blank plates, since they include small screws that hold the plate firmly in place. Bosch also sells a throat plate designed to accommodate a wide stack of dado blades. If you're making your own blank plates, make a couple of extras for this purpose.

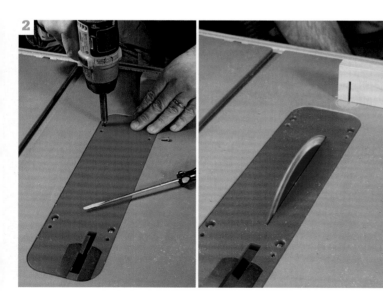

build a
workbench
tool cabinet

WHETHER YOU BUILD
the workbench featured in Chapter 1 or
some other design, putting a tool cabinet
in the base is a great idea. The one we'll
build in this chapter is large enough to
store all of the hand tools you're likely to
own, keeping them safe, dust-free, and
within arm's reach, with plenty of room
left over for bench accessories and a host
of other tools and supplies.

This cabinet is designed to slip neatly
into the base of our bench, but you can
customize it to fit any workbench without changing the overall design. Like the
workbench itself, the tool cabinet can
be built with very basic tools and
techniques, while looking and working
great for decades. As a bonus, it
will teach you a number of handy
cabinetmaking techniques, which you
can use on many other projects.

To match the benchtop, I'm making
the cabinet out of Baltic-birch plywood,
with the same stripey edges. But you
can make yours out of any type of plywood or MDF that looks good to you and
fits your budget. The keys here are the
overall design and techniques, which are
relatively straightforward and effective.
You'll learn how to cut the big cabinet
parts accurately plus an easy way to
assemble them. Once you've built the
case, I'll show you a straightforward,
fun approach to good-looking,
smooth-sliding drawers.

GOOD-LOOKING AND HARDWORKING. This
workbench storage cabinet features smooth-
sliding drawers in two sizes, with enough
space to stow a pile of tools and accessories.

DADO SETS

A dado set—a.k.a. "stack dado" or "dado blades"—consists of two outside blades, designed to cut the edges of the notch crisply and cleanly, and "chippers," specialized blades that get stacked between the outside ones, determining how wide the notch will be. Between those blades go thin spacers, called shims, that let you fine-tune the width of the notch by the tiniest increments.

A dado set removes a lot of wood in one pass, so you have to take it slow with your workpieces, and sometimes make a cut in several passes, raising the blades a little higher each time. You'll need to use a different throat plate with your dado blades, one with a much wider slot in it. You can start with a blank throat plate and use the dado stack to cut its own slot in the plate or buy a ready-made plate with the wide slot in it already.

The notches you can cut with your dado set are all variations of the same thing, but they have different names. A three-sided slot is called a "dado" if it runs across the grain. These are used most often to create shelves in bookcases and cabinets. Run that same slot in line with the grain and it's just called a slot. When you cut the slot at the very edge of a workpiece, that two-sided notch is called a rabbet, no matter which way the grain is running. These are used most often to attach cabinet tops and bottoms to cabinet sides, or in our case, along the back edges of a cabinet to hold the back panel.

The names aren't really important, but now you'll know what other woodworkers are talking about (maybe even better than they do).

DADO SET OPENS UP A WORLD OF TABLESAW JOINERY

In this project, we'll be taking the tablesaw to the next level with a dado set, which is a stack of blades used in various combinations to cut clean, precise notches, opening up a world of helpful joints (see the sidebar on p. 55). We'll use the dado set to slot the sides of the cabinet for the drawers and notch the back edges to accept the cabinet back.

Our simple drawers feature overlapping bottoms, which fit into those slots in the sides. This is a simple way to make smooth-sliding drawers. The slots show up at the front edges of the cabinet, but on a shop project like this, they look just fine.

SMART APPROACH TO ASSEMBLY

There are a handful of ways to assemble big cabinet parts like these, but once again we'll choose the straightest path, using screws alone to create strong connections. You'll see the screws at the top and bottom edges of the cabinet, at least at first, but not after you insert the cabinet into the base of the workbench. Using screws without glue also lets you disassemble the cabinet if necessary, in case you forget a slot or two, or something else goes wrong.

If you've had bad experiences using screws in the past, it's probably because you didn't use both clearance holes and pilot holes, two essential but often misunderstood elements of a rock-solid screw joint. Leave out the clearance holes, and the two parts you're joining could end up with a space between them that you can't close; get the pilot holes wrong, and you'll likely either strip the screws or split the wood. Check the drawing below for the simple but essential components of a strong screw joint.

The trick when using screws alone to join big cabinet parts is keeping the parts perfectly in line while drilling the holes and driving the screws. So we'll be making a pair of simple clamping blocks to hold the parts in position (see p. 63). They're easy to make and they work like a charm, completing our rock-solid cabinet-making system.

THE SECRET TO SUPER-STRONG SCREWS

Drill the right-size clearance holes and pilot holes, and your screws will be incredibly strong. A countersink at the top lets the screw heads sit flat.

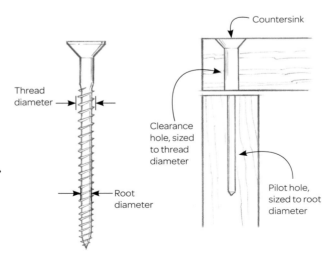

Thread diameter

Root diameter

Countersink

Clearance hole, sized to thread diameter

Pilot hole, sized to root diameter

PROJECT Nº.

tool cabinet made easy

For almost all furniture that contains drawers, woodworkers build the case first, then measure its interior and cut drawer parts to fit. That's because drawers rely on pretty tight tolerances to slide smoothly, and you don't want to pre-cut a bunch of parts only to have them end up too small, or pre-make drawers that end up a little too big.

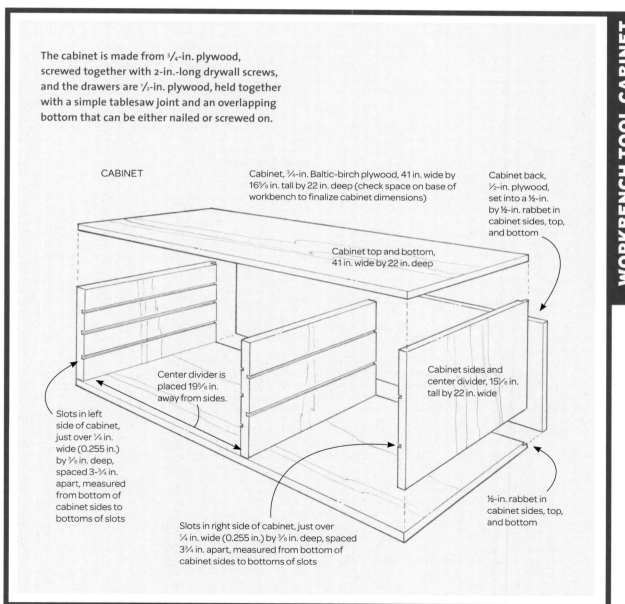

WORKBENCH TOOL CABINET

The cabinet is made from ³/₄-in. plywood, screwed together with 2-in.-long drywall screws, and the drawers are ¹/₂-in. plywood, held together with a simple tablesaw joint and an overlapping bottom that can be either nailed or screwed on.

CABINET

Cabinet, ³/₄-in. Baltic-birch plywood, 41 in. wide by 16⁵/₈ in. tall by 22 in. deep (check space on base of workbench to finalize cabinet dimensions)

Cabinet back, ¹/₂-in. plywood, set into a ¹/₂-in. by ¹/₂-in. rabbet in cabinet sides, top, and bottom

Cabinet top and bottom, 41 in. wide by 22 in. deep

Center divider is placed 19⁵/₈ in. away from sides.

Cabinet sides and center divider, 15¹/₈ in. tall by 22 in. wide

Slots in left side of cabinet, just over ¹/₄ in. wide (0.255 in.) by ³/₈ in. deep, spaced 3-³/₄ in. apart, measured from bottom of cabinet sides to bottoms of slots

½-in. rabbet in cabinet sides, top, and bottom

Slots in right side of cabinet, just over ¹/₄ in. wide (0.255 in.) by ³/₈ in. deep, spaced 3³/₄ in. apart, measured from bottom of cabinet sides to bottoms of slots

TOOL CABINET MADE EASY

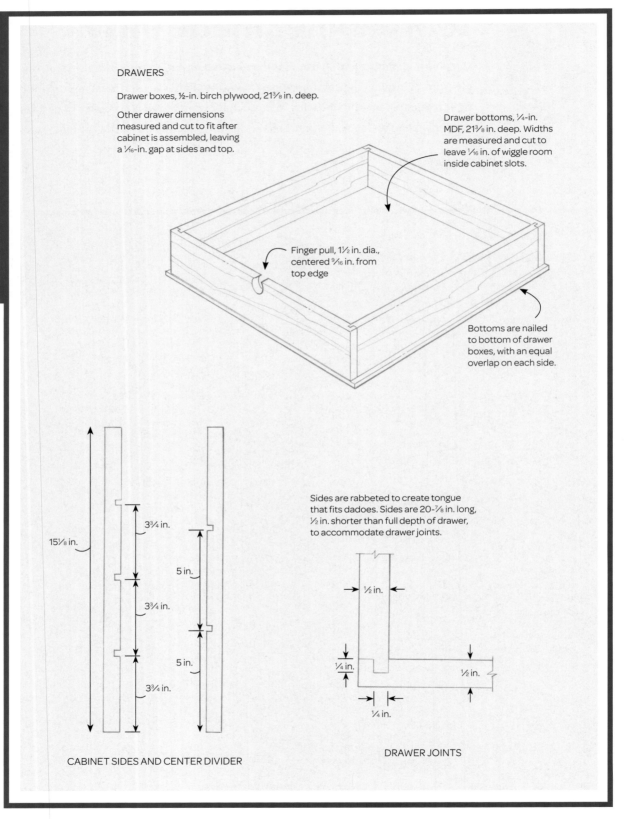

DRAWERS

Drawer boxes, ½-in. birch plywood, 21⅜ in. deep.

Other drawer dimensions measured and cut to fit after cabinet is assembled, leaving a ¹⁄₁₆-in. gap at sides and top.

Drawer bottoms, ¼-in. MDF, 21⅜ in. deep. Widths are measured and cut to leave ¹⁄₁₆ in. of wiggle room inside cabinet slots.

Finger pull, 1½ in. dia., centered ⁹⁄₁₆ in. from top edge

Bottoms are nailed to bottom of drawer boxes, with an equal overlap on each side.

15⅛ in.

3¾ in.

5 in.

3¾ in.

5 in.

3¾ in.

CABINET SIDES AND CENTER DIVIDER

Sides are rabbeted to create tongue that fits dadoes. Sides are 20-⅞ in. long, ½ in. shorter than full depth of drawer, to accommodate drawer joints.

½ in.

¼ in.

½ in.

¼ in.

DRAWER JOINTS

CUT OUT THE CABINET PARTS

As we did for the workbench top, we'll start by breaking down a full sheet of plywood into slightly oversized parts, using a circular saw and saw guide. Those parts will be much easier to handle on the tablesaw, where we will rip them to final width.

1 MARK SQUARE LINES. Place your combination square on both sides of the parts to mark square lines.

2 USE YOUR CIRCULAR SAW TO MAKE THE CUTS. Use the saw guide featured earlier in this book to cut all the parts to size.

3 TABLESAW CAN HELP. The sides and center divider are short enough to crosscut on the tablesaw. Cut them extra wide at first, then mark a square corner and be sure to run that against the rip fence to be sure the other edge ends up square too.

MATERIALS & SUPPLIES

- (½) 4x8 sheet of ¾-in. Baltic-birch plywood (or a single 5x5 sheet if you can find it)
- (1) 4x8 sheet of ½-in. birch plywood (doesn't have to be Baltic birch)
- (1) 4x8 sheet of ¼-in. MDF (medium-density fiberboard)
- Box of 2-in.-long drywall screws
- Small screws, brads, or finish nails for attaching cabinet back and drawer bottoms
- Minwax Tung Oil Finish

DADO THE CABINET SIDES

An 8-in. dado set is a versatile stack of blades that can make precise notches up to $^{13}/_{16}$ in. wide. We'll use it here to slot the cabinet sides for the drawer bottoms, and later to notch the cabinet parts to hold the back. You can lower or remove the blade splitter to use the dado set.

1 SET UP THE DADO BLADES. We'll only need the outside and inside blades here, with a thin spacer between. The dado set includes a number of these thin shims in various thicknesses. After tightening the blades in place, measure across the teeth with your dial calipers. You are shooting for about 0.255 in.

2 TRUTH IS IN THE TEST CUTS. Make a test cut in a piece of scrap, and slide a piece of the $^{1}/_{4}$-in. MDF (for the drawer bottoms) in it to make sure it slides smoothly without too much wiggle. Adjust your dado blades if necessary by replacing the shims (spacers) or adding another. Adjust the blade height so the dadoes end up $^{3}/_{8}$ in. deep. Note that I replaced the standard throat plate with one that has a wider slot in it.

3 CUT THE DADOES. Lay out the edges of the cabinet sides and center divider for the correct slot spacing. Mark the bottom edge of each slot, and mark an "X" above the line to be sure you cut on the correct side of it.

4 DOUBLE-CHECK THE DADO LOCATIONS. Stack all the vertical cabinet parts to make sure all of the dadoes line up. Note the triangle I marked to indicate the top edge of the parts and their correct orientation.

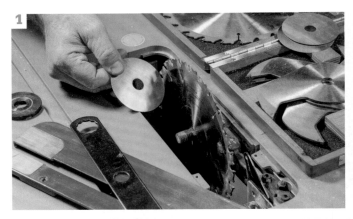

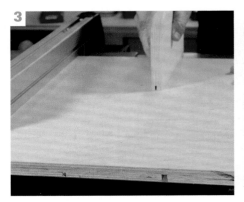

ADD AN AUXILIARY RIP FENCE FOR RABBET CUTS ━━━

To cut rabbets on a tablesaw, there can't be any gap between the dado stack and the rip fence. It's nearly impossible to have the blades spinning against the fence without damaging it, so woodworkers add an extra wood fence to the rip fence and usually bury the blades in it slightly. It sounds tricky but it's not. You just clamp on the auxiliary fence, lower the blades fully, bring the wood fence slightly over the top of them, and then turn on the tablesaw and crank the spinning blades up into the fence.

Once the dado blades have cut a little pocket out of the fence, you'll be able to move the fence around to fine-tune the size of the rabbets. Follow the photos at right and on p. 62 to see how it all works. We'll also be using rabbets and dadoes for the handy drawer joint coming up next.

1 ADD CHIPPERS THIS TIME. Chippers are special blades that go between the inside and outside blades of a dado stack, to make it any width you require. Add a couple of these, plus a few shims, to make the stack a little over ½ in. wide.

2 ADD AN AUXILIARY FENCE TO YOUR RIP FENCE. We'll need to bury the dado blades slightly in this fence to cut our rabbets. Any piece of plywood or MDF will serve as this extra fence. Place the clamps high enough that the workpieces will slide under them.

3 DIAL IN YOUR RABBETS. With the auxiliary fence clamped on and the blades adjusted upward to almost touch its bottom edge, adjust the rip fence so the dado blades will create a ½-in.-wide rabbet and lock it there.

4 RAISE THE BLADES. Now raise the spinning blades up into the bottom of your plywood fence. Turn them off and check the height. You want it to be ½ in.

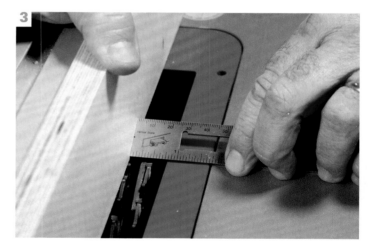

5 PERFECT RABBETS. Press your cabinet parts firmly against the table and fence to form accurate rabbets. Be sure to keep your hands clear of the blades where they emerge at the back edge.

6 SUPPORT LONG WORKPIECES. Use a work stand or outfeed table to support the parts as they come off the back of the table. This will let you focus on keeping your hands safe.

7 DON'T FORGET TO TRIM THE CENTER DIVIDER. The center divider is ½ in. narrower from front to back, to accommodate the cabinet back. Use the rabbeted parts to set the rip fence (center right) and then trim the center divider (bottom right).

GET READY TO ASSEMBLE THE CABINETS

All we need are long screws to assemble this cabinet. To keep the parts aligned perfectly while we drill them and drive the screws, we'll use a pair of handy shop-made clamping blocks.

1 MARK THE PARTS. Draw lines on the top and bottom panels to mark the location of the center divider as well as the inside edges of the cabinet sides.

2 DRILL CLEARANCE HOLES. The clearance holes need to be the same size or just a hair larger than the outside diameter of the screws. Place the top and bottom on some scrap wood and drill five holes along each edge, and five more for attaching the center divider. You can countersink the holes afterward or use a combination drill-countersink as I did.

3 MAKE A PAIR OF CLAMP BLOCKS. Cut out the square parts, drill the clamping holes, and then angle your miter gauge at 45 degrees to cut the angled edges as shown.

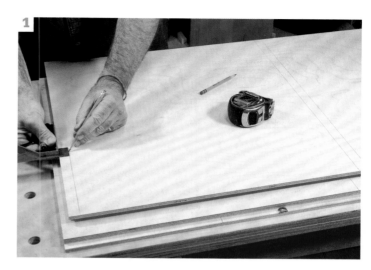

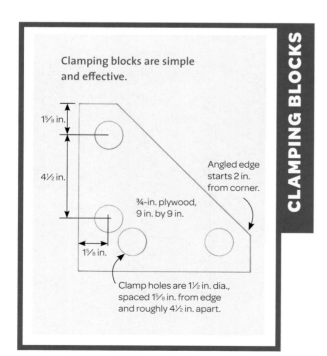

Clamping blocks are simple and effective.

1⅝ in.

4½ in.

Angled edge starts 2 in. from corner.

¾-in. plywood, 9 in. by 9 in.

1⅝ in.

Clamp holes are 1½ in. dia., spaced 1⅝ in. from edge and roughly 4½ in. apart.

CLAMPING BLOCKS

ASSEMBLY IS STRAIGHTFORWARD

The clamping blocks ensure that the parts are perfectly aligned, and they let you tackle one joint at a time.

1 ATTACH A BLOCK. Start by clamping a block so it lines up with the end of one of the cabinet sides. Your fingers will tell you if it's flush.

2 CLAMP IT TO THE CABINET BOTTOM. Line up the side and front edges of the parts and lock down the block.

3 DRILL A PILOT HOLE. Pick a drill bit that's roughly the same diameter as the root diameter of the screw, measure between the threads, and then reach up through the clearance hole in the bottom panel to drill a pilot hole in the cabinet side.

4 DRIVE A SCREW. Drive a screw into the hole you just drilled. Now you can remove the clamp block at this end and go to work on the opposite edge of the same side panel.

5 LOCK DOWN THE OTHER END. Rotate the cabinet on the workbench and clamp the block at the opposite edge, drilling a pilot hole there and driving another screw.

6 TIP IT UP AND FINISH THE JOB. With the two ends of the side panel locked in place, you can tip the cabinet on edge to finish drilling pilot holes and driving screws in the other three locations. Repeat this process to attach the vertical divider and the other side of the cabinet to the bottom panel.

7 ADD THE TOP. Tackling one joint at a time, using both of your clamping blocks to align the parts, drill pilot holes and drive screws to finish assembling the cabinet.

8 SAND THE EDGES. I'm using my all-time-favorite sanding block here—the "Preppin' Weapon"—along with 150-grit sandpaper to smooth the edges of the cabinet and make a tiny 45-degree bevel on all the sharp corners. After sanding, apply a coat of oil finish to the areas that will be visible under the bench.

9 SLIDE YOUR CABINET INTO PLACE. If you sized the parts correctly, your new cabinet should slide easily into place, with minor gaps at the top and sides. Lock it in place by driving a couple of screws into the front legs as shown. Be sure to countersink them so they don't get in the way of the drawers.

10 NAIL IN THE BACK. Cut a piece of ½-in. plywood to fit in the rabbets, prefinish it, and nail on the back. I'm using an air-powered brad nailer here, with 1¼-in.-long brads, but small screws or finish nails would also work. No glue is necessary.

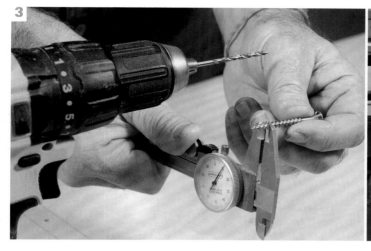

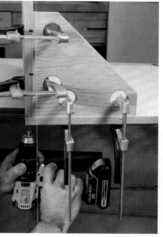

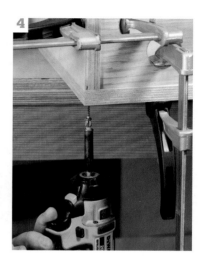

CUT THE DRAWER PARTS TO SIZE

Once you've got your cabinet assembled and slid into place, you're ready to measure for the drawer parts. You'll understand pretty quickly why we waited to make the drawers. It's difficult to get that middle divider panel perfectly centered in the cabinet, so the drawer widths are likely to be ever-so-slightly different on each side. It's also nearly impossible to divide the vertical space so evenly that every drawer on each side is exactly the same height. No worries. It's very easy to size each set of drawer parts for its unique opening.

Start by cutting the $\frac{1}{4}$-in. MDF drawer bottoms to fit their slots. The slots are already sized to fit the thickness of the MDF, so all you have to do is cut the parts to the right depth and width. The depth of all of the drawers is the same: roughly $\frac{1}{8}$ in. less than the interior depth of the cabinet. That will leave the drawers inset slightly, which looks nice. So start by ripping all of your MDF to that depth dimension. You can use your saw guide and circular saw to cut the full sheet down a bit first or buy the MDF in 2-ft. by-4-ft. panels.

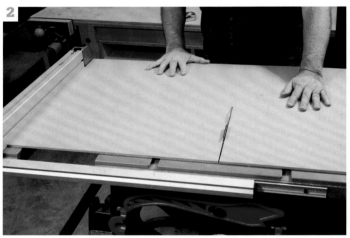

1 START WITH THE DRAWER BOTTOMS. All of the $\frac{1}{4}$-in. MDF bottoms are the same depth, but their widths will vary. The bottom ones are narrower, because they don't slide in slots at all, and they also need $\frac{1}{16}$ in. of wiggle room on each side. To measure the rest, measure from one end of a slot to another, and cut the bottom $\frac{1}{8}$ in. narrower than that total width.

2 2X4 PANELS ARE EASIER TO HANDLE. You can buy MDF in 2-ft. by-4-ft. panels at your local home center. Rip these to the universal drawer depth, and then crosscut them as shown.

3 RIP THE PARTS TO HEIGHT. The spaces between the drawer bottoms will vary slightly. Cut each set of four drawer parts to the same height, to fit neatly above their MDF drawer bottom with a $\frac{1}{16}$-in. gap above them.

4 NOW CROSSCUT THEM TO LENGTH. The fronts and backs should fit into their openings with a $\frac{1}{16}$-in. gap at each end, and the sides should be cut $\frac{1}{2}$ in. shorter than the final drawer depth to accommodate the corner joints coming up next.

USE YOUR DADO SET TO MAKE A COOL JOINT ▬▬▬

As with almost every other woodworking task, there's more than one way to tackle it successfully, depending on the tools you own. To build these drawer boxes, for example, small biscuits would work nicely, so if you have a biscuit joiner, go for it. But we'll be using a really slick tablesaw joint, made with the dado set I just introduced.

The drawer joint is made by cutting a small dado in the fronts and backs of the drawer boxes, and then rabbeting the sides to create a small tongue that fits into those little dadoes, as seen in the drawing on p. 58 and photos at right and on p. 68. Test cuts on extra pieces of the same plywood are the key to dialing in each part of the joint for a perfect fit.

1 SET UP A ¼-IN. DADO STACK. The birch plywood I used is exactly ½ in. thick, and you want your dadoes to be exactly one-half as wide. Because these dadoes go across the grain, they will be prone to chipping, so I inserted a blank throat plate in the tablesaw and brought the spinning blades up through it to create a zero-clearance slot that will prevent splintering.

2 GET THE DEPTH RIGHT TOO. Raise the blade height until your slots are exactly half as deep as the material is thick, in this case, ¼ in. deep.

3 NOW DIAL IN THE LOCATION. Use the handy depth gauge at the end of your dial calipers to set the rip fence so it's ½ in. from the outside edge of the dado blades, or the exact thickness of your drawer parts.

4 CUT A DADO AND CHECK IT. Use your miter gauge to support the parts, with the rip fence acting as a stop. Then tuck another piece of plywood against one edge of the dado to see if the outside edges line up.

5 DADO ALL YOUR PARTS. With your setup dialed in, it only takes a few minutes to dado all of the drawer front and backs.

6 SET UP THE SAW FOR THE OTHER PART OF THE JOINT. You should be able to leave the blade height right where it is, add an auxiliary fence to your rip fence, and bring it over so it just kisses the side of the dado blades.

7 MAKE A TEST CUT. To cut these small rabbets, you'll once again support the parts with your miter gauge and use the rip fence as a stop.

8 DIAL IN THE FIT. If the fit is too loose or too tight, adjust the blade height as needed. If you need a wider rabbet, just widen your stack of dado blades, bury them partly in the fence as we did earlier, and adjust the rip fence as needed. Once the tongue fits well and the parts line up nicely, ditch your test pieces and rabbet all of your drawer sides.

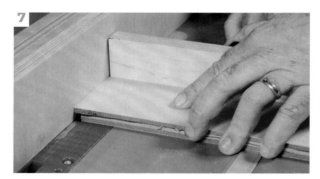

PREP THE PARTS FOR ASSEMBLY

There are a few easy steps before you're ready to assemble your drawers and celebrate. One of my favorite drawer pulls is nothing more than a largish hole drilled at the top of each drawer front, slightly overlapping the edge. These partial holes are simple but stylish, and a Forstner bit handles the job perfectly on the drill press. If you don't have a drill press, feel free to attach any pull you like.

1 DRILL THE FIRST FINGER PULL. Use the dimensions in the drawing on p. 58 to mark one of the holes and set up a fence to drill with a Forstner bit as shown. Be sure to have a sacrificial piece of wood underneath to prevent chipout.

2 DRILL THE REST. Place the drill in the first hole to set up a stop block (far left in the photo) for locating all of the rest. Drilling those will go quickly now.

3 SAND AND FINISH THE FRONTS. The fronts are all you'll see in the finished cabinet, so they are the only drawer parts you need to sand and finish. Sand the front faces, top edges, and ends for comfort and good looks, using 150-grit paper, but leave the bottom edges square, so they mate up with the drawer bottoms nicely. Then wipe oil finish on those same surfaces.

TIPS FOR TROUBLE-FREE DRAWER ASSEMBLY

Start every glue-up (woodworking slang for any glued assembly) with a dry-fit, to be sure everything comes together and you have the right clamps before you start spreading glue. Fine-tune the joints now if necessary. I'll be attaching the drawer bottom with 3/4-in.-long air-powered brads, but you could also hand-drive screws or small finish nails to do so.

If you go with hand-driven nails, predrill the drawer bottoms first, so the nails are easier to drive without shifting the parts. If you go with screws, use the same principles you used to screw together the cabinet parts: clearance holes, pilot holes, and a small countersink to make sure the screw heads sit flush.

1 JOINT GETS A LIGHT LAYER OF GLUE. Working on one drawer box at a time, squeeze a narrow bead of Titebond III into each dado, spread it evenly with a small brush, and then use the excess to paint a light layer onto the rabbeted ends of the joint.

2 CLAMP THEM UP. Assemble the joints by hand, as best you can, and then clamp them fully together with whatever clamps you have. Whichever you use, be sure they are centered on the joints, so they don't pull the box out of square. Give the boxes an hour in the clamps.

3 START ATTACHING THE DRAWER BOTTOM. Begin by setting your combination square to create an even overlap at each side of the drawer. Then, starting at a front corner, line up the front edges of the drawer box and bottom, set the overlap at that edge, and drive a nail near the corner.

4 CONTINUE ALONG THE FRONT EDGE. Even out the front edges of the box and bottom, and drive nails all the way across to lock the front end of the drawer bottom in perfect position. Angle the nails slightly inward so they don't accidentally emerge on the outside of the box.

5 NOW THE BACK EDGE. Spin the drawer around, flex the drawer a little to be sure the overlap is correct there too, checking it with your combination square, and hold the bottom in place while you fire nails along the back edge.

6 SIDE EDGES ARE LAST. Use the same combination-square setting to draw lines that mark the outer edges of the drawer box and use those to guide you as you shoot nails about 1/4 in. away from the line.

7 ADD LINERS AND TOOLS. I like to place rubber-mesh drawer liner material in my tool drawers. This cabinet is large enough to store all of the hand tools you are ever likely to own, as well as bench accessories and more.

FINISHING TOUCHES

Before applying a simple oil finish, I sanded all the parts with 150-grit sandpaper, held on a sanding block, and softened the sharp corners with the same block. To put a light bevel (called a chamfer) on sharp edges, I take a specific amount of strokes along each edge—between 8 and 12, depending on how much of a chamfer I want—with the block held at 45 degrees.

After that, just as I did on the benchtop, which is made out of the same birch plywood, I applied a coat of the same Minwax Tung Oil Finish, which adds a bit of warm color that pairs nicely with the color of the construction lumber.

4

build a tablesaw crosscut sled

YOUR SAW COMES with a special jig for making crosscuts, called a miter gauge, which we covered in Chapter 2. It's lightweight and handy, and will do an admirable job on smaller workpieces, especially if you make the improvements recommended in that chapter.

But the miter gauge isn't the best tool for all crosscuts. For a start, it can't handle wide workpieces safely. Those force you to pull the fence off the front of the table, making the miter gauge wobbly and unsafe. Secondly, the miter gauge essentially drags workpieces across the table, which works fine for small parts but not so great when that little jig is trying to keep a long, heavy workpiece square to the blade.

For these reasons and more, most woodworkers make a custom crosscut sled for their saw. There are a few commercial versions, but you can make a better sled than you can buy, and you'll save money in the process.

Your shopmade sled will cover the entire table and then some, carrying both parts of your workpiece safely past the blade. It also includes two miter runners, which slide in both of your saw's miter slots, ensuring that the sled works smoothly and accurately for years to come. The only downsides to a sled (vs. a miter gauge) is that the sled is heavier and more awkward to move on and off your saw, and you have to make it. But like everything else in the previous chapters, it will pay dividends for a decade or more.

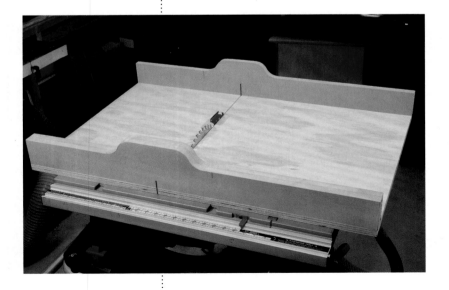

WHY A CROSSCUT SLED BEATS A MITER GAUGE. Unlike the miter gauge included with your tablesaw, a crosscut sled is guided by two runners and both of your saw's miter slots. It also has a longer fence and carries workpieces smoothly past the blade instead of dragging them over the table.

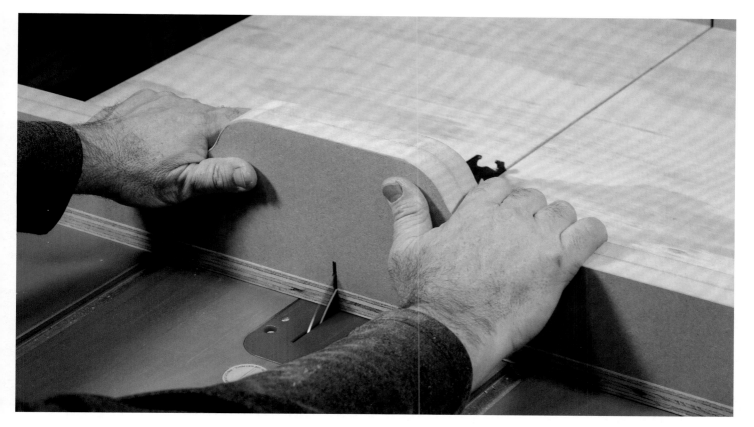

THREE REASONS FOR THE BUMP. The big bump in the fences is a physical reminder to keep your hands clear of the blade slot. It also keeps the fences strong even if you cut through the sled at full blade height, and it makes the rest of the fence shorter, for easier clamping and work-holding.

There are a number of ways to make a crosscut sled, but the following is one of the easiest, using only the tablesaw you already own. The trickiest tasks are cutting precise hardwood runners and attaching them to the sled so they slide perfectly in the miter slots, and then attaching the front fence perfectly square to the blade. But no worries—I've got slick tricks for each of those challenges.

Because of how a crosscut sled is built—with two runners vs. one, and a base that carries the work past the blade—it's also generally more accurate than even the best miter gauge, which is why woodworkers prefer the sled for their most important crosscuts. Better yet, the sled not only has a zero-clearance slot in its front fence but also one in the base, ensuring clean cuts with no chipping on either the rear or lower edge of a workpiece.

A crosscut sled is also the best platform for a number of cool joinery cuts, including miters, notches, and box joints, opening up a new world of project possibilities. Some of those joinery setups require angling the blade or using the sled in conjunction with a dado blade, both of which will widen that neat, zero-clearance slot in the base and fence, but both surfaces are easy to refresh. You just use double-stick tape to attach a layer of 1/4-in. MDF to the base and fence, put your normal blade back on the saw, set it to 90 degrees, and make another clean cut through the sled. Presto, your zero-clearance blade slot is restored.

CUT THE BASE TO SIZE

I recommend making your first sled as deep, front to back, as your saw will support, because you never really know what you'll be cutting on it. That said, there's a limit to how much sled you'll want to lug around your shop and onto the saw. I'll make this version as large as our compact Bosch tablesaw can safely handle, or about 24 in. by 36 in. That size not only fits the saw nicely but also means we'll be able to make the base and fences from 2-ft. by 4-ft. pieces of plywood and MDF available at home centers. Those smaller panels are easier to transport and easier to handle on the tablesaw.

Speaking of plywood and MDF, both are great choices on their own, but we'll be using a smart combo of the two. We'll make the base out of 3/4-in. plywood, because it is lighter than MDF, making the whole sled lighter, and provides better gripping power for the short screws that will attach the runners. Then we'll use 3/4-in. MDF for the fences, since MDF tends to be very flat and straight.

The base panel is already the right width for the project—24 in.—but I would still take a whisker off both of the long edges, just to clean them up. You can do this with rip cuts on your tablesaw. To cut the base to length, lay out a square, accurate cut and make it with your circular saw and saw guide, as shown in the workbench chapter (Chapter 1). For the fences, you'll need three strips of MDF, which you can simply rip off your 2x4 panel on the tablesaw and then cut to length on your miter saw (or with your circ saw again).

SLED HANDLES WORKPIECES OF ALL SIZES. The long fences and generous depth of the sled (front to back) accommodate everything from big cabinetry panels to long boards.

GET SERIOUS ABOUT DUST COLLECTION

We've made it this far without talking about wood dust, so I'm guessing it's piling up on the floor at this point. Wood dust is not only a nuisance for woodworkers but also a hazard, with the finest particles hanging longest in the air and penetrating deepest into your airways.

You can sweep up after you work, but that gets tedious, and it won't keep dust out of your lungs. The best solution by far is collecting dust at the source.

All power tools and machines have a dust port on them, often with a small dust bag attached. Put the bag aside—it's almost worthless—and connect a powerful shop vacuum or true dust collector to each of your tools. You'll save time on cleanup, and your lungs and sinuses will be happier too.

A shop vacuum will work for all of your handheld power tools—like sanders—and many of your benchtop machines too, like our stationary sander and miter saw. Look for a vac with HEPA filtration.

Larger machines like a tablesaw are a different deal. These need a lot more air moving through them to collect all the dust and chips they produce, and the small hose on a shop vac just can't move that much volume.

A true dust collector has a lot more power and a bigger hose, able to grab a higher volume of larger chips. These come in a wide range of sizes, but a smaller ¾-hp or 1-hp model will do just fine if you keep it relatively close to the machine.

far left: MACHINES NEED A TRUE DUST COLLECTOR. This ¾-hp, wall-mounted unit from Rockler has a canister filter that collects dust down to 1 micron in size. Team it up with one of Rockler's "Dust Right" expandable hoses and it will reach every machine in your shop, starting with the tablesaw.

left: SHOP VACS ARE GREAT FOR POWER TOOLS. Connect a shop vac to your sander, and it will not only be dust-free but actually work better too. Without a pile of dust under the disk, the sandpaper will last longer and work better.

3

crosscut sled, an indispensable tablesaw helper

Almost every woodworker ends up making a crosscut sled like this one for their tablesaw. It's not hard to build, and it will deliver furniture-quality crosscuts on workpieces of all sizes.

ANATOMY OF A SOLID SLED

Almost all crosscut sleds include the same basic elements, but there are a number of ways to execute them and attach them accurately. I've combined the best of the best, to make things as easy as possible.

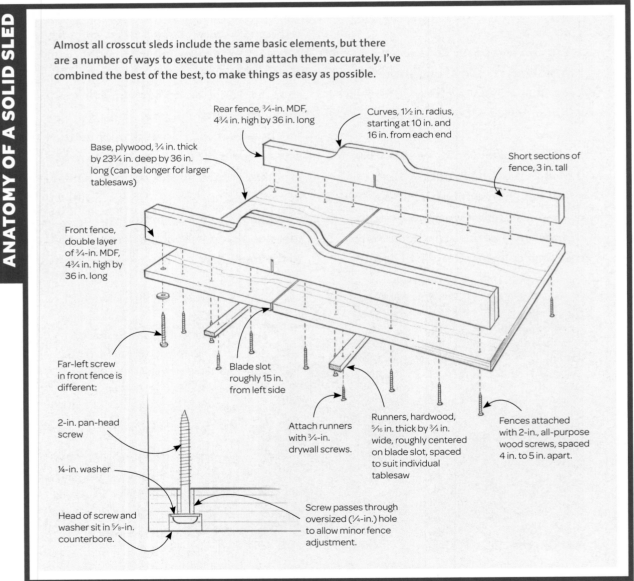

Rear fence, ¾-in. MDF, 4¾ in. high by 36 in. long

Curves, 1½ in. radius, starting at 10 in. and 16 in. from each end

Short sections of fence, 3 in. tall

Base, plywood, ¾ in. thick by 23¾ in. deep by 36 in. long (can be longer for larger tablesaws)

Front fence, double layer of ¾-in. MDF, 4¾ in. high by 36 in. long

Far-left screw in front fence is different:

2-in. pan-head screw

¼-in. washer

Head of screw and washer sit in ⅝-in. counterbore.

Blade slot roughly 15 in. from left side

Attach runners with ¾-in. drywall screws.

Runners, hardwood, ⁵⁄₁₆ in. thick by ¾ in. wide, roughly centered on blade slot, spaced to suit individual tablesaw

Fences attached with 2-in., all-purpose wood screws, spaced 4 in. to 5 in. apart.

Screw passes through oversized (¼-in.) hole to allow minor fence adjustment.

HOW TO MAKE ACCURATE HARDWOOD RUNNERS ━━━━

The runners are the first tricky part of this project, but we'll make short work of them with a few cool tips and techniques. The runners on a crosscut sled need to slide nearly perfectly in the miter slots. The width of the slots—³/₄ in.—is what matters most, as that is what keeps the slide on track with no sideways wobble. The depth of the slots—³/₈ in.—isn't as critical; you just need the runners to be a little thinner than that dimension so they don't bottom out.

The best material for the runners is any type of hardwood, so you'll need to find a straight, flat, smooth board that's at least ³/₄ in. thick and 4 in. wide. If you are a more advanced woodworker, you'll be able to joint and plane a smooth, straight board like that yourself. If not, you'll need to find one at your local lumber supplier. There are hardwood retailers almost everywhere that will be glad to help out. Maple and oak are great candidates for runners, but pretty much any hardwood will work, and even some tougher softwoods like alder and poplar.

If you have access to a thickness planer, the best way to fine-tune the hardwood strips for a perfect fit is to plane the faces of a board until its edge drops into the slots, and then rip off the thin strips you need from the edge of that board. We haven't introduced the planer yet, so I'll show you a way to create perfect runners using the tablesaw only.

1 **TRIM THE EDGE OF A BOARD TO FIT.** Stand your hardwood board on edge, and make light trimming cuts, keeping the board vertical against the fence and your fingers out of harm's way. Start at the edge of the board and work your way inward with successive cuts until the edge of the board fits perfectly in the miter slots, sliding smoothly with minimal slop.

2 **SLICE OFF THE RUNNERS.** Make them about ⁵/₁₆ in. thick, so they won't bottom out in the ³/₈-in.-deep miter slots.

HOW TO ATTACH THE RUNNERS ACCURATELY

The next trick with the runners is to get them screwed onto the bottom of the sled base in the perfect position, so they slide perfectly in the two parallel miter slots. Because they fit the slots so well already, there's almost no margin for error.

We'll attach the runners with ¾-in.-long drywall screws, so the first step is to drill five evenly spaced clearance holes in each runner, and countersink them so the screws end up flush at the bottom. The way most woodworkers position the runners accurately is to keep them in their slots while attaching them to the base. We'll do the same, but we'll add an extra step—driving little brads down into the runners from above the base—to make sure they don't shift a little as we screw them on permanently. Follow the photos on the facing page and it will all make sense. The careful, step-by-step process will pay off with a very durable, smooth-sliding sled.

1 DRILL CLEARANCE HOLES. Back up the runners with a piece of scrap wood, to prevent splintering on the bottom side, and make the holes just large enough for the ¾-in. screws to pass through cleanly. Space out five holes across each runner and countersink the holes so the screw heads will sit just below the surface.

MATERIALS & SUPPLIES

- (1) 2-ft. by 4-ft. panel of ¾-in. smooth, flat plywood
- (1) 2-ft. by 4-ft. panel of flat ¾-in. MDF (medium-density fiberboard)
- Straight, flat piece of hardwood, at least ¾ in. thick by 4 in. wide
- (10) ¾-in. drywall screws, for attaching runners
- (20) 2-in. general-purpose screws, for attaching fence
- 2½-in. pan-head screw for adjustable end of front fence
- Bottle of Titebond III glue

2 MAP OUT THEIR LOCATIONS. Sit your freshly trimmed base on top of the saw, with the blade located as shown in the drawing (15 in. from the short edge of the sled) and slide the base slightly forward and back to see where the miter slots are. Draw lines at the edges of the slots.

3 INSERT THE RUNNERS. If either one doesn't slide smoothly in its slot, feel free to sand the edge lightly with a block or lightly against the flat side of your benchtop sander. Then position the runners in their slots, flush with the front edge of the table. They are a bit thinner than the miter slots are deep, so you should also boost them up flush with the top of the saw table by putting dimes or pennies below them.

4 CLAMP DOWN THE BASE. The key here is aligning the base with the front edge of the table, which will position it relatively square to the blade.

5 LOCK THE RUNNERS IN PLACE WITH NAILS. An air-powered nailer works best here, along with ¾-in. brads. Set the nailer to drive the brads deep into the plywood, so they will be sure to stick out the bottom into the runners. If you don't have an air nailer, you can hammer in brads or finish nails, but you'll need to drill slightly smaller pilot holes to make them easy to drive.

6 DRIVE SCREWS IN THE ENDS OF THE RUNNERS. Slide the sled backward just enough to reach the first screw at the end of each runner. The nails and miter slots will keep the runners aligned as you do this. Then slide the sled forward to drive screws in the other end of the runners.

7 FLIP THE SLED AND DRIVE THE OTHER SCREWS. With the nails and the two end screws in each runner, they should stay locked in position as you drive the last three screws.

8 WAX THE BOTTOM. Apply any kind of furniture wax to the edges of the runners to help them slide smoothly without binding. If they are too tight in their slots at this point, you can sand the edges with a block, or even remove them to sand them more.

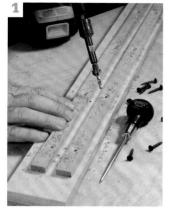

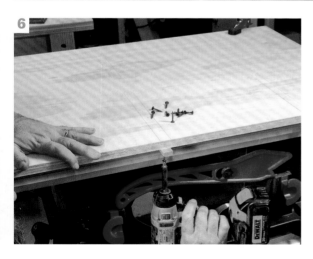

EASY WAY TO MAKE SOLID FENCES

The front and back fences have two main jobs on a crosscut sled. First, they work together to keep the two halves of the sled connected once the sawblade cuts through the base. The front fence also serves to hold workpieces square to the blade, so it's even more critical than the back one.

To support workpieces accurately, the front fence not only has to be perfectly straight but also perfectly plumb—in other words, attached square to the base vertically. There are a number of ways to build a fence that stays perfectly upright, but the easiest is simply to laminate (glue together) two layers of the 3/4-in. MDF, creating a 1 1/2 -in.-thick fence. The thicker fence will not only stay straighter but will also be easy to mount squarely and solidly to the base.

The next step is to shape the fences as shown in the photos on the facing page and the drawing on p. 76. There are a couple of reasons for that bump where the blade passes through. The main one is that it allows the blade to cut through the sled at full height without compromising the strength of fences. We could make the fences that same height along their full length, but it's nice to have the top edges lower where possible to allow your hands to reach over more easily to control workpieces. The lower sections also make it easier to clamp things to the front fence, which will come in handy later in the book.

The other great thing about the bump on the front fence is that it serves as a physical warning to keep your hands away from the spot where the blade pops out. It's really easy to forget about that and leave your fingers in harm's way. Some folks even attach a box or large chunk of wood at that spot, or paint a big red stripe there, to be sure their fingers never stray into the danger zone. Feel free to add that extra measure of safety.

1 RIP STRIPS FOR THE FENCE. Use the tablesaw to rip your 4-ft.-long panel of MDF into 5-in.-wide strips. Then chop them to the 36-in. length required for this sled, using a miter saw or circular saw.

2 DOUBLE UP THE FRONT FENCE. Spread glue evenly on one of the layers and apply clamp pressure evenly. Don't worry about getting the edges perfectly even at this stage.

3 TRIM THE EDGES OF THE FRONT FENCE. Let the glue cure for two hours or so, remove the clamps and scrape off any glue squeeze-out, and then make light cuts along each long edge to clean them up and make them square, cutting the fence down to 4 3/4 in. wide in the process. Cut the rear fence to the same width also.

4 MAKE STOPPED CUTS UP TO THE CURVES. Mark lines 14 in. and 9 in. from each end, set the rip fence for a 3-in. cut, and cut up to each line. After reaching the line, hold the piece in place while you turn off the saw, and wait until the blade stops to remove it. You'll need to flip the fences end for end to make the two stopped cuts, so your stop marks will need to be on opposite sides.

5 CUT THE CURVES. Lay out the curves as shown in the drawing on p. 76, and then clamp the pieces to the workbench and cut the curves with a jigsaw. A bandsaw will also work great.

6 SAND THEM SMOOTH. Use your benchtop sander or sand by hand to smooth your jigsaw cuts. This isn't absolutely necessary, but it will make the sled easier on the eye and hand.

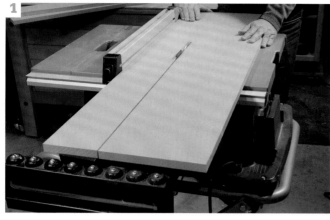

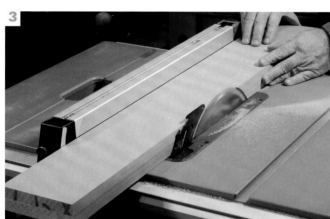

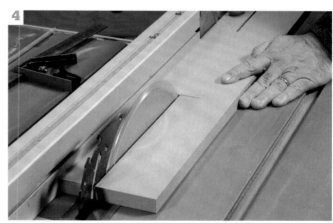

ATTACHING THE FENCES

To attach the fences solidly to our sled, we'll be relying on the principles of a super-strong screw joint, covered earlier on in the book (see p. 56). That means clearance holes in the base of the sled and pilot holes in the MDF fences. MDF is prone to both splitting and stripping, so it's critical to get those pilot holes just right and drill them to the full depth of the long screws we are using.

Just as we did with the runners, we'll also be countersinking the clearance holes in the base, so the heads of the screws sit below the surface and don't cause problems. After drilling, it's easy to attach the back fence. But the front fence is trickier. That's the one that needs to hold your workpieces perfectly square to the blade, so the fence has to be attached perfectly square to the blade too. Here's one of the easier ways to do that.

We'll use the same long screws to attach the front fence, with one exception. The left-most screw will be a pan-head-style screw, which has a flat bottom, and we'll drill an oversize hole for it, letting us shift that end around to fine-tune the fence position. So we'll start with just one normal screw at the right edge and our one special screw in an oversized hole on the left. Then we'll make some test crosscuts until we know the fence is perfectly square. The oversized hole and special screw will let us shift the fence angle slightly.

1 DRILL CLEARANCE HOLES. With the exception of one special screw at the end of the front fence, all of the screws that attach the fences are the same. Flip over the base of the sled, mark the edges of the fences to help locate your screw holes, and then drill clearance holes for all of the normal, 2-in.-long screws.

2 LAST SCREW IS DIFFERENT. The left-end screw in the front fence has a "pan-head" to allow it to slide back and forth in its oversized hole. Drill a $5/8$-in counterbore about $1/4$ in. deep, using a Forstner bit if you have one (or a normal bit), and then follow it with a standard $1/4$-in. bit—which will follow the center of the larger hole—drilling through the base.

3 ATTACH THE FRONT FENCE WITH JUST TWO SCREWS. Clamp the front fence in place, aligned with the front edge of the sled. Then drive a normal 2-in. screw at one end, into a normal countersunk clearance hole, and the pan-head screw into the larger hole at the other end, along with a washer under the screw head. Be sure to drill accurate pilot holes for all of the screws so the MDF doesn't split.

4 CUT THROUGH THE SLED. After attaching the rear fence with normal screws along its full length, flip the sled, place the runners in their miter slots, and make a cut through the whole thing.

USING YOUR NEW CROSSCUT SLED

You'll notice that the sled has a shorter side to the left of the blade and a longer side to the right. That's because most saw tables are also wider to the right of the blade. So you'll make most of your crosscuts with the workpiece on the right side of the sled, giving you the support of the longer part of the fence. That long side of fence is also a great place to clamp stop blocks for repeat cuts. If your workpiece reaches past the end of the sled, make a hook-style stop as shown on pg. 85.

Give your new sled a try. You'll be amazed at how much control it gives.

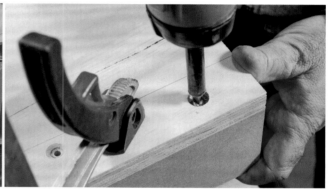

DIAL IN THE FRONT FENCE FOR PERFECT CUTS ━━━━

Because the front fence is aligned with the front edge of the sled, it should be pretty close to square with the blade, but it's probably not perfect just yet. That's why we've only attached it with two screws so far, with one allowing some back-and-forth movement.

1 CHECK IT WITH A SQUARE. Start by placing a square against the fence and blade as shown. Make sure the square isn't touching the blade's teeth. If the fence isn't square to the blade, adjust it now.

2 LOOSEN THE SPECIAL SCREW TO ADJUST THE FENCE. The pan-head screw, passing through an oversized clearance hole, allows you some adjustment fore and aft. It helps to mark a pencil line along the inside edge of the fence to record its current position before moving it.

3 THE TRUE TEST. The square will get you close, but this test will help you eliminate the slightest inaccuracy. Rip a piece of plywood about 8 in. to 10 in. wide, mark a squiggle line on top, and use the sled to crosscut it. Then flip one of the pieces, pull both of them against the fence, and see if the cut edges come together without a gap. If they don't, the fence needs a little more adjustment, and you'll need to repeat the test.

4 DRIVE THE REST OF THE SCREWS. Once your latest squareness test looks good, flip over the sled and drive the rest of the screws, locking it permanently into position.

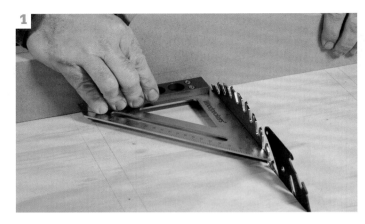

EXTENDED STOP IS A BONUS ━━━━━

You can clamp a stop block anywhere along the front fence, as we did on the miter gauge in Chapter 2, but this type of extended stop can be built to accommodate workpieces of any length.

1 EASY TO SET UP. Just hook your measuring tape into the blade slot in the sled, and line up the hook stop with your desired dimension. Notice how the overlapping part on top keeps the stop level as you position it.

2 CUT MULTIPLE PARTS TO THE SAME LENGTH. Cut one end of your workpiece clean and square, place that end against the stop, and cut the piece to perfect length. Always control the part that's trapped between the blade and stop. The waste piece will vibrate freely out of the way.

This simple stop will accommodate workpieces up to 28 in. long or so, but you can size yours as needed, or make more than one.

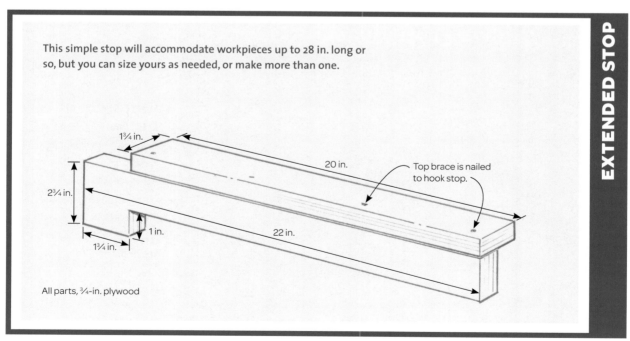

1¾ in.

20 in.

Top brace is nailed to hook stop.

2¾ in.

1 in.

1¾ in.

22 in.

All parts, ¾-in. plywood

EXTENDED STOP

dowel joints are quick and strong

BY NOW YOU'VE GOT your workspace set up, complete with a sweet new workbench, a dialed-in tablesaw, and an accurate crosscut sled. So let's put all of that to use and start making projects. Many of the projects pitched to beginning woodworkers fall down in one of two ways: They are either not as doable as advertised, or they are too lame to really be worth doing in the first place. The books in this series take you step-by-step through durable, useful, good-looking projects that you can actually build with basic tools and skills.

If you've worked your way through the chapters to this point, you have the ability to cut wood to size, and then drill and shape it in various ways. The next trick is learning how to join those workpieces together in a durable way. The rest of this book focuses on joinery methods that are both strong and simple, with cool projects to go along with each new joint. We'll kick it off with, dollar for dollar, the best basic joinery device I've found: a simple doweling jig, available on Amazon for $20—an unbelievable price considering how versatile and accurate this little gizmo is.

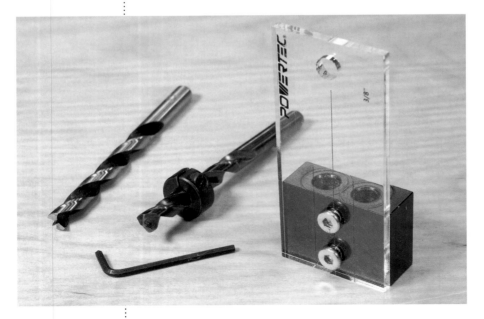

SIMPLE, STRONG, AND AFFORDABLE. Just $20, this simple doweling jig can be used in a wide variety of ways, on an endless array of projects. The kit includes a bit and a stop collar used to set the drilling depth.

TWO TABLES ARE JUST THE BEGINNING

We'll build two tables in this chapter: a side table with a floating top, which can serve as an end table, plant stand, nightstand, or whatever you need; and a cool coffee table with a natural-edge walnut slab atop a clean, geometric base. Although the tables are very different, our little jig handles every joint.

I took my time on the designs for these tables, but don't feel compelled to build them exactly as they are shown here. The great thing about woodworking is that you are in control. I used hemlock for one table and walnut for the other, but you can go with any nice wood you can get your hands on. If you can't find it in the thicknesses or sizes specified in the drawings, feel free to change things up. If you don't love the design details, change those too. The important lessons here are the techniques. Once you see what you can do with dowels, you'll start dreaming up all sorts of projects you can build with them.

For the top of the coffee table, I reused a nice walnut slab from a different project in Book 1. Natural-edged slabs are all unique, so you are pretty unlikely to find one that's the exact same size and thickness as

SIDE TABLE WITH A FLOATING TOP.
We'll start with this versatile side table, which features a floating top and tapered legs. I made this one from hemlock, but you can use any nice hardwood or softwood that strikes your fancy. You'll learn the basics of table joinery in this project, plus how to glue up a beautiful top from separate boards.

NATURAL-EDGED COFFEE TABLE. We'll use the doweling jig in still other ways to build a clean, geometric base for a natural-edged walnut slab.

ADVICE ON FINDING THE RIGHT LUMBER

For the projects in this chapter, and some of the others in the book as well, you'll need hardwood (or nice softwood) lumber planed to specific thicknesses. If you have access to a jointer and planer—machines used to mill lumber to specific thicknesses, leaving it flat, straight, and smooth—you can buy your hardwood in any condition and mill it to the thicknesses you need.

If you don't own these big machines, no worries. I didn't either for the first few years I worked with wood, and there are easy work-arounds. I always tell new woodworkers to start at their local home center. I'm often surprised with all the great project material I find there. Depending on where you live, you're likely to find smooth, flat, project-ready wood in a handful of species. Try both Lowe's and Home Depot, as each differs slightly in what they offer. Lowe's, for example, has a wide variety of thin strips and also wide panels made of multiple boards, saving you the trouble of joining and leveling those boards to get material of a similar width.

Home-center and hardware-store wood is limited, though, especially in the most attractive varieties, so your next step should be a Google search

LOOK FOR PRESURFACED WOODS. When you're just starting out, you won't have the big milling machines necessary to smooth and straighten your own lumber, so shop around locally for hardwood suppliers that sell presurfaced wood, or are willing to plane rough boards to the thicknesses you need. If the boards are already planed smooth, make sure they're straight before you bring them home.

for local lumberyards and hardwood retailers. Next, I highly recommend that you call them on the phone and explain what you are looking for. Most will be glad to help, since they want your business. If you don't know something, just admit it and ask.

DOWEL JOINTS ARE QUICK AND STRONG

lumber lingo

Here are some key concepts you'll encounter at the lumberyard. Some hardwoods are sold "rough," with deep saw marks on them. Depending on where you live, some rough lumber is planed along most of its surface (but not all), which is called "hit-or-miss" planing. If you buy rough lumber, you'll need the lumberyard (or a friend) to surface it for you. Many lumber retailers are quite happy to do this for a small charge and will plane down your wood to any specific dimension you need in the process.

The other thing you'll find at some lumberyards is fully surfaced material, which is sold as S4S (surfaced on both faces and both edges, or all four "sides") or S2S (surfaced on its two main faces). There are usually fewer species of wood available in this form, and only a few standard thicknesses—mostly ¾ in. but also thicker pieces sometimes.

By the way, lumber thicknesses are measured in quarters of an inch, based on how thick they are when they are sawn off a log. So 4/4 (pronounced "four-quarter") starts off at 1 in. thick, and is then dried and planed to yield ¾-in.-thick boards; 5/4 lumber ends up yielding 1-in.-thick material; and so on.

Also, lumber is sold in a variety of grades, from construction-grade to cabinet-grade. Avoid construction lumber—like 2x4 studs—for furniture and other nice woodworking projects. It will have lots of knots and other defects, and only be dried partially if at all, leaving it prone to shrinking and warping. The nice stuff, with the straightest grain and fewest defects, will be called "Select" and graded A, B, C, or D. If you want the knotty look, go for No. 1 or No. 2 Common.

But the bottom line is to go to the lumberyard, make friends with the staff, and start looking through the bins and racks for what you want. Most experienced woodworkers do just that, picking boards one at a time. Good wood isn't cheap, so you don't want to take any chances. If you want to stay friends with the staff, always put the boards back just the way you found them.

Last but not least, I do not recommend buying cheaper woods and staining them to resemble something fancier. It's extremely hard to fake good material, and you're very likely to end up with a blotchy appearance that looks like a hot mess. Beautiful woods, on the other hand, need only a basic, clear finish to look amazing.

Good hardwoods and select softwoods can be pretty expensive, but you are making things to last a lifetime, and you don't want to wrestle with warped lumber, or have to live with a bad stain job for as long as your project lasts.

the one I used. That's just fine. Get whatever you can, in any sort of wood, and then adjust the size of the base to suit it. You can even just glue together a series of boards to make a rectangular top, just like we are doing for our floating-top side table.

The only non-negotiable part of these projects is starting out with smooth, flat, straight boards, already planed to the right thicknesses—before heading to the tablesaw to cut out the various parts. If you have access to a jointer and planer, and you know how to use them safely, you'll be able to mill your own stock to perfect thickness. If not, no problem: Check out my short guide on ready-to-use material, "Advice on finding the right lumber," on pp. 88–89.

AN ELEGANTLY SIMPLE JIG

The doweling jig is made by Powertec. We'll go with the 3/8-in. size (model no. 71497), which I find to be the most versatile, but there are also 1/4-in. and 1/2-in. models. Due to the size of the dowels and the maximum depth of the holes you can drill with a 3/8-in.-dia. drill bit, the 3/8-in. version of the jig is appropriate for small- to medium-sized furniture like the pieces in this chapter. But if you buy the jig designed for a 1/2-in. drill bit, you can make everything up to the largest dining tables and biggest beds.

The jig is really nothing more than a block of metal that guides a 3/8-in.-dia. drill bit, with a tough, clear plastic fence attached. The fence locates the jig on a workpiece and provides a surface for clamping solidly in place. The kit also includes a drill bit, along with a stop collar that controls drilling depth. The simple design makes the jig cheap to produce but incredibly versatile—as you'll see in this chapter, where we'll use it as intended and then teach it (and you) a few extra tricks.

In its basic form the jig lets you drill two clean, 3/8-in. holes, spaced exactly 3/4 in. apart, which then accept two 3/8-in. dowels. Drill those in two mating

pieces, squirt some glue in the holes, tap in the dowels, clamp the parts together, and they are joined for life. This basic ability lets you join parts at 90 degrees for all sorts of projects, from door and picture frames to the base of a table. This versatile jig can also be used to join pieces side by side, aligning them perfectly with each other at the same time. We'll do this to create a lovely tabletop from separate boards.

a few helpful tips for this jig

I've been using this jig with students for a few years now, and I have a number of helpful tips to share. For a start I always replace the standard 3/8-in. drill bit that comes with the kit with a 3/8-in. brad-point bit. You can get a good one for less than $10 on Amazon. Compared to the twist drill included in the kit, a brad-point bit will create a more accurate hole and a cleaner entry rim. It will also make drilling faster and easier. At $10 this simple upgrade is a no-brainer.

You'll also need a couple of small clamps for quickly attaching and detaching the jig from a workpiece. Avoid spring clamps and Quick Grip-style clamps, which just don't hold tightly enough. Go with clamps that ratchet or screw down solidly.

As for the dowels themselves, you could use standard wood dowels, sold at the home center and hardware store in 2-ft. or 3-ft. lengths, and cut them to the length you need. But I find that those dowels vary a lot in diameter—some ending up a little loose in their holes and others too tight. Instead, I recommend that you buy precut dowels made for the dowel joinery, in whatever size and length you need, from a woodworking retailer like Rockler or Woodcraft. These not only offer a consistent fit, but they also have little slots on their sides to let glue and air escape when you tap them into their holes.

Last, if you happen to drill the dowel holes in the wrong spot, sometimes you can just glue a dowel into the wrong hole(s), let it dry, saw and sand it flush, and then re-drill in the right spot.

Before you clamp on your dowel jig and start drilling, there are few things you need to do.

REPLACE THE STANDARD DRILL BIT. The kit comes with a standard twist drill (right). These cut a little bit roughly in wood, so replace yours with a high-quality brad-point bit (left). It will cut much more quickly, smoothly, and cleanly, and make more accurate holes.

DOWELS 101. Best dowels from left to right. The best type (left) is sold specifically for dowel joinery and tends to be very accurate, with spiral grooves that allow glue and air to escape when you drive them in. The middle type is also sold for doweling but doesn't create quite as strong a glue bond. On the right is a dowel cut from long hardware-store dowels. These tend to vary a lot in size. Whichever dowels you use, make sure they fit OK in the holes your drill bit makes.

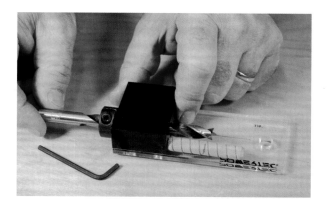

SET THE DEPTH. You want to drill just 1/8 in. or so deeper than necessary, to give extra glue a place to go and make sure the joint will close completely. In this case, I drew a line halfway along the dowel I'm using and made sure the bit passed the line by a little, before locking the stop collar on the drill bit.

SET THE DRILL FOR DRILLING, NOT DRIVING. While tightening the bit in the chuck, make sure your drill is set in drilling mode, which is indicated by the little drill-bit icon.

DOWEL-JIG BASICS

Before we get started on our projects, let's take a look at how this jig works. It's pretty straightforward to use, but a bit of practice on some scrap wood will help you get a feel for attaching the jig and drilling.

1 **MARK A LINE ACROSS THE JOINT.** This only needs to be roughly centered by eye.

2 **THE JIG CLAMPS ON QUICKLY.** Clamp the workpiece in your vise as shown, so it's near the middle of the jaws, and then clamp on the jig. In this case I'm using the jig's centerline for alignment. Make sure it's right on the mark and clamp the jig firmly in place. Often two clamps are better than one.

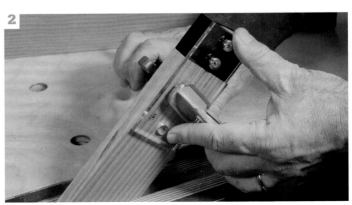

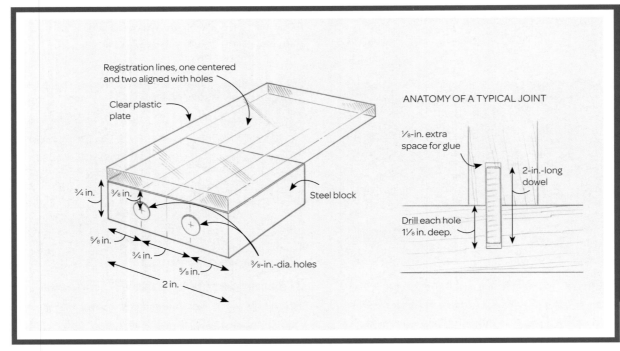

Registration lines, one centered and two aligned with holes

Clear plastic plate

¾ in.
⅜ in.
⅝ in.
¾ in.
⅝ in.
2 in.

Steel block

⅜-in.-dia. holes

ANATOMY OF A TYPICAL JOINT

⅛-in. extra space for glue

2-in.-long dowel

Drill each hole 1⅛ in. deep.

ANATOMY OF THE DOWEL JIG

DOWEL JOINTS ARE QUICK AND STRONG

3 DRILLING TIPS. Place the drill bit in the hole before squeezing the trigger and drill until the stop-collar hits the jig. It helps to pull the bit partway out of the hole at least once as you drill, to help clear the wood chips. Use both holes in the jig.

4 DRILLING THE OTHER PART. In this case, the vise can clamp the jig and workpiece at the same time. Alignment and drilling are the same as before, and just as fast.

5 GLUE IN THE DOWELS. Squirt some woodworking glue in the holes and use a small stick or brush to spread it evenly. Then just tap in your dowels. You don't need to apply glue to them.

6 ASSEMBLY IS QUICK AND EASY. Spread some glue in the other pair of holes, and just push the parts together. Add some clamps to hold them tightly together as the glue dries.

AN ELEGANTLY SIMPLE JIG

They don't tell you all of this in the instructions, but here's how to make your dowel jig even more useful.

1 OFFSET THE JIG. If you place a thin piece of plywood or MDF between the guide block and the plastic fence, you can offset the holes by any amount. You'll need slightly longer screws to attach the fence.

2 DRILL AS USUAL. In this case, I am lining up the jig with the top edge of each part, instead of using the alignment lines.

3 THREE ARE BETTER THAN TWO. To create joints with more than two dowel holes, place a dowel in the last hole you drilled, and place the jig on that dowel to line up the next hole.

4 REMOVE THE SPACER FOR THE OTHER PART. Drill the mating part without the spacer in the jig. Note that the jig is lined up with the top of the rail, to be sure the parts align perfectly.

5 PERFECT TABLE JOINT. Now we have three dowels in this table leg and rail, for added strength, and the parts are offset nicely. This is how you would make a standard table base.

DOWEL JOINTS ARE QUICK AND STRONG

OTHER GREAT LESSONS IN THIS CHAPTER TOO

Dowel joinery isn't the only important lesson in this chapter. The two projects featured here include a number of other fundamental furniture-making methods, including tapering and beveling parts safely on the tablesaw, gluing up a beautiful tabletop, and trouble-free assembly.

safe, smooth tapers

Tapers are a nice way to make legs more interesting and elegant, and there are lots of ways to cut them, including the bandsaw or jigsaw. Those tools leave a slightly rough surface, one that's only as straight as your aim is true. To clean them up, you'll need to do some careful sanding—or hand planing, if you have that skill in your locker—and it can be tough to end up with adjacent tapers that match each other perfectly.

That's why we'll be cutting our leg tapers on the tablesaw, using a really cool sled that will teach you a lot about jig-making (see the drawing on p. 105). Like most woodworking machines, the tablesaw is a platform for all sorts of techniques, and jigs and sleds are how you unlock its versatility. Our jig will quickly and safely cut clean, matching tapers on two adjacent faces of each leg, requiring only the slightest amount of sanding to clean them up.

gluing up panels

Whether you're making door panels, cabinet sides, or a tabletop, you'll need to know the fundamentals of a good panel glue-up. Making a wide panel means gluing multiple boards into one flat, pretty surface. That can be tricky, but our tuned-up tablesaw and handy doweling jig will make it easy.

The tablesaw will cut square edges on the boards, so they can be glued together with no visible gaps. And we'll insert dowels in the edges to keep them perfectly aligned, which means you'll only have to do a minor amount of sanding to bring the boards level to each other and make the joints invisible.

clean, safe bevel cuts

Our tabletop gets a 30-degree bevel along its bottom edge, and we'll use another fundamental tablesaw setup to do that safely. Your first thought might be to run one edge of the top along the rip fence, with the angled blade cutting the opposite edge, but this can be a little dicey. That's because the wood will be trapped between the angled blade and the fence, meaning any wobbles will ruin the cut, or worse, cause the panel to kick back.

Instead, we'll bury the angled blade in an auxiliary fence, like we did earlier in the book when we cut rabbets with a dado blade. With this setup, you could accidentally let the board wander away from the fence and nothing bad would happen. That's because you'd be leaving too much wood behind, not too little, and all it takes to smooth the cut is another pass over the blade.

assembly and finishing

Making real furniture is where woodworking starts getting complicated, and part of the challenge is assembly. But the glue-up stage doesn't have to be stressful if you follow a few tips. These include dry-fitting, choosing the right clamps, aligning them properly, and taking the job in stages.

All of those methods are covered in this chapter. As I've said many times over, the point of this book isn't so much the specific projects as it is the lessons built into each one.

side table with a floating top

This table base includes internal rails that elevate the top to make it appear to float. A "side" table like this can be used as a night-stand, plant stand, end table, and lots of other things. Most importantly, it includes wood-working lessons that will prove very useful.

ANATOMY OF SIDE TABLE

Internal rails, ¾ in. thick by 3 in. wide by approximately 12½ in. long (measure actual table base to determine length)

Underbevel, 30 degrees by ¾ in. high, leaving ½ in. of the square edge intact

Top, 1¼ in. thick by 16 in. square

Rails are set ¼ in. below top of legs.

Legs, 1½ in. square by 25 in. long

Rails, ¾ in. thick by 3 in. wide by 11½ in. long

6 in.

Leg tapers, 6 in. long by ½ in. deep, on inside faces of each leg

Table base, 14½ in. sq. overall

INTERNAL RAILS

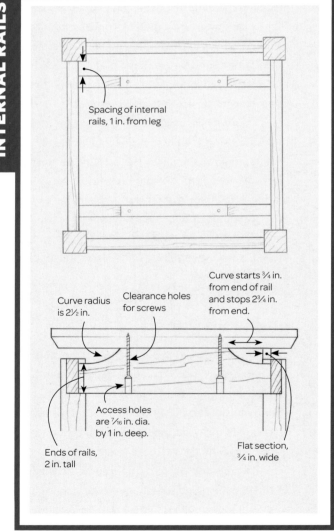

Spacing of internal rails, 1 in. from leg

Curve radius is 2½ in.

Clearance holes for screws

Curve starts ¾ in. from end of rail and stops 2¾ in. from end.

Access holes are ⁷⁄₁₆ in. dia. by 1 in. deep.

Ends of rails, 2 in. tall

Flat section, ¾ in. wide

DOWEL JOINTS ARE QUICK AND STRONG

CUT UP YOUR PARTS

You'll need to start out with your materials already planed to the right thickness. See "Advice on finding the right lumber" (p. 88–89) for more on that. Then you can head to the tablesaw and cut your parts to size. Make a couple of extra legs, if possible, in case you mess up the joinery or tapering.

1 RIP THE PARTS TO WIDTH. Remember from Chapter 2 that your boards need at least one straight edge to run against the rip fence, in order to make these cuts safely.

2 THEN CUT THEM TO LENGTH. Start by trimming one end clean and square with your crosscut sled, marking those good ends as you go. Then set up a stop block to trim the other ends to perfect length.

3 HOW TO HANDLE THE LEGS. Use the extended stop from Chapter 4 to cut the legs to length. Be sure to cut one end square first, before placing that end against the stop to cut the other.

MATERIALS & SUPPLIES

- (50) wood dowels, ⅜ in. dia. by 2 in. wide
- (4) ⅜-in. dowel centers
- (4) 3-in.-long wood screws
- Pint of wood finish of choice
- Bottle of Titebond III wood glue
- Smooth, surfaced boards in the following thicknesses:
- ¾ in. thick, for the rails
- 1¼ in. thick, for the top
- 1½-in. thick, for the legs

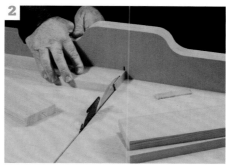

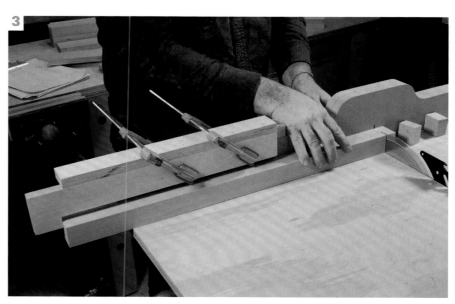

SIDE TABLE WITH A FLOATING TOP

DRILL THE DOWEL JOINTS

Use the techniques shown earlier in this chapter to make these joints. There are a few new wrinkles, covered below.

1 DRILL THE RAILS. Use the jig as usual, without the spacer, lining it up with the top edge of the rail to drill the first two holes. Note the arrow that marks the top front corner of the part. Then relocate the jig as shown to cut a third dowel hole.

2 MARK THE TOPS OF THE LEGS. The rails meet the legs $1/4$ in. down from the top end, so mark the legs for locating the dowel jig. Note the arrow that points to the outside corner of the legs. That will help you remember where the dowel holes go.

3 SET UP THE JIG. Add the $1/4$-in. spacer to the jig this time, so there is an offset between legs and rails. It helps to place a narrow board in the bottom of the vise, so the leg can rest on that when you are clamping everything in place. Note how the jig is also aligned $1/4$ in. from the top end of the leg, at the marks we just made.

4 ADD THE EXTRA DOWEL HOLE. After drilling the first two holes, use the dowel trick to position the jig for drilling a third.

5 ALWAYS DO A DRY FIT. Assemble the joints you've cut so far to make sure all the parts come together fully. Because of the way the dowels hit each other inside the legs, you'll discover you need to drill the dowel holes a little deeper in the rails. You can do this without the jig, following the holes that are already there.

DOWEL JOINTS ARE QUICK AND STRONG

MAKE THE INTERNAL RAILS

These need to be measured after the base is assembled (without glue at this point), so you can determine their precise length.

1 MARK THE RAILS. Clamp the base tightly together in both directions, place a square end of each rail against the inside of the outer rails, and then mark the other end for trimming on your crosscut sled.

2 SNEAK UP ON A TIGHT FIT. Don't cut right to the pencil line at first. Keep taking little whiskers off, returning to the table to try the fit until it just drops in, as snug as possible. But don't stress if you overcut the parts by a whisker.

3 LAY OUT ONE OF THE PARTS. Use your combination square and compass to mark the curved ends of these rails.

4 CUT AND SAND TO THE LINE. Cut just outside the lines with your jigsaw (or bandsaw), and then use the benchtop sander to sand up to the line.

5 USE THE FIRST RAIL TO LAY OUT THE SECOND. Transfer the layout with a sharp pencil, and then saw and sand to the line as before.

JOIN THE INTERNAL RAILS TO THE BASE

As we did on the workbench project, we'll be using dowel centers here to transfer dowel locations from one piece to another.

1 DRILL THE ENDS. These get two dowel holes each. Line up the dowel jig with the top (curved) edge of the rail, as shown.

2 INSERT DOWEL CENTERS. Stick $3/8$-in. dowel centers into the rails as shown and make a 1-in.-wide spacer for the next step.

3 TRANSFER THE HOLE LOCATIONS. With the ends of these internal rails pressed against the spacer, and also aligned with the top edge of the outer rails, press down firmly.

4 PRESTO. The dowel centers leave two little dimples right where you need to drill.

5 DRILL CAREFULLY. Set up the stop collar so the drill bit only goes about $5/8$ in. into the rails. You don't want the bit popping out the other side!

6 DRILL HOLES FOR ATTACHING THE TABLETOP. Start with the access holes, which are larger than the through-holes that follow. Mark the depth on the outside of the rail, and set the depth stop on your drill press. Clamp a fence to the drill press to control the workpieces as you drill and make sure the holes are centered.

HOW TO MAKE A TABLETOP

Unless your tabletop is one big slab of wood, you'll be assembling it from multiple boards. The dowel jig helps you do that cleanly and easily.

1 **PICK A NICE ARRAY AND MARK THE BOARDS.** Starting with the boards a little oversize in length and width, with clean edges on both sides of each one, flip them around until you like the look of your tabletop. Draw a big triangle to record their orientation, and then make little marks across the joints for aligning the dowel jig.

2 **DRILL THE EDGES FOR DOWELS.** Make sure to orient the jig against the top face of each board and use one of the registration lines on the jig to line up one of its holes with your pencil mark. Set the drilling depth at approximately 1⅛ in. for these 2-in.-long dowels.

3 **ALWAYS DO A DRY FIT!** Make sure the joints all come together cleanly before proceeding. Drill the holes a little deeper if necessary.

4 **SPREAD GLUE ON EACH EDGE.** Both edges of each joint need a thin layer of glue. Place a small bead along each one, and then spread it with a small brush. You don't need to put glue in the holes; the dowels are for alignment only. Inexpensive "acid" brushes make great glue brushes, and you can rinse them out afterward.

5 **CLAMP IT UP.** Any sort of long clamps work fine here. I like these lightweight aluminum bar clamps (from Woodcraft) because they don't interact with the glue and stain the wood. Alternate the bar clamps to help keep the panel flat, and then place clamps at the ends of the joints to make sure those surfaces stay flush.

6 **CHISEL OFF THE SQUEEZE-OUT.** You're supposed to get a nice little bead of glue along each joint on assemblies like this. That shows that you applied enough glue to each one. After the clamps come off (leave them on for at least an hour), you can use the bevel side of a chisel to pare away these extra beads of glue without damaging the wood below.

7 **RIP AND CROSSCUT.** Make a rip cut along both edges of the top, to bring it to final width. Then crosscut the end-grain edges to the same width, cleaning them up in the process.

DOWEL JOINTS ARE QUICK AND STRONG

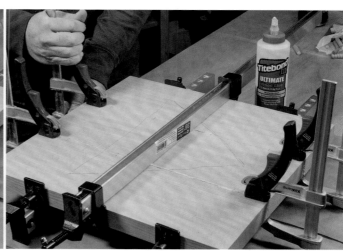

SIDE TABLE WITH A FLOATING TOP

SAFE BEVELING ON THE TABLESAW

Here's how to bevel an edge safely on the tablesaw. You'll need to clamp an auxiliary fence on the rip fence, and bury the blade in it slightly, similar to the rabbeting technique shown earlier in the book.

1 BURY THE BLADE. Start by lowering the riving knife or removing it, so it's not in the way. Then tilt the blade to 30 degrees, attach an auxiliary fence as shown, and bring the spinning blade up into the fence so the tip is buried.

2 MAKE A TEST CUT. On a board that's the same thickness as the tabletop, draw a line marking the top edge of the cut and make a test cut. You'll probably have to move the fence to get it to line up properly, and that might require lowering the spinning blade and raising it back up into the fence.

3 CHECK YOUR WORK. The cut should end right at the 1/2-in. mark. If it doesn't, adjust the fence slightly (with the blade spinning), flip your test board, and make another test cut until it's just right.

4 BEVEL THE REAL THING. Start on the end-grain edges, which are prone to chipping. The next cuts on the long-grain edges will remove any of that splintering. Watch out for the small sliver of wood trapped under the blade. Once it comes free, it can shoot out toward you, but not dangerously.

TABLESAW JIG MAKES CLEAN LEG TAPERS ▬▬▬▬

There are a number of ways to cut the taper on the legs, but this tablesaw jig will do it cleanly, quickly, and safely. The jig is easy to make, and you can adjust it for different tapers in the future.

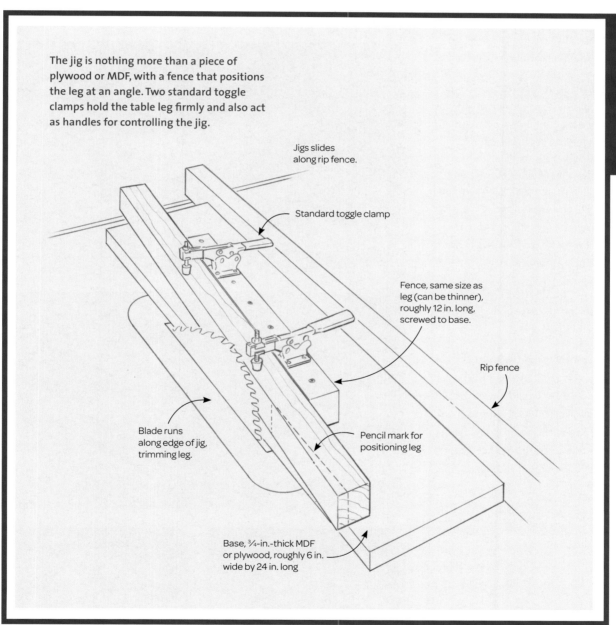

The jig is nothing more than a piece of plywood or MDF, with a fence that positions the leg at an angle. Two standard toggle clamps hold the table leg firmly and also act as handles for controlling the jig.

Jigs slides along rip fence.

Standard toggle clamp

Fence, same size as leg (can be thinner), roughly 12 in. long, screwed to base.

Rip fence

Blade runs along edge of jig, trimming leg.

Pencil mark for positioning leg

Base, ¾-in.-thick MDF or plywood, roughly 6 in. wide by 24 in. long

1 ATTACH THE FENCE. Start by marking the starting and stopping point of the taper on one of the legs and use those marks to position the leg and fence on the jig. Then screw the fence to the base, making sure to drill clearance holes in the fence first.

2 MARK THE END LINE. This is all you need to position each new leg in the jig.

3 ADD THE TOGGLE CLAMPS. This type of clamp is invaluable for jigs of all kinds, holding work firmly in place and keeping your fingers clear of the blade.

4 ADJUST THE CLAMP PRESSURE. The little clamp posts are adjustable up and down, and forward and back. Place a leg in the jig and adjust the lock nuts above and below the horizontal beam to create firm clamping pressure.

5 LINE UP THE RIP FENCE. Adjust the rip fence until the edge of the jig is just grazing the blade.

6 TAPER AWAY. Only the inside faces of the legs get tapers. Those are the ones with dowel holes on them. Keep the jig snugly against the rip fence as you push it past the blade, using the clamp handles as a control points. Cut tapers on both inside faces of each leg.

PRE-SAND ALL OF THE PARTS

It's much easier to sand and smooth furniture parts before they are assembled. You can always do some touch-up sanding afterward, but it's good to get the heavy lifting done now. I'll cover this in more depth in Chapter 9 on finishing, but here are some highlights.

1 COMBINATION OF POWER AND HAND. A random-orbit sander speeds things up on large surfaces, and a sanding block gives great control on narrower ones.

2 DETAILS MATTER. I used the hard side of my cork-lined, MDF sanding block to sand crisp chamfers on the tops of the legs, and the soft side of another block to gently round the rest of the edges, making them look and feel much better. Chamfer the bottom of the legs also, so they don't splinter over the years.

ASSEMBLE IN STAGES

Be sure to do a dry-fit of the entire table before putting glue in the dowel holes for the real assembly. Titebond III glue will give you extra working time, but it still starts getting stiff after 15 or 20 minutes, so assemble the table in stages.

1 CUT SOME MINI-DOWELS. Cut the 2-in. dowels in half for attaching the internal rails. A handsaw is the safest tool for cutting these little parts.

2 JOIN ONE END OF THE TABLE AT A TIME. Join two legs and one rail as shown, making sure to use the rails with the extra dowel holes in them for the internal rails to come later. Center the clamp on the joints and tighten until there are no gaps between the parts. While you're at it, glue the little half-dowels into the rails.

3 CONNECT THE TWO SIDES. Leave the two sides in their clamps for a couple of hours, and then add the two last outer rails and the two internal rails to complete the table. It might take a bit of wiggling and tapping to get the parts lined up with their dowels.

4 FINAL CLAMPING. Clamp the two halves of the table together as shown, with any long clamps you have. I threw clamps across the internal rails also, to close any tiny gaps at their ends.

5 FINISH THE TOP AND BASE SEPARATELY. They are much easier to finish this way (see Chapter 9 for more on how I finished this table). Note how this lovely hemlock only requires a clear finish to look amazing. Avoid cheap woods that need staining.

6 ATTACH THE TOP AND YOU'RE DONE. Elevate the top on blocks and a protective cloth so you can even out the overhang on all sides of every leg and clamp the top in that position. That way the screws won't shift the top as you drive them.

DOWEL JOINTS ARE QUICK AND STRONG

PROJECT Nº.

slab-topped coffee table

We'll use our versatile little doweling jig in new ways to craft a strong, handsome base for a natural-edge slab.

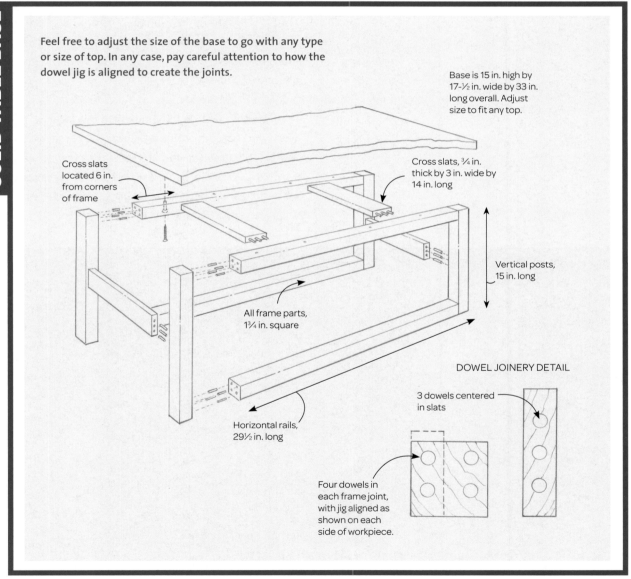

SOLID TABLE BASE

Feel free to adjust the size of the base to go with any type or size of top. In any case, pay careful attention to how the dowel jig is aligned to create the joints.

Base is 15 in. high by 17-½ in. wide by 33 in. long overall. Adjust size to fit any top.

Cross slats located 6 in. from corners of frame

Cross slats, ¾ in. thick by 3 in. wide by 14 in. long

Vertical posts, 15 in. long

All frame parts, 1¾ in. square

Horizontal rails, 29½ in. long

DOWEL JOINERY DETAIL

3 dowels centered in slats

Four dowels in each frame joint, with jig aligned as shown on each side of workpiece.

SLAB-TOPPED COFFEE TABLE

/ **109** /

ADVICE ON HANDLING NATURAL-EDGED SLABS ━━━

Big, thick wood slabs have enduring appeal. Rustic yet refined, they tell the story of the tree, especially if the edges of the log are left intact. But big slabs can be tricky to handle. They tend to warp as they dry and flattening them is beyond the capacity of common woodworking machines. There are huge router jigs you can make to flatten them, but those are hard to

justify if you only work with slabs once in a long while, and the flattening process takes a lot of time. Hand-planing also works, but it's tricky to flatten a big slab by hand, making that approach best for hand-tool lovers with a lot of experience.

That's why most of us take our slabs to a local woodworking shop that owns a wide-belt sander, a big, expensive machine designed for this exact task. For less than $100, one of the shop pros will run the largest slab through the sander on both sides until it is dead-flat and very smooth, leaving you just a little bit more sanding to do with finer grits before it's ready for a nice wood finish.

I took my slab to my local millwork shop for flattening. And now that I belong to a local woodworking club with that same type of machine, I'll be able to flatten future slabs there for a few dollars-worth of shop time. Using a wide-belt sander saves a lot of time and frustration, leaving you more time and energy to devote to the rest of the project.

MATERIALS & SUPPLIES

- (56) wood dowels, ⅜ in. dia. by 2 in. wide
- (8) 3-in.-long wood screws
- Pint of wood finish of choice
- Bottle of Titebond III wood glue
- Smooth, surfaced boards in the following thicknesses:
- 1¾ in. thick, for the frames
- ¾ in. thick, for the cross-slats
- plus a 1½-in.-thick top of your choosing

RENT A WIDE-BELT SANDER. Most big millwork shops will rent out time on their big wide-belt sanding machines at a reasonable rate and provide a skilled staff member to handle the process. It cost me about $60 to get my slab sanded smooth and flat.

COOL WAY TO CLEAN UP NATURAL EDGES. Strip off any bark first, as it will only pop off over time. If the edges are too sharp or damaged, you can reshape them. Draw a line along one of the grain lines, set your jigsaw to a less acute angle, and follow your line to reshape the edge. Sand away the saw marks and everyone will think the curvy new edge is original.

BUILD THE BASE TO FIT

You can adapt this clean design—including the strong dowel joinery—to suit any-size slab you find, or a more traditional tabletop made from multiple boards, such as reclaimed planks with built-in character.

1 MILL AND MARK THE MAIN FRAME PIECES. After ripping these to width from a 1¾-in.-thick board, line them up so they look their best and mark across the joints to record their positions. A white pencil works great on walnut.

2 DRILL THE POSTS. Mark the outside face of each post with an arrow to be sure you drill on the inside face. Line up the jig with the end of the post as you position it on each side to drill the four holes.

3 DRILL THE RAILS. The jig is positioned the same way—on two opposite faces of the workpiece—to drill into the ends of these pieces. Make sure you are lining up the end of the jig with the outer face of the rail each time, so the rails and posts end up flush at the corners.

4 MARK CENTERLINES FOR THE SLAT JOINERY. The three dowel holes are centered on the slats, so we can work from a single centerline this time. Mark those centerlines on the ends of the slats and the outside faces of the rails and posts.

5 DO THE THREE-DOWEL TRICK. Line up one of the holes with your centerline and drill it and its neighbor. Then drop a dowel into that center hole and use it to position the jig for drilling the hole on the other side of the centerline. Do this on the slats and the frame parts, making sure to drill the frame parts on the sides that will face inward.

6 ASSEMBLE THE FRAMES. Once again, do a dry-fit first to make sure everything comes together OK, before spreading glue in the holes, tapping in the dowels, and assembling the frames. If you have trouble assembling the parts due to tight dowels, pull them together with clamps. That tends to work better than a rubber mallet on tight joints.

7 ADD THE SLATS FOR A STRONG, ELEGANT BASE. Use whichever long clamps you have on hand—the stronger the better—to draw these joints together. Turn to Chapter 9 for advice on sanding and finishing.

8 ATTACHING THE TOP IS EASY. Long screws pass through the frame parts and hold the thick slab securely.

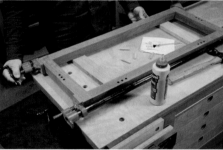

SLAB-TOPPED COFFEE TABLE

master the miter, and open a world of new projects

ELEGANT IN ITS simplicity, a miter joint is formed by cutting two parts at matching angles. Miters have been used for centuries by carpenters and woodworkers alike, on everything from small boxes to picture frames, window trim, cabinetry, and fine furniture.

The beauty of the miter joint is how one part flows into the next. Any decorative details—whether molded or inlaid into those parts—also meet up perfectly. You can see how this works on picture frames, letting you round or notch a long strip of molding, cut it into four pieces, miter their ends and glue them together, and watch the lovely detail flow around all four corners. Cut grooves in the inside edges—to hold a box lid or bottom, for example—and those meet up perfectly, too.

The visual payoff is high for clean miters, but gaps are obvious. And cutting precise 45-degree angles can be trickier than it seems. On a box or frame, you also have to make opposite sides the same length, or those pesky gaps show up again. Last but not least, once you spread glue on the joints, miters can be slippery buggers to clamp together firmly and accurately.

Don't get psyched out, though. I'll show you how to produce clean, accurate miters on all sorts of workpieces, as well as a variety of sure-fire techniques for clamping. The projects in this chapter will open the door to a hundred others.

LITTLE TEA BOX IS PACKED WITH TECHNIQUES. You'll learn simple ways to cut box miters, glue them together, add decorative splines, and insert a liner that holds the lid in place—lessons you can use to build boxes of all sizes.

BOX MITERS ARE JUST THAT

There are two families of miters—box miters and frame miters—and I'll cover both here, with projects for each type. We'll kick off the chapter with box miters, the long beveled edges used to put all sorts of containers together, from small decorative boxes to full-size furniture.

The larger the mitered box, the more challenging it is to get the joints to come together seamlessly, so we'll start with a soup-to-nuts strategy for small boxes. The main project here is a charming little tea box that's so easy you can build it in batches. I sized it to hold standard, paper-wrapped tea bags, which makes it a useful gift. But it can be scaled up for all sorts of cargo. To prove that, I'm using the same approach to make a small cabinet for a Bluetooth speaker kit from Rockler.com.

This little tea box holds an entire approach to box-making, from cutting perfect joints on the tablesaw to clamping them together in the easiest way you can imagine. We'll build the box as a closed object, and then cut it apart on the tablesaw to form a matching box and lid. After that, I'll show you how to line the

inside so the lid pops on and off easily and lines up perfectly. And that's not all. I'll use a slick tablesaw jig to cut slots in the corners of the box, for inserting little splines that strengthen and decorate the box at the same time. All of these are techniques you can use again and again.

FRAME MITERS MAKE OTHER PROJECTS POSSIBLE

Frame miters are cut in the other direction on the ends of boards, to make any sort of flat frame. These frames can hold pictures, of course, but they can also cover the front of a plywood cabinet, surround a tabletop, frame a window or door, and lots more.

We'll start off with a couple of nice picture frames. Then I'll expand on that concept to make a unique frame that hides a pocket for an album cover, turning your vintage vinyl records into wall art. The same concept could be used to make a pocket for an obsolete tablet computer, for example, turning it into an interactive sign.

The tablesaw will do a fine job on frame miters, but we'll cut ours with less fuss on the miter saw, thanks to a couple of tricks uniquely suited to that tool. And we'll clamp these miters in a few new ways. But let's get started with our little tea box, which is packed full of valuable techniques.

CUSTOM PICTURE FRAMES. Use any wood you have on hand to make unique frames for your favorite photos and artwork. You'll also learn easy ways to mat your photos and hang the frames.

DISPLAY YOUR VINTAGE VINYL. A built-in pocket lets you slide album covers in and out of this cool frame project (see p. 146), turning them into wall art.

OLD MEETS NEW. The slotted detail on the fronts of these projects makes them a nice pairing, highlighting the combination of old and new technology.

MASTER THE MITER, AND OPEN A WORLD OF NEW PROJECTS

7 tea box project

You can load up this box with tea and give it as a gift or keep it as a nice way to offer guests their brew of choice. As with some of the other projects in the book, you'll need to start out with flat, smooth wood in the right thickness. But any wood will do, and you can make it thicker than the ¼ in. specified here. Lots of home centers and craft stores have thin wood strips, so it shouldn't be hard to find something suitable. If you own some woodworking machines not covered in this book—such as a jointer, planer, and bandsaw—you can saw and plane your own thin panels from any wood in the world. I made my box from quarter-sawn white oak, which has an especially nice grain pattern.

What's a little different about this box is the thin plywood used for the top, bottom, and liner pieces. It's ⅛-in. craft plywood, available at most craft stores. What I love about this thin material is that it's very close to the thickness of many tablesaw blades, meaning you might be able to cut a single blade slot near the top and bottom of the box sides and slip the plywood in perfectly. The plywood probably won't be thinner than your saw blade, but there's a chance it might be thicker. If that's true, all you have to do is make a second pass to widen your slots.

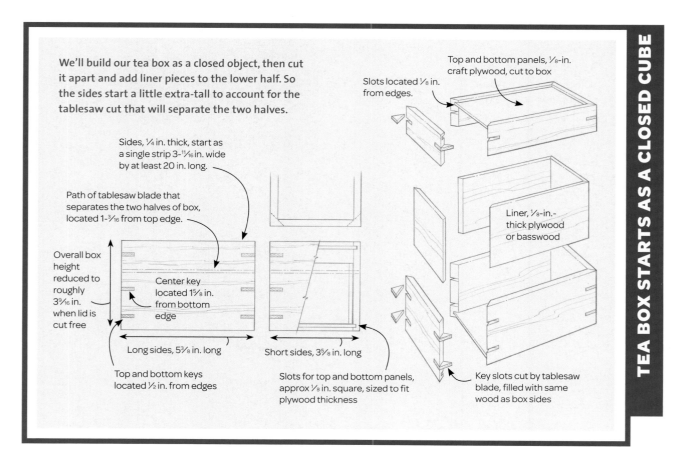

We'll build our tea box as a closed object, then cut it apart and add liner pieces to the lower half. So the sides start a little extra-tall to account for the tablesaw cut that will separate the two halves.

Top and bottom panels, ⅛-in. craft plywood, cut to box

Slots located ⅛ in. from edges.

Sides, ¼ in. thick, start as a single strip 3-11⁄16 in. wide by at least 20 in. long.

Path of tablesaw blade that separates the two halves of box, located 1-3⁄16 from top edge.

Liner, ⅛-in.-thick plywood or basswood

Overall box height reduced to roughly 3-9⁄16 in. when lid is cut free

Center key located 1⅝ in. from bottom edge

Long sides, 5⅜ in. long

Short sides, 3⅝ in. long

Top and bottom keys located ½ in. from edges

Slots for top and bottom panels, approx ⅛ in. square, sized to fit plywood thickness

Key slots cut by tablesaw blade, filled with same wood as box sides

TEA BOX STARTS AS A CLOSED CUBE

PREP THE SIDES

The first step in this project is making the box sides, which start as a 20-in.-long strip, so the grain will wrap around the box nicely. Rip it to the width specified in the drawing on p. 118, and then—before chopping it up and mitering the ends—cut those slots for the top and bottom of the box.

1 RIP AND SLOT THE SIDES. After ripping the strip to width, lower the blade and cut slots ⅛ in. from the edges.

2 CHECK THE FIT OF THE TOP AND BOTTOM. The top and bottom panels are made from ⅛-in. craft plywood, which might be a tiny bit thicker than your tablesaw blade. If it is, just adjust the rip fence and make another pass through the slots to widen them slightly, until the fit is just right.

MATERIALS & SUPPLIES

- ¼-in.-thick hardwood for box sides
- ⅛-in.-thick plywood (available at craft stores) for box top and bottom
- ⅛-in.-thick plywood or basswood (available at craft stores) for box liner
- Tablesaw crosscut sled
- (2) straight-line toggle clamps, rockler.com
- Blue painter's tape, wide roll if possible

MASTER THE MITER, AND OPEN A WORLD OF NEW PROJECTS

SET UP FOR PERFECT BOX MITERS

Each chapter in this book (as in the first book) builds on the previous ones, letting you build up your tools, skills, and jigs as you go. The crosscut sled you built in Chapter 4 stars again here, becoming a mitering sled for our box parts. Mitered boxes won't come together cleanly unless the sharp ends of the parts are square to each other, and the sled ensures they will be.

The first step is to tilt the tablesaw blade to 45 degrees. You'll need to install the original throat plate to do that, as it has a wide slot that lets the blade tilt. Then you'll need to make a new cut through your crosscut sled. This will chop a long triangular chunk out of the sled base, but don't worry. We'll fix that with a technique I've been planning the whole time. Any time the zero-clearance slots in the base and fence of your sled get blown out or otherwise altered by angling the blade, using a thick stack of dado blades, or changing the blade to a slightly thicker one, for example, there's an easy way to refresh the sled.

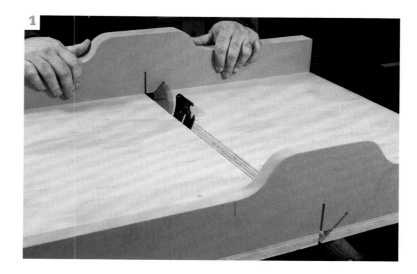

1 CUT A SLOT THROUGH YOUR SLED. Tilt the blade to 45 degrees, raise it about 2 in. above the table, and cut a new slot through your crosscut sled. You'll be removing a long triangle of wood from the base, but we'll address that next.

2 REFRESH THE BASE. To restore the zero-clearance support around the blade, use double-stick tape to attach a piece of ¼-in. MDF to the base, and then cut through it with the blade again.

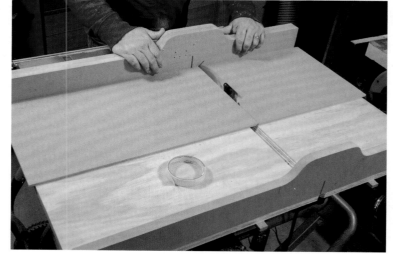

3 HANDY GIZMO. This digital angle gauge is under $30 on Amazon and will set your blade angle far more precisely than the pointer in the front of the saw. Zero it out on the base of the sled, and then stick it on the blade (it's magnetic) to dial in the exact angle. Make sure it's aligned vertically on the blade for best accuracy.

4 CUT A FEW MITERS TO BE REALLY SURE. Cut a strip of plywood and use the techniques on the following pages to cut four equal sides. If there are tiny gaps in the joints, your blade angle needs a tweak or two.

5 ADD TWO TOGGLE CLAMPS. To keep your fingers away from the blade when cutting small pieces, add a few straight-line toggle clamps to the sled's fence. I screwed on a block to push them outward a bit and adjusted their tips for a firm hold on the ¼-in.-thick box sides.

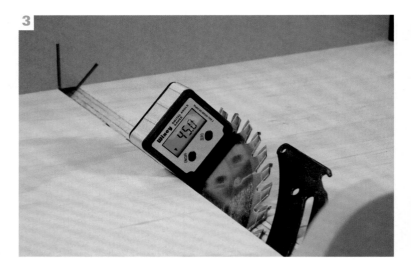

MASTER THE MITER, AND OPEN A WORLD OF NEW PROJECTS

CUT YOUR BOX PARTS

To make sure you have nice continuous grain all around your box, start by mapping out and numbering the sides on your long strip of wood, so you keep them in order as you cut them: short side, long side, short side, long side. The next step is to miter one end of each side, working your way down the strip. This will leave a miter pointing the right way on one end of each piece, and one pointing the wrong way.

Next, you'll need to set up a stop on the sled for the other end of the sides, or at least one set of the sides, as there are two different lengths in this box. The good end of each piece will go against that stop while you miter the other properly, cutting it to the right length at the same time. Go slow when cutting miters on pieces this thin. The areas around the slots (for the top and bottom of the box) are fragile, so take it slow and easy. After that, set up a stop for the other set of sides and cut those to length, mitering them at the same time. Follow the step-by-step photos, and it will all make sense.

1 LAY OUT THE SIDES. Decide which face of your strip is the prettiest, and then mark the rough position of the sides on that face, placing them in the order they wrap around the box. That will help you put them back in the right order later. A white pencil works well on darker wood.

2 MITER ONE END OF EACH PIECE. Using your rough layout lines as a guide, chop up your long strip, cutting a clean miter on one end of each part in the process. Your sled setup ensures clean, accurate, safe cuts.

3 SET UP A STOP TO MITER THE OTHER ENDS. Clamp a strip of wood to your sled and place the sharp point of the good miters against it to cut the other end to length, mitering it properly in the process. It helps to cut a test piece to dial in your stop position for the two different side lengths.

CUT THE TOP AND BOTTOM TO SIZE AND ASSEMBLE

One major lesson of furniture making is to build projects one stage at a time, usually working outside-in, so you can fit interior parts to whatever you've just put together. The classic example is waiting to build drawers until a cabinet is fully built and assembled. The bottom line is that you never know exactly what size something is going to be until you build it. And that's just fine. You can use what you've built to measure and mark the next pieces directly, instead of relying on math and your tape measure.

In this case, we waited until now to cut the top and bottom panels to size. No matter how carefully you set your stops on the crosscut sled, the sides are unlikely to come out at the exact length you were shooting for. So we'll use the actual sides to determine the size of the top and bottom.

Now you're ready to assemble the box. One of the things I love about mitered boxes is how easy they are to glue and clamp together, using nothing more than blue painter's tape. A roll of blue tape provides all the clamping you need. One of the reasons this works so well is that blue tape has some stretch to it, which works to pull the corners tightly together.

Bear in mind that miter joints are end-grain joints, and end grain sucks up glue like a thousand tiny little straws. So you'll notice the glue slowly disappearing before you've had a chance to wrap up the box and close the joints. That can leave the joints starved of glue, which can weaken the joints and allow them to pop open later. To make sure each joint has a thin layer of yellow glue on it, take a last look and apply a little more right before you close up the box.

MASTER THE MITER, AND OPEN A WORLD OF NEW PROJECTS

1 HOW TO SIZE THE TOP AND BOTTOM PANELS. You can drop the panels into their slots to determine the right size to cut them. When there's a little room at both ends of each slot (as shown here), your panels are the right size.

2 DRY-FIT THE BOX. A dry-fit is the only way to know a project will come together properly before you spread glue and clamp it up.

3 A BIT OF SANDING TO DO. Now is the time to sand the inside edges of parts that will be hard to access later. Here, I'm sanding only the areas that will be inside the lid. The lower half of the finished box will be covered by the liner.

4 STRETCH TAPE ACROSS THE JOINTS. Flip the parts so the outside faces are up, and hold them against a long strip of wood to keep them aligned as you pull them tightly together with tape.

5 SPREAD GLUE IN THE JOINTS. Try to keep the glue toward the inside of the miters to minimize the amount that squeezes into the interior of the box. These end-grain joints will drink up glue, so make sure there's a visible coating on each joint before closing the box. A little acid brush makes a great glue spreader.

6 WRAP IT UP. Spread some glue in the slots and insert the top and bottom panels. Then wrap the sides around them to close the box.

7 TAPE THE LAST CORNER. Close the open corner by stretching more tape across it. Pull the tape firmly to close the joint tightly and leave the box to dry for a few hours.

SEPARATE THE TOP AND BOTTOM

Leave the tape on for a few hours, letting the glue cure. Then peel it off, and you're ready to cut your box apart. Set the rip fence to cut the box apart at the right place (see the drawing on p. 117), and then set the blade height as shown in photo 1.

You're going to be making cuts along each side of the box. The key here is to set the blade height so it cuts *almost* through each side, but not quite. If you set it too high, you'll cut through the sides, and the box will be unstable as you cut through the fourth side. But if you leave just a whisker of wood at the inside edges, the box will stay together while you cut it but come apart easily afterward, by running a chisel or screwdriver inside the seams.

1 SET THE BLADE HEIGHT CAREFULLY. Set the blade so its tip is just a hair shy of the thickness of your box sides. To separate the lid at the right point, set the rip fence to the dimension shown on the drawing.

2 CHECK THE DEPTH. Make one cut along one side of the box and push a chisel or screwdriver into it. The tool should break through the remaining wood with a little bit of pressure. If it won't, raise the blade a little. If the slot is wide open, lower the blade a bit.

3 CUT YOUR WAY AROUND THE BOX. With the blade height dialed in, you can make cuts around each side of the box. Keep the box flat on the table and tight to the fence as you make each cut. Note that the lid side runs against the rip fence.

4 ONE BECOMES TWO. Push a screwdriver or chisel into the blade slots to break the last slivers of wood.

5 MAKE A SANDING PLATFORM. Spray contact cement onto the back of two sandpaper sheets (150- and 220-grit) and adhere them to a flat piece of plywood.

6 SAND THE JOINTS. It's easier to keep the parts flat on the sanding platform, rather than sanding them with a handheld block. The same goes for the outside of the box (see p. 131). Start on the rougher paper, then move to the finer grit.

7 CLEAN OUT THE SQUEEZE-OUT. There will be some glue squeeze-out along the inside corners of the box. Now is the time to chisel it away carefully.

MASTER THE MITER, AND OPEN A WORLD OF NEW PROJECTS

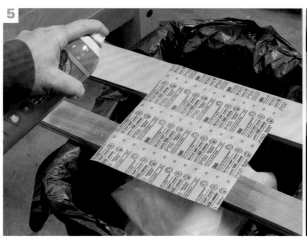

ADD THE LINER PIECES

The liner pieces can be made from the same ⅛-in. plywood used for the top and bottom. If you don't like the seams of the plywood showing, craft stores also sell ⅛-in.-thick basswood, which is a very nice option. Hinges can be tricky to install perfectly, but this box doesn't need them! The liner pieces are taller than the bottom of the box, so they stick up a little. That creates a nice little lip that the top fits onto perfectly. Because the bottom of the box is made from the same thin plywood, the liner pieces create an all-white interior.

1 MITER ONE END. Rip a strip of the ⅛-in. plywood (or basswood) to the right width and then cut a miter cut at one end. No clamps or stops are needed here.

2 MARK AND CUT THE OTHER END. Place the mitered end against one end of the box to mark the miter at the other end. The zero-clearance slot on the sled fence helps you line up the cut. Stay a hair away from the line on the first cut.

3 CREEP UP ON A PERFECT FIT. Nibble away at the last end of each part until it just slides into the box. Fit the parts one by one until all four are nestled together in the box.

4 LITTLE BIT OF SANDING. Gently round and smooth the top edges of the pieces before gluing them in.

5 GLUE AND CLAMP. Spread a little bit of glue inside the box before re-inserting each piece of the liner. Clamp as necessary to make sure each piece is tight against the sides of the box as the glue dries.

MASTER THE MITER, AND OPEN A WORLD OF NEW PROJECTS

WHAT TO DO IF A JOINT POPS OPEN

If some of the joints were a little starved for glue, or you didn't wrap the blue tape tightly enough, you might pop one of the joints open when you're pushing liner pieces into place. Don't panic. Knowing how to fix mistakes is the most important skill of all. In this case, just work more glue into the joint and rewrap that corner with tape. Let it dry a few more hours and it will be just fine.

MAKE A JIG TO CUT SLOTS FOR DECORATIVE KEYS

At this point you can simply sand the box on all sides, round the sharp edges lightly, and apply a finish. But stopping there not only leaves the box a little plain looking, it also means you'll miss out on another great woodworking jig, one you can use for mitered boxes and frames far into the future.

The jig cradles any box or frame and carries it over the table-saw blade, letting you cut a slot through the corners. Insert little tabs of wood in those slots, saw and sand them flush, and you've not only made your project prettier but also made the joints stronger at the same time.

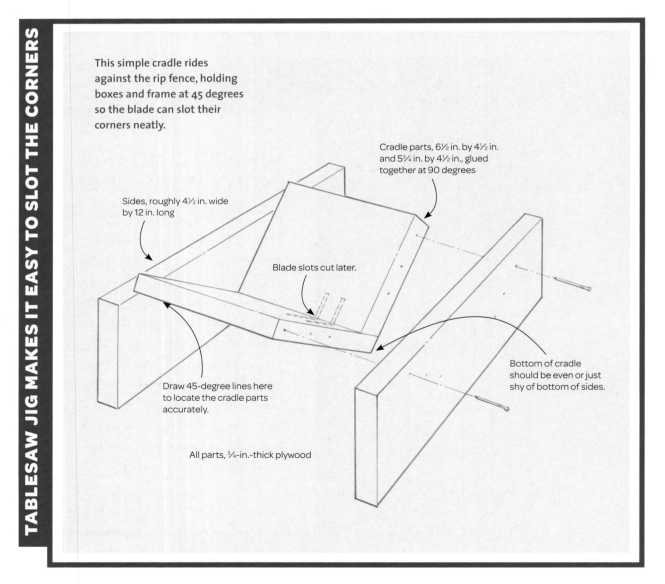

TABLESAW JIG MAKES IT EASY TO SLOT THE CORNERS

This simple cradle rides against the rip fence, holding boxes and frame at 45 degrees so the blade can slot their corners neatly.

Cradle parts, 6½ in. by 4½ in. and 5¾ in. by 4½ in., glued together at 90 degrees

Sides, roughly 4½ in. wide by 12 in. long

Blade slots cut later.

Draw 45-degree lines here to locate the cradle parts accurately.

Bottom of cradle should be even or just shy of bottom of sides.

All parts, ¾-in.-thick plywood

MASTER THE MITER, AND OPEN A WORLD OF NEW PROJECTS

1 GLUE AND NAIL THE JIG TOGETHER. Start by making the center of the cradle, joining the two parts at 90 degrees with glue only (nails or screws could hit the tablesaw blade later). Then mark 45-degree lines on the sides to locate the cradle accurately as you glue and nail or screw on the sides. Keep the nails away from the lower corner of the cradle, where the blade could hit them.

2 SET THE RIP FENCE. Measure as shown to locate the first slot cut 1/2 in. from the bottom and top of the box. You'll slot both halves of the box at this setting.

3 SLOT ONE CORNER AND CHECK THE DEPTH. Set the blade height so the slots are just shy of 1/2 in. long. This will ensure that the blade doesn't cut all the way through to the box interior.

4 SLOT ALL CORNERS. Hold the bottom of the box against the fence side of the jig as you slot each corner. Do the same with the lid, with its top side toward the fence.

5 RESET THE FENCE FOR THE MIDDLE SLOT. To cut the upper slot on the lower part of the box, just reset the rip fence.

MITER KEYS ARE EASY TO INSERT AND TRIM

You can use any wood you like for these decorative keys, but I like to make them from the same wood I used for the rest of the box (you'll need a board that's at least ½ in. thick). You'll notice that the ends of these little keys end up a little darker, because you are seeing their end grain, and that creates subtle contrast with the sides. For even more contrast, go with a darker wood.

1 SIZE THE STRIPS TO FIT. Start with a piece of scrap wood and rip strips as shown, tweaking the rip fence until the strips slide into the miter slots with no slop. Once they do, switch to the real wood you're using for the actual miter key and rip a few long strips.

2 CHOP OFF THE KEYS. Place your strips in a little stack and chop off short pieces with your miter saw. Hold the long end of the strips, not the short pieces, as you make the cuts.

3 GLUE IN THE KEYS. Spread a little bit of glue in the slots, and then press the keys into place. Leave them for a couple hours to dry.

4 SAW OFF THE EXCESS. Use any sharp handsaw to gently cut away most of the excess material, staying just clear of the sides of the box.

5 BLOCK PLANE COMES IN HANDY HERE. If you have a sharp block plane (these are covered in the next chapter), use it with a fine blade setting to trim the keys flush with the sides of the box. If you don't own a block plane, you can simply sand the keys flush.

MASTER THE MITER, AND OPEN A WORLD OF NEW PROJECTS

APPLY A LOVELY FINISH

Oil finishes will stay smelly on the inside of the box, even after they dry, so we'll be using shellac here. Flip ahead to the last chapter to see how to apply this awesome finish.

1 SAND THE BOX SMOOTH. Sand the exterior of the box and lid on your sanding platform, starting on the 150-grit paper and finishing up on the 220. Then gently round the sharp edges with your sanding block.

2 SHELLAC AND WAX ARE THE PERFECT FINISH. A simple shellac finish is great for small boxes. Each coat dries in 10 or 15 minutes, so you can apply all the coats you need in a single day. Finish up with wax to give each box a soft glow and feel. The details are in Chapter 9.

3 LID FITS PERFECTLY. The lid slips perfectly over the liner, holding the two halves together nicely.

SOLID TOP ELEVATES THE LOOK. I made this top from the same white oak used for the sides. It's rabbeted to fit into its slots. It will shrink and expand with humidity changes, so don't glue it in.

MAKE YOUR OWN UNIQUE BOXES

Once you get a feel for the techniques, you can start varying the dimensions and details of your boxes. To give you a small taste of what's possible with these box-making methods, I've added two cool variations. The first is a solid-wood top, made from the same wood used for the outside of the box. The second is a Bluetooth speaker (see p. 134). Unlike the plywood, which is dimensionally stable, solid wood shrinks and expands with seasonal humidity changes, especially across the grain. So you have to let a solid-wood top float in its little slots, rather than gluing it in.

The top is the same thickness as the box sides— $\frac{1}{4}$ in.—but it fits into the same $\frac{1}{8}$-in.-wide slots as the plywood. The way you do that is by cutting small rabbets around the edges of the top, leaving $\frac{1}{8}$-in. tongues that fit neatly into the slots. Cut those rabbets on the tablesaw, using a small stack of dado blades and an auxiliary fence, just like we did for the rabbets at the back of the workbench cabinet (see pp. 61–62).

That's one pretty variation, but you shouldn't stop there. Want to make a bigger box? Just make the sides thicker. The top and bottom can be thicker too, both made from solid wood. I went with a square rabbet on my solid-wood top, but the top can be shaped and detailed all sorts of ways, as can the sides. And when you're ready to try setting hinges, those will take your boxes to a new level. Just be sure to use high-quality, machined brass hinges, the kind that need to be mortised into place (set into little notches).

MASTER THE MITER, AND OPEN A WORLD OF NEW PROJECTS

BLUETOOTH SPEAKER TAKES BOX MITERS EVEN FURTHER

These boxes are so quick and easy to make, I couldn't stop at our little tea containers. Rockler makes a nice little Bluetooth speaker kit, so I designed a handsome mitered cabinet to hold it. I used walnut—one of my favorite hardwoods—for the sides and made the front and back from fir plywood. But any solid wood will do for the sides, and any plywood for the front and back.

The reason I'm using plywood for the fronts and backs on this project, and the top and bottom of the tea box, is that it doesn't expand and contract with changes in humidity, the way solid wood does. That lets me glue those parts into place, strengthening the boxes. Solid-wood panels, on the other hand, have to be left floating in their slots, with a little extra room for expansion.

One bit of design advice for mixing contrasting woods like the walnut and fir I'm using here: Less is more. When you discover the amazing variety of colors and grain patterns at the lumber store, it's easy to get carried away trying to make a big impression. But subtler contrast will be more pleasing in the long run.

The front fits into slots in the sides, just like the top on the tea box, but the back is different. This box isn't cut in half to create a lid, and you'll need access to the interior after you build it, in order to insert the electrical components and the dividers between the speakers. So I cut rabbets at the back of the box, cut the back to fit inside them, and used small screws to attach it.

I thought about all sorts of ways to make the plywood front more interesting, settling on a series of shallow slots, cut in minutes on the tablesaw, which gives the box a retro look. But you can do whatever you like.

You get another bonus technique with this box: learning to use an amazing hole-cutting device that's been around for a century or more. It's the General

Tools No. 55 circle cutter, and it cuts holes from $1^3/_4$ in. up to $7^7/_8$ in. dia. Solid and effective, it's only $20 on Amazon, making it one of the best woodworking deals ever. See "Equip your drill press with these 5 bits" on p. 138 for more on this and other essential drilling tools. The Bluetooth speaker kit also includes a small controller unit that fits onto the back of the box. Rockier made it round, just like the speakers, so it's just as easy to insert.

> When mixing woods like the walnut and fir I'm using here: Less is more. When you discover the amazing variety of colors and grain patterns at the lumber store, it's easy to get carried away.

boost the acoustics

From past speaker projects I've learned a couple of tricks for improving speaker performance. One is adding dividers inside the cabinet. These stop the speakers from "cross-talking" as they resonate and move air, which would muddy the sounds you hear. We'll hold ours in place with hot glue, which couldn't be easier. Another important move is filling the space behind each speaker with a chunk of upholstery foam (or any medium-density foam). This stops the sound from bouncing around inside, making it significantly more crisp and punchy. Try these tricks and you'll be surprised at how great your little Bluetooth unit sounds.

8

bluetooth speaker

Use the same box-making techniques to build a cool cabinet for a Bluetooth speaker kit. Most of the techniques were covered in the tea box project. The rest are shown on the following pages.

The sides are mitered the same way as the tea box and slotted similarly to accept the front of the cabinet. But the back of this cabinet is screwed into a rabbet in the sides so it can be inserted after the box is built, making it possible to add the electronic components. I've included the dimensions I used, but those are really up to you.

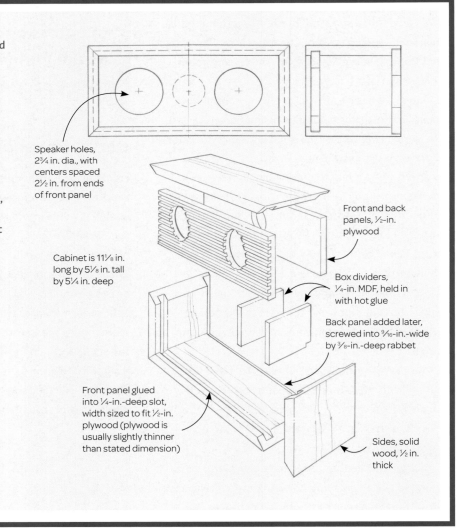

Speaker holes, 2¾ in. dia., with centers spaced 2½ in. from ends of front panel

Cabinet is 11⅛ in. long by 5⅛ in. tall by 5¼ in. deep

Front and back panels, ½-in. plywood

Box dividers, ¼-in. MDF, held in with hot glue

Back panel added later, screwed into 9∕16-in.-wide by ⅜-in.-deep rabbet

Front panel glued into ¼-in.-deep slot, width sized to fit ½-in. plywood (plywood is usually slightly thinner than stated dimension)

Sides, solid wood, ½ in. thick

This mitered box is assembled just like the tea box, but the front panel needs a few extra steps and the interior gets two simple dividers.

1 DRILL LARGE HOLES FOR THE SPEAKERS. Use a hole saw or circle-cutting tool like this one (see "Equip your drill press with these 5 bits" on p. 138) to cut 2-3⁄4-in.-dia. holes in the front panel.

2 SLOT THE FRONT. Evenly spaced slots on the front panel give the project a retro look. Cut them on the tablesaw by setting the blade 3⁄16 in. high and moving the rip fence 1⁄4 in. after each pass.

3 BUILD THE BOX. Choose a nice board and cut a deep, wide slot for the front panel (see the drawing on the facing page) and a rabbet for the back, using your dado set and the techniques covered earlier in the book. Then miter the parts, add glue to the miter joints and front-panel slots, add the front panel only, and wrap up the box with blue tape as you did for the tea box.

4 ADD DIVIDERS. Cut a piece of 1⁄4-in. MDF to fit into the box and use it to create two dividers that wall off the speaker areas. These will prevent the speakers from interfering with each other. Attach these with hot glue and be as messy as you want. Note the small notches left for the speaker wires.

MATERIALS & SUPPLIES

- Stereo Wireless Speaker Kit, $35, Rockler.com
- Smooth, flat piece of solid wood, 1⁄2 in. thick by 5 1⁄4 in. wide by 35 in. long
- 1⁄2-in.-thick plywood for front and back panels
- 1⁄4-in. MDF or plywood for internal dividers
- Hot-glue gun
- 4-in. black drawer pull with screws
- 1-in. anti-skid foot pads, Everbilt, HomeDepot.com
- 3⁄4-in. wood screws for attaching back
- Small piece of thick upholstery foam

ADD THE BACK AND FINISH THE BOX

The back holds the control unit for this speaker kit. Install the speaker components in the front and back panels while the box is open, and then screw in the back and add the other finishing touches.

1 MAKE THE BACK. Cut the back to fit snugly in its rabbets, and then use a Forstner bit in the drill press to center a $1^7/_8$-in. hole for the Bluetooth control unit. You can also cut this hole with a circle cutter.

2 ATTACH THE HARDWARE. Apply your favorite finish to the box and then add a handle to the top and foot pads to the bottom. I used a short driver bit on its own to reach into the tight cabinet when attaching the handle.

3 POP IN THE SPEAKERS. If you drilled the holes precisely, the speakers will press in and stay put. If not, add some 15-minute epoxy to the edges of the holes to hold them in place.

4 FINISH OFF THE BACK. Drill and countersink small holes $1/_4$ in. from the edges, apply some wood finish, and push the Bluetooth control unit into place.

5 CONNECT THE WIRES. The speaker wires are color coded where they connect to the control unit.

6 ONE MORE ACOUSTIC IMPROVEMENT. Push a chunk of upholstery foam into each speaker compartment. This will kill any echoes and make the sound clearer and more punchy.

7 SCREW IN THE BACK. Use $3/_4$-in.-long screws to attach the back and your speaker is done.

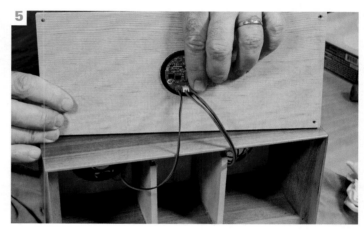

EQUIP YOUR DRILL PRESS WITH THESE 5 BITS

This book adds a benchtop drill press to your workshop, and it's time we talked about the woodworking bits you'll want to use with it. I'll describe them in the order I think you should buy them.

twist drills

First up is the humble twist drill. These are the standard drill bits most people know about, with a V-shaped tip. Some have hex-shaped shanks and others round, but both will fit into the chuck on your drill press. These are the least expensive type of bit, and they work fine for all sorts of general drilling tasks, both in your cordless drill and drill press. They are so inexpensive that you'll be able to afford a big set in lots of sizes up through ½ in.

countersink bit

The next essential bit is the humble countersink, used to inset the heads of screws so they end up flush with the surface, or slightly below it. You can countersink your holes after you drill them, using a dedicated bit, or buy a small set of combination bits that drill and countersink in a single step.

THREE ESSENTIAL BITS. Start with a set of basic twist drills (right). And then add a set of brad-point bits (center) for cleaner drilling when it counts. Next, buy a set of Forstner bits (left), which will drill clean holes with flat bottoms, up to 2 in. dia.

TWO WAYS TO COUNTERSINK. Countersink your screw holes with a specialized bit (right) or drill the hole and countersink in one step with a combo bit (left).

brad-point bits

Twist drills were originally designed for cutting metal and, as a result, do not always make the smoothest holes in wood. For a cleaner entry and more consistent hole diameters, woodworkers turn to brad-point bits, the kind I recommended for your doweling jig. You won't need a full set of these right away, but you should buy a set as soon as you can. Brad-point bits have a sharp point at the tip, which is easier to line up with a pencil mark or, better yet, the small dimple made with an awl. They also have sharp spurs at their edges, which cut a clean rim as they enter the wood.

Compared to the brad-point bit, the twist drill is literally a blunt instrument. But hold onto those basic twist drills. Wear them out on noncritical drilling jobs and save your pricier brad-points for times when perfection is paramount. A good set of brad-point bits goes up to ½ in. Buy as much quality as you can afford, in 1/64-in. increments if possible.

forstner bits

For everything larger than ½ in., your next drilling purchase should be a set of Forstner bits. These are even pricier than brad-points, but they are well worth the money. The Forstner bit is a unique creature. It has a sharp point and sharp spurs, like a brad-point bit, with similar benefits, but the similarities end there.

A Forstner bit has horizontal cutting edges at the bottom, which makes the bottom of its holes very flat too. That works great for all kinds of holes, especially counterbores, those larger holes that let you inset the head of a screw or bolt below the surface of the wood. Forstners also have flat sides,

which keep them marvelously on track, meaning you can drill holes at an angle or even partial holes at the edge of a board. All other types of bits will wander in those situations. Mostly though, Forstner bits are just phenomenal at drilling large holes super-cleanly and accurately, up to 2 in. or more. Buy as large a set and as much quality as you can afford. Better bits will be sharper, more accurate, and longer lasting.

circle cutter

I love the General Tools No. 55 circle cutter. Unlike a hole saw, which is really a contractor's tool designed to cut rough holes in framing lumber, the General No. 55 cuts very clean holes in sizes up to a whopping 7⅞ in., picking up where your Forstner bits leave off.

A circle cutter is infinitely adjustable, letting you bore perfect holes for vacuum hoses, for example. That adjustability lets you add dust-collection ports to router-table fences and other fixtures. It also let me cut perfect-sized holes for the speakers in my Bluetooth kit. Even cooler, when you reverse the cutting bit in the No. 55, it will cut smooth circles just as well, letting you make wheels for wooden toys and smooth disks of all sorts. Flip to the next page to see how to use this versatile tool safely and accurately.

USING A CIRCLE CUTTER SAFELY

With its long, whirling arm, the General Tools No 55 circle-cutter scares some folks. Here's how to use it safely, with a healthy respect but no worries. First, it must be used in a drill press only—NEVER in a handheld drill—with the drill press on its slowest speed. Second, the workpiece must be clamped in place securely. And last, keep your hands clear of the whirling arm. Follow those rules, and you'll love the No. 55 circle cutter.

1 SET THE DRILL BIT. It should extend about ⅛ in. farther than the cutting bit. Lock it there and leave it.

2 SET THE HOLE DIAMETER. The heavy-duty swing arm adjusts in and out to cut holes and circles up to 7⅞ in. diameter.

3 SLOW THE SPEED. My drill press is a vintage Delta, but all models have a way to reduce their RPMs. Choose the slowest setting.

4 LOCK DOWN THE WORKPIECE AND KEEP YOUR HANDS CLEAR. This tool must be used in a drill press, with the workpiece clamped to the table.

5 AMAZING RESULTS. Go slow and steady, and the circle cutter will bore a super-clean hole. Reverse the cutting bit and it will cut clean circles, for toy wheels, for example.

GET READY FOR FRAME MITERS

When you cut angles in the other direction, to form a flat frame, you're cutting frame miters. These can be cut with a variety of tools, but I think the miter saw offers the easiest approach. As I've pointed out before, the miter saw is a contractor's tool and needs some help to do fine woodworking. The first step is to replace the standard blade with a higher-quality, smoother-cutting crosscut blade. You'll find these at home centers, designed for miter saws. Look for one designed for fine-finish cuts and expect to spend $50 or more for a decent one. The next step is dialing in the angle setting on your saw, and then creating zero-clearance surfaces where the blade exits the wood. On this tool, that's the base and fence, where we will add fresh pieces of 1/4-in. MDF.

Cutting with an angled blade can push parts sideways, which can make a cut slightly curved instead of flat. The solution is simple. Stick some sandpaper (120-grit) onto the back fence, and the pieces will stay put. This sandpaper trick works in other situations too, on other tools and jigs.

After you miter one end of your workpieces, you'll need to set a stop to ensure that the parts come out at the same length as you miter the opposite ends, just like we did for the box parts. There are lots of ways to create a stop on the miter saw; check the bottom photo at right for one of the easiest.

1 DIAL IN THE SAW ANGLE. Start by moving the blade to the 45-degree position, and then check its accuracy by cutting four equal parts and dry-fitting them. If there are gaps, adjust the 45-degree setting. Read the manual to learn how to do that on your saw.

2 BETTER CUTTING SURFACES. Use double-stick tape to attach pieces of 1/4-in. MDF to the base and fence of the saw, and then cut through it to create a zero-clearance blade slot. Last, use spray adhesive to attach 120-grit sandpaper to the fence, so parts don't slip sideways as you cut them.

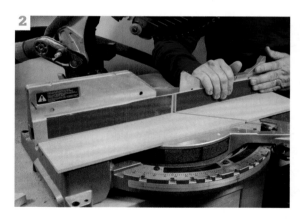

3 ADD A STOP SYSTEM. Screw a long strip to the upper part of the fence to hold a stop that we'll clamp on later.

TWO FUN PROJECTS WITH FRAME MITERS

To get you familiar with cutting and clamping these miters, we'll build a couple of custom picture frames. It can be pretty pricey to have your favorite photos and artwork framed and matted at your local frame shop. Doing it yourself not only saves money but also lets you make your pictures more personal.

My first trick is a great way to get the mat board and glass you'll need. I learned from a friend to go to a dollar store and look for cheap frames with the mat and glass (or acrylic plastic) included, sized for standard photo formats. You can also buy mats and glass at a framing shop or cut them yourself if you have the right tools. I went with a square frame and a rectangular one, to fit a couple of keepsake photos I have, but the size of the photos, mats, and frames is up to you. The techniques shown here will cover them all.

With a couple of picture frames under your belt, you'll be ready for another cool frame, which turns an album cover into wall art (see p. 146). The thin frame you see up front is flat and simple. Then you just glue thin MDF strips to a thin MDF or plywood panel to create a pocket in the back. The top of the pocket is left open to let you slide record covers in and out and change your wall art whenever you want.

PICTURE FRAMES 101

The first step in any picture-frame project is finding nice wood with enough length to wrap around your artwork, including the mat if you're using one. Almost any width greater than about $3/4$ in. will do, and any thickness greater than $5/8$ in.

The next step is deciding on a molding style for your frame. I kept it simple here, keeping both of my frames flat. One has a small step cut on the tablesaw along its inside edge. I textured the other by slicing the frame parts to thickness on my bandsaw and leaving the cuts bumpy, giving them just a light sanding

afterward. I know many of you won't have a bandsaw yet, but the point is that anything goes. I didn't even touch the router, which opens up an endless variety of other molding profiles, powered by the infinite array of router bits.

On the frame for the album covers, I cut a series of shallow, evenly spaced slots, like the ones on the front of the bluetooth speaker, using the same tablesaw technique.

Picture frames need a rabbet on the back side, to hold the glass, mat board, art, and a thin backer board, which can be made from stiff cardboard or $1/8$-in. plywood. I make these rabbets about $7/16$ in. deep, and then use picture-framing "points" to hold in the contents, driving them in with an inexpensive set of "picture frame pliers."

For all of the projects in this chapter, I went with shellac, a wonderful finish that cures super-fast, letting you apply all the coats you need in a single day. For all three of the beautiful, straightforward wood finishes featured in this book—oil, polyurethane, and shellac—flip ahead to the finishing chapter.

CUSTOMIZING FRAMES. I added a shallow rabbet to the frame above and a rough bandsaw cut to give the frame at right a rustic touch.

MASTER THE MITER, AND OPEN A WORLD OF NEW PROJECTS

PROJECT N⁰.

custom picture frames

Use the following techniques to make unique picture frames for any artwork. Use any wood you want, make the sides as wide as you like, and mold or texture the front as desired.

MATERIALS & SUPPLIES

- Framing mats, if desired
- Glass or acrylic plastic in same size
- Thin backer board in same size (cardboard or thin plywood)
- Band clamp
- Window glazing or framer's points
- Picture-framing pliers
- Sawtooth hangers

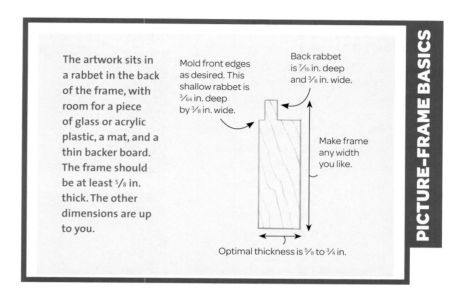

PICTURE-FRAME BASICS

The artwork sits in a rabbet in the back of the frame, with room for a piece of glass or acrylic plastic, a mat, and a thin backer board. The frame should be at least $5/8$ in. thick. The other dimensions are up to you.

Mold front edges as desired. This shallow rabbet is $3/64$ in. deep by $3/8$ in. wide.

Back rabbet is $7/16$ in. deep and $3/8$ in. wide.

Make frame any width you like.

Optimal thickness is $5/8$ to $3/4$ in.

PREP YOUR FRAME STOCK

For the best appearance, make each frame from a single, long strip of wood.

1 MOLD OR TEXTURE THE FRONT. I decorated one frame with a shallow rabbet along the inside edge. Use double-stick tape to attach an auxiliary fence to the rip fence, bury the blade in it slightly as we did earlier in the book, and then run your long piece of stock on edge to cut a clean rabbet.

2 RABBET THE BACK FOR THE CONTENTS. Now bury your dado blades in the auxiliary fence to rabbet the back to hold the glass, mat, artwork, and backer board.

CUSTOM PICTURE FRAMES

MITER THE PARTS

As with the box parts we cut earlier, miter one end of each part first. Then set that end against a stop to miter the other ends to the right length.

1 MITER ONE END OF EACH PIECE. As you chop the long strip into four pieces, you'll be mitering one end of each part properly. Put the outer face down against the saw table for these cuts. Hold the workpiece tight against the fence as you bring the blade slowly down. Let it come to a full stop before lifting it.

2 INCREDIBLE CUTS. The MDF panels prevent chipping along the bottom edge, the sandpaper prevents side-slipping, and the results are clean and crisp.

3 CHEAP SOURCE FOR FRAMING MATERIALS. Check out your local dollar store for cheap frames that contain a nice piece of glass, a mat, and a thin backer board. You can also find those materials at craft stores and framing stores.

4 USE THE CONTENTS TO SIZE THE SIDES. Set the mat or backer board into the back rabbet, leaving a little extra at each end of the rabbet as you mark the other end for mitering. Carry that mark around to the front of the frame.

5 USE THE MARK TO LINE UP THE CUT. Note how the blade slot in the fence helps you line up your pencil mark. Also, the blade angle stays right where it is, and the workpiece flips over for the second cut.

6 SET YOUR STOP. I made the stop L-shaped as shown, so I could clamp it to that upper strip I attached to the saw earlier.

7 CUT TWO SIDES AT THAT SETTING. Miter the other end of two opposite sides, and then reset the stop for the other set of sides.

MASTER THE MITER, AND OPEN A WORLD OF NEW PROJECTS

GLUE UP THE FRAME AND FILL IT WITH ART ━━━

Use a simple band clamp to glue together frames like these. Then add a finish, tack on a hanger, and use framing points to hold the contents in place.

The band clamp I like best is made by Rockler and is just $20. Its ratcheting handle is easier to use than the ones on typical tie-down straps.

1 GET THE BAND CLAMP READY. Start by winding the strap around the ratcheting spindle a few times. Then wrap it loosely around the frame, thread the loose end into the other part of the clamp, and pull it snug but not tight.

2 SPREAD A THIN LAYER OF GLUE. The miter joints are end-grain joints, so they want to drink up the glue at first. Spread a little more right before you close the joints.

3 TIGHTEN YOUR BAND CLAMP. Center the strap on the edges of the frame as you draw it tight. The ratcheting handle makes it easy to tighten. If the joints aren't staying level with each other, pinch the faces with traditional clamps.

4 ADD A HANGER. I like sawtooth-style hangers for small- to medium-sized frames. Mark the exact center of the top side of the frame and center the hanger on that line. For larger, heavier frames, I place a small eye hook on each side of the frame and string "picture wire" between them.

5 HOW TO HOLD IN THE ARTWORK. Place the glass, mat board, photo/art, and a thin backer board into the rabbet. Then drive framer's "points" around the edges, using a framing pliers. I like to use "glazier's points" here, designed for setting glass in windows.

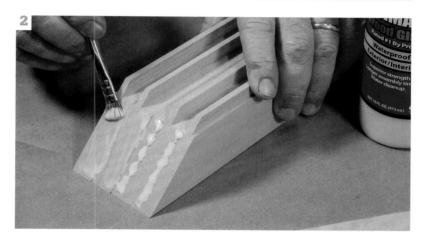

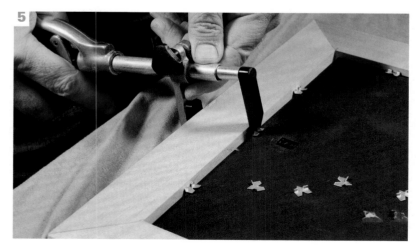

10

album-cover holder adds a pocket to a standard frame

There's something about vinyl records that I still love. Aside from the warm, full sound, there's the tactile appeal of the record jackets, liner notes, and discs themselves, harking back to a time when so much care was taken to produce an album and buying one was a big deal. As an analog antidote to digital music, vinyl records have drawn in a new generation of fans. But you don't have to be a collector to enjoy this interactive album holder. Find a few vinyl records at a flea market or antique store, and you're ready to create this interactive art piece.

If you can make a mitered frame, you can build this project. I started by determining the size and thickness of a typical album. Many of my favorites are double albums, so I added extra space in the pocket for those. You can follow the dimensions provided in the drawing on the facing page, or just lay an album down on a thin back panel, build up strips around it to form the sides and bottom of the pocket, and then size your frame to just cover the edges of the album cover.

The size and style of the front frame is up to you, though I make mine thinner than the picture frames, since there is no rabbet needed at the back. I gave this frame the same series of grooves I used on the Bluetooth speaker, making the two items a nice marriage of yesterday and today.

After mitering the parts, all you have to do is glue and clamp them together. That brings up a third miter-clamping method, the easiest one yet, perfect for thin frames like this one. Blue painter's tape stars again, with its inherent stretchiness, but we'll be stretching it across each individual joint this time—front and back.

This thin frame will only be so strong on its own, but it gains additional rigidity from the pocket that's glued onto its back. Follow the step-by-step photos for the whole process. And once again, turn to the final chapter for easy finishing advice. Welcome to the world of miters. These projects are only the beginning of what you can do with this elegantly simple joint.

TURN VINTAGE VINYL INTO WALL ART. This frame has a pocket in back that allows you to slip album covers in and out.

This project has a thin frame up front, which hides a pocket for a favorite album cover. The pocket is sized to fit common cover dimensions, with extra thickness for double albums, and it's open at the top so you can change the display whenever you want.

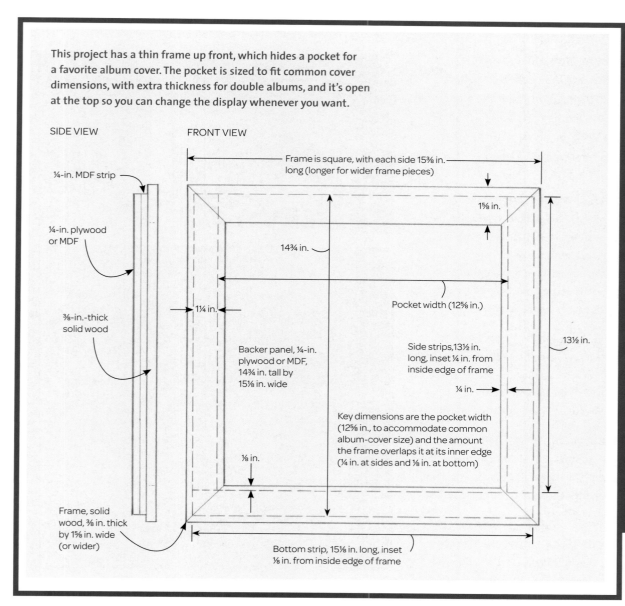

SIDE VIEW

FRONT VIEW

¼-in. MDF strip

¼-in. plywood or MDF

⅜-in.-thick solid wood

Frame, solid wood, ⅜ in. thick by 1⅝ in. wide (or wider)

Frame is square, with each side 15⅜ in. long (longer for wider frame pieces)

1⅝ in.

14¾ in.

1¼ in.

Pocket width (12⅝ in.)

Side strips,13½ in. long, inset ¼ in. from inside edge of frame

¼ in.

13½ in.

Backer panel, ¼-in. plywood or MDF, 14¾ in. tall by 15⅛ in. wide

Key dimensions are the pocket width (12⅝ in., to accommodate common album-cover size) and the amount the frame overlaps it at its inner edge (¼ in. at sides and ⅛ in. at bottom)

⅛ in.

Bottom strip, 15⅛ in. long, inset ⅛ in. from inside edge of frame

Start by making a thin flat frame, and then add the pocket to the back by simply gluing on strips and a thin panel. The frame parts are a bit thin for our band clamp, so we'll use another cool trick for clamping them.

1 DIFFERENT WAY TO CLAMP MITERS. Draw pieces of wide blue painter's tape across the joints. Be sure each joint is aligned as you stretch tape tightly across it. Then flip the frame over, stretch tape across the other side of each joint, and pinch the joints with clamps to make sure they stay level with each other.

2 MAKE A FEW LAYOUT MARKS. Mark the correct insets for aligning the pocket strips. Mark these at the top and bottom of the frame, so you can line up the strips properly.

3 GLUE DOWN THE STRIPS. Start with the bottom strip and one side strip, aligning them with your layout marks and each other. Add extra strips of plywood on top to spread the clamping pressure.

4 GLUE ON THE LAST STRIP AND THE BACK PANEL. The last strip goes on first, clamped like the others. Give an hour to dry and then glue on the back panel, using plywood strips again to spread the clamping pressure.

5 DRILL A HOLE AND YOU'RE DONE. All you need for hanging the frame is a small hole, drilled near the top edge of the backer panel, and centered across its width. Make the hole slightly larger than the head of a drywall screw. To prevent splintering, place a strip of wood in the pocket before drilling, and make sure to stop after drilling through the thin panel.

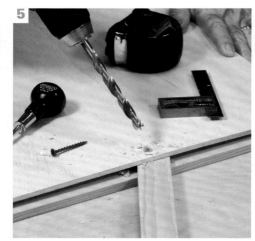

7

foolproof sharpening

CHISELS, HANDPLANES, and handsaws are the holy trinity of hand tools, used by woodworkers to take their work to a new level of precision and refinement. So far in these books, however, I've limited my hand-tool use mostly to a single handsaw (see p. 152). Razor sharp and ready to use out of the box, it's perfect for beginners and intermediates alike.

The reason I've steered clear of chisels and handplanes until now is that they need to be sharpened really well to work their magic. And magic is exactly what they perform, helping you do a wide range of indispensable tasks with no setup required, other than the occasional sharpening session. Sharpening is the gateway to this new way of working. If you never quite master the process, your chisels and handplanes will feel more like enemies than friends. If you follow the instructions in this chapter, you'll pass gleefully into hand-tool heaven. It's really that simple.

I've seen every sharpening technique under the sun...and tried most of them. While there are a number of tools and techniques that will get you to nirvana, I'll be offering up a straightforward path that anyone can follow. That's what these books are all about. In that vein, we'll be building a simple, effective sharpening station that includes everything you need to put a razor edge on all of your hand tools. Once you learn how to use it, you'll be ready for the project in the next chapter, a classic Shaker bench that will put your sharp new hand tools to use.

A SOLID CHISEL SET. These are standard "bench chisels," all-purpose performers that can handle a variety of tasks. This WoodRiver set arrived in good shape, but the backs needed flattening and polishing before I was able to hone the bevel side. Higher-end chisels will show up with flat, polished backs and need just a light honing to be razor sharp and ready to go.

WoodRiver Low-Angle, $130, Woodcraft.com

Stanley 6-in. Bailey Low-Angle, $48, HomeDepot.com

Veritas DX60, $220, LeeValley.com

THREE LEVELS OF BLOCK PLANES. These three models represent the low, middle, and high end of the market. All are potentially great performers, but the low- and middle-end planes need extra work to reach their potential. Other than a light blade honing, the Veritas is ready to go out of the box and is an amazing tool. The WoodRiver's blade needed flattening and polishing as well as honing, and the Stanley needed a complete overhaul. But all three worked great in the end.

MOST HAND TOOLS NEED SHARPENING, BUT SOME DON'T

In this book, our main hand tools consist of the aforementioned handsaw, a basic set of chisels, a small marking knife (see next chapter), and the first handplane I recommend for any woodworker: the nimble, versatile, relatively affordable block plane.

Not all of these tools need sharpening. The pullsaw (see the photo on p. 152) is a good example. While Western-style handsaws cut on the push stroke and need sharpening from time to time, pullsaws come with hardened teeth that are razor sharp and made to stay that way for years of use. This type of saw is also easier to use and less prone to binding in the cut.

As for the marking knife, I'm going with an affordable, effective X-Acto knife with a snap-off blade (see p. 188 in the next chapter), which lets you expose a new razor-sharp edge whenever the tip gets dull, meaning no sharpening is required.

I'll be focusing my sharpening talk here on chisels and plane blades (or "plane irons"). Although both work a little differently, the way you sharpen them is the same. Learn it and you'll be ready to sharpen and use all sorts of hand tools in the future. That includes larger handplanes that let you prep surfaces much faster than sandpaper can do, spokeshaves that smooth curves just as quickly, and specialized planes designed to fit joints perfectly to each other.

A SHARP EDGE IS THE JUNCTION OF TWO POLISHED SURFACES

Every one of these exciting tools requires a razor-sharp blade to do its thing, and the two components of that edge will be the same in every case: a flat back and an angled bevel, both honed to a mirror polish. Neglect either of those two intersecting planes, and the edge won't be truly sharp.

In practice, the vast majority of your sharpening work will happen on the bevel side of the blade; but before you tackle the bevel, you have to flatten and polish the back. That can be both tricky and time-consuming, depending on the quality of the manufacturing and the way you approach the process, but, luckily, it's a job you only have to do once. After that, your sharpening process will consist of grinding and honing the bevel, which goes relatively quickly.

Just like a tablesaw, even the best chisels and plane blades will not be ready to use out of the box. While the most expensive will arrive with their backs ground perfectly flat and at least partially polished, the rest won't, leaving you a fair bit of work to do on the backs before you can move on to the bevels. So we'll cover the whole sharpening process here, letting you save some money on your first few hand tools.

A BUYER'S GUIDE TO CHISELS AND HANDPLANES

The best chisels and handplanes not only require less work to sharpen, especially up front, but their blades are made of better steel, meaning they hold a sharp edge relatively longer, letting you spend more time woodworking and less sharpening. Equally important, every mechanical part of the best handplanes will work smoothly and positively, making adjustments a cinch.

So there's definitely a case to be made for investing in quality at the outset, as chisels and handplanes are designed for a lifetime of use. But there's also a good case for bargain hunting at the beginning of your woodworking career. First, you don't want to invest too much in a hobby you might not end up pursuing long-term. Second, you don't need a shop full of perfect tools to get started, and getting started is the most important step of all. And last, you'll learn a lot by tuning up less-than-perfect power tools and hand tools, from how they work to how to maintain them in the future.

But all of these paths are just fine. The bottom line is that you can end up with great hand tools without emptying your bank account.

path 1: invest in quality up front

If you are ready to invest now in a block plane and chisel set that will offer the highest level of performance over a lifetime of use, you really don't have to look any farther than two companies—the Coke and Pepsi of the high-quality hand-tool market. One of those companies, Lie-Nielsen Toolworks, has taken the best hand-tool designs of the past and made them better. The other, Lee Valley—specifically their Veritas line of hand tools—has completely re-invented many of the classics. But you won't find anything but amazing quality and performance up and down either company's catalogs. There are other great makers that specialize in one thing or the other, but those two companies are a great place to start.

path 2: sweat equity

Due to an explosion of interest in woodworking in the 1970s and '80s, we have more hand tools than ever to choose from. Not surprisingly, both Lie-Nielsen and Lee Valley were founded right after that initial explosion. Soon after, many other brands—made all over the globe—jumped into the market, offering

SOME TOOLS SHOW UP READY TO GO. I strongly recommend buying a handsaw that cuts on the pull stroke. Start with an inexpensive yet effective model like this Irwin model (bottom), available at your local home center. Later, add a Japanese dozuki saw (top), which will make a faster, finer cut.

woodworkers a range of choices in new tools. For the block plane and chisels in this book, I went with nice mid-range models—Woodcraft's WoodRiver brand—that show up in relatively good shape, need a moderate tune-up at the outset, and deliver very solid performance after that.

To help you save even more, I'll show you how to rehab a plane that needs even more work (see "Handplane clinic" on p. 170). This process takes a bit more time but opens you up to less-expensive new planes and gently used vintage models. The used market has also exploded, with tool collectors snapping up vintage models, rating their condition and offering them for sale on websites and in person at yearly gatherings around the U.S. and Europe.

There are pluses and minus to buying new or used. With a new tool, you know what you're getting and where to get it. In other words, you'll receive a rust-free, brand-new tool, a short time after you order it, from any number of online retailers. The used market is a Wild West by comparison. You might strike gold on a classic handplane or chisel that's incredibly well made, with little to no rust. Or you might buy something that was never very good in the first place,

is irreparably rusted or damaged, and/or has missing parts, etc. But if you're careful on eBay or at your local flea market or hand-tool sale, you can come up with incredible deals.

One great source for high-quality, pre-owned hand tools is your local woodworking "guild." These hobbyist clubs hold estate sales when members pass away, and also offer a way for members to sell tools to each other.

you can make most planes and chisels perform well

When I was starting out, I bought used tools almost exclusively. Those included less-expensive new models and vintage tools worth saving. In both cases, all it took was some extra work to get these tools to perform wonderfully.

One easy step you can take to improve the performance of an inexpensive new plane or a used vintage model is replacing the standard blade with an aftermarket one from Hock Tools, Lee Valley/Veritas, Lie-Nielsen Toolworks, or a variety of other great online sources. These blades will have a flat back, leaving

THE SHARPENING PROCESS

The first stage on most chisels and plane blades is flattening and polishing the back of the tool. The good news is you only have to do this once. The rest of the work happens on the bevel side of the tool.

FLATTENING AND POLISHING THE BACK. The most-expensive chisels and plane blades won't need this, but most tools will. This is best done on sandpaper, adhered to a dead-flat surface of some kind. After that you'll move to you waterstones, bringing the back to a high polish. Note that the whole back doesn't need this treatment, just the portion near the tip.

GRINDING THE BEVEL. You'll do this on sandpaper at your sharpening station, using your honing guide.

HONING THE BEVEL. By raising the angle of the tool in the guide, you'll be honing just a small section near the tip, bringing it to a mirror polish on your waterstones.

THE THREE MAIN STAGES

A sharp edge is the junction of two highly polished surfaces. The best way to get there is the following three steps.

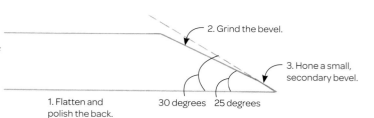

2. Grind the bevel.

3. Hone a small, secondary bevel.

1. Flatten and polish the back.

30 degrees 25 degrees

you next-to-no work to do on it, are made of excellent steel, and are often thicker than stock blades, meaning they will be much more solid in use. After that, you can rehab the plane itself, using the simple techniques shown in "Handplane clinic" on p 170.

So there's no reason to wait until you have enough money for the highest-end hand tools. If you're short on cash, dig around for deals, learn how to rehab and sharpen them, and start enjoying what hand tools can do.

> I've boiled down the essential gear as far as I can, but there's no escaping a small investment in essential sharpening equipment.

SHARPENING IS A THREE-STEP PROCESS

As I mentioned previously, a sharp edge is the junction of two polished surfaces. On plane blades and chisels, one of those surfaces is the entire flat back of the tool and the other is a short bevel that's ground onto the other side. When the blade shows up in your hands, it will already have its back ground relatively flat and its bevel formed. If you buy the very best new hand tools, the backs of the blades might arrive both perfectly flat and sufficiently polished for you to move on to the bevel. But I'm going to assume they're not, as they weren't on my WoodRiver plane blade and chisels and aren't on 90% of the hand tools out there.

After the back is flat and polished, you can move on to the bevel. You'll attack the bevel in two stages, grinding and then honing. The grinding stage produces a flat, even bevel at 25 degrees or so. That's

your starting point, and most chisel and plane blades come with a nice bevel already formed. After that you'll move on to finer abrasives for the honing stage. The really cool trick here is to raise the angle of the tool a little for honing, so you're polishing only the tip, creating what's called a "secondary bevel" or "micro-bevel."

The genius of the secondary bevel is that it requires you to hone only a small area. The fine abrasives used for honing cut more slowly, and it would take a long time to bring the entire bevel to a mirror polish. Luckily, you don't have to, because only the very tip of the blade needs to be sharp.

I said three steps, but there are really three and a half. Grinding and honing the bevel will leave a tiny little whisker of metal—often called a "wire edge"—rolled over onto the back side of the blade. That needs to be removed to leave the tip truly sharp. It's easy to do: You just flip the tool over onto its back and rub it a little on your finest honing stone (8,000 grit) at the very end of the process. It only takes a few seconds.

After you've honed that first little secondary bevel, you can rehone it a number of times to resharpen the blade, without needing to grind a whole new bevel. But eventually the "micro-bevel" won't be very micro anymore and will be too wide for efficient honing. That's when you have to regrind the whole bevel at 25 degrees again, so you can hone a small new secondary bevel. This will all make more sense when we start working through the steps. But first let's talk about the sharpening gear you'll need.

ESSENTIAL ABRASIVES

I've boiled down the essential gear as far as I can, but there's no escaping a small investment in essential sharpening equipment. For our rougher abrasives, used for flattening backs and grinding bevels, we'll use common sandpaper. For polishing those backs and honing the bevels, you'll need to spend significantly more.

INVEST IN SOME ESSENTIAL SHARPENING EQUIPMENT

You'll need some abrasive stones, a honing guide, and some simple shopmade equipment to get yourself set up for successful sharpening and a lifetime of happy hand-tool use.

Basic honing guide, $16, Amazon.com

Waterstone: Norton, 1,000/4,000 grit, $105, Woodcraft.com

Waterstone: Norton, 8,000 grit, $120, Woodcraft.com

Diamond stone: DMT 10-Inch DuoSharp Bench Stone, Coarse/Extra-Coarse, $97, Amazon.com

HEART OF THE SYSTEM. Old-school oilstones have been supplanted by Japanese-style waterstones, which cut efficiently and use only water for lubrication. You'll need three different waterstones: the one at left is a combination stone with two abrasives; the one in the middle is a single-abrasive stone; the diamond plate at right is used to flatten the waterstones before each use. On top of the single-abrasive stone is the simple honing guide we'll use throughout the sharpening process.

CARE AND FEEDING. Buy a small plastic tub and keep your waterstones in it, submerged in water. They'll also need an occasional spritz of water in use.

A SANDING PLATE FOR FLATTENING. You'll need a dead-flat substrate for sandpaper, to be used for flattening the backs of chisels and plane blades. This piece of Corian came from the sink cutout in a countertop, and I got it for free. Another affordable source for a flat plate is a large marble or granite tile (not a ceramic one).

MAKE A SHARPENING STATION. After the backs of your plane blade and chisels are flat and polished, you'll be able to do all of your future sharpening at this handy sharpening station. Read on for how to build and use it.

You can do your fine honing on all sorts of abrasives, from sandpaper to exotic ceramic stones, but 8,000 grit is the magic number for producing a truly sharp edge. To get there I strongly recommend a set of waterstones in the following grits: 1,000 (or 1,200), 4,000, and 8,000. Woodworkers in North America and Europe once relied on naturally quarried stones, lubricated with oil, and those Arkansas stones and other types still work fine. However, once we discovered waterstones, used by Japanese woodworkers, most of us never looked back.

waterstone basics

Waterstones are lubricated with water, making them less messy. They are also softer and easier to flatten than oilstones, which exposes fresh abrasive and keeps them working efficiently. Combination stones, actually two different waterstones laminated back-to-back, are a good way to save money. But no matter which way you slice your stones, you're likely to spend around $200 for the set. Norton is a good brand made in the U.S., and there are a bunch of great brands manufactured in Japan. There are also some lower-quality models, so beware of half-price "bargains."

Waterstones, especially the lower grits, dish out relatively quickly and need to be flattened regularly. Otherwise, they'll hone a slightly curved edge onto your blades, and you'll never really know if the finer abrasive on the next stone is reaching the tip of the tool.

As for storage, your waterstones should be kept in a water bath, so they are always saturated and ready to go. That just means buying a little plastic tub with a cover, filling it partway, and dropping the stones in. After a while the metal and stone dust from the waterstones will dirty up the tub, so you'll want to give it a wash and some fresh water. Also, you always want a little bit of water on the surface of your waterstones when you're using them, so buy a small spray bottle and keep it with your sharpening gear.

diamond plate flattens waterstones

There are specialized stones made for flattening waterstones. Most of those work fine, but my favorite flattening stone for this purpose is a diamond plate, or more precisely a metal and plastic plate with diamonds embedded in it. DMT is one good brand but there are others. Look for one that's 10 in. long with 45-micron diamonds ("325 mesh") on it. Those will flatten your waterstones relatively quickly while leaving the surface smooth.

Specialized flattening stones are cheaper than diamond plates, so go for one of those if you want. But I like the fact that I can also sharpen kitchen knives quickly on my diamond plate, and it stays sharp for many years of occasional use.

honing guide is another must-have

As you move through the various grades of sandpaper and the three waterstones you'll be using to grind and hone your bevels, it's critical that you keep the tool at the same precise angle for every pass. Otherwise, you'll never know if each new abrasive is reaching the tip of the tool and replacing the rougher scratches from the last one. A basic, affordable honing guide is the answer. It clamps onto your chisels and plane blades, with a small wheel on the bottom that rides over the abrasive surface and keeps the tool at a fixed angle the whole time.

Pro woodworkers of the past (and a few in the present) were able to hone their blades effectively without a guide, relying on muscle memory and constant practice to keep the tool at a consistent angle. But this is a dicey move for the rest of us, who don't sharpen hand tools on a daily basis. And since a honing guide is so cheap, and so quick to clamp onto a tool, it's a no-brainer. Better yet, you only need the simplest type of honing guide to get the job done. Basic models are available for under $20 online, and they work great on both narrow chisels and wide plane blades.

One of the keys to using a honing guide is clamping the blade or chisel with a precise amount of blade protruding from the front of it, creating the exact angle you're after. Higher-end models have clamp-on attachments that set the protrusion for a variety of common angles. My favorite of these is the Veritas Mk. II honing guide from Lee Valley Tools, which also has a wide roller on the bottom for excellent stability. But you don't need a fancy guide like that one. Our sharpening station has a row of stops that dial in your setup in seconds.

SHARPENING STATION CONTAINS EVERYTHING YOU NEED

The featured project in this chapter is one of my favorites, and it forms the center of a sharpening class I teach at my local woodworking club. It was inspired by a somewhat similar platform designed by Deneb Puchalksi of Lie-Nielsen Tools, which was featured in *Fine Woodworking* magazine when I was working there.

I simplified Puchalski's design a bit and made it out of melamine-covered particleboard instead of plywood to help it stay flat and resist water. But you should still wipe it dry after each use. I also added extra space for sticking down a full sheet of sandpaper. Like many advanced woodworkers, Puchalski uses a bench grinder to form fresh bevels on his chisels and plane blades, before honing them on waterstones. But we'll be using sandpaper for grinding, and our same basic honing guide. That lets us fit the whole sharpening process onto one compact sharpening platform, which you can stow away easily on a shelf. Grinding on sandpaper also means you won't need to buy a bench grinder for now or learn how to use it effectively without overheating your blades and softening their hardened steel.

Here are the key components of our handy sharpening station (see the drawing on p. 158). Along one edge is a series of stops for positioning tools in the honing guide. We'll be grinding our bevels at 25 degrees and honing the secondary bevels at 30 degrees, and there are stops for both of those angles. There are actually two stops for each angle, since the honing guide holds chisels in a lower position than wide plane blades, which changes the geometry a little.

Next to those stops are four little cleats for holding two waterstones in place, so they don't slide around in use. I left just two positions for our three waterstones, assuming one of them will be a combo stone, but you can easily make the platform a little wider and build in a spot for a third stone.

Next to that is an open area for a full sheet of 220-grit paper. You already know from earlier chapters how to use spray adhesive to attach sandpaper to a flat surface, but here are the key steps. Spray the contact cement only on the back of the paper, working somewhere the overspray won't be a problem. Let the wet adhesive dry and get sticky for a minute or two before pressing the paper down evenly onto your flat substrate. Keep rubbing gently for another minute or so to make sure it doesn't curl up and there are no bubbles, and then leave it another 10 minutes to dry before using it.

Another important tip is to replace the sandpaper often; otherwise the grinding process will slow significantly. Just peel it off, wipe away the leftover contact cement with paint thinner, wipe the surface dry, and then stick on another sheet. It's fast and easy. That does it for the main equipment you'll need. Now let's get into the process.

STEP ONE IS
LAPPING THE BACK

"Lapping" refers to flattening the back of a chisel or plane blade and also honing it to a high polish—without losing that flatness. This is the fussiest part of the sharpening process, but it's essential to success. After that, the back will always be flat and polished, and you can focus your sharpening efforts on the bevel side of the edge.

The easiest way to flatten the back of a chisel or plane blade is by simply adhering sandpaper to a flat surface and rubbing the tool on it. We used a version of this technique when sanding the small boxes in Chapter 6. But the plywood we used there isn't quite flat enough for tool backs.

two great options for a flattening plate

Flattening backs relies on just that: flatness. If the surface doesn't stay perfectly flat during the process, and gets even slightly rounded at the edges, for example, we'll have that same old problem of not knowing if each new, finer abrasive is actually reaching the tip of the tool.

For chisels, a rounded back creates another problem. Chisels require a perfectly flat, straight back to make the straight, precise paring cuts you are looking for. If the back is rounded ever-so-slightly, the chisel won't travel in a straight line, and your cuts will be unpredictable and frustrating.

So I highly recommend that you find something flatter and more warp-proof than plywood to use as your lapping surface. There are specialized granite "surface plates" that are dead-flat and very expensive, but there are also much-less-spendy options that work just as well. One is any stone tile—made of marble or granite, for example—ground and honed dead-flat. Go to your local tile shop or home center and buy just one. Make sure it's not a normal ceramic tile, as those are not very flat at all. If you get the 12x24-in. size, you'll be

able to stick two full sheets of sandpaper on the top side of the tile. If the bottom side is just as smooth and flat, you can stick two more there.

Another great option for a flat lapping surface is the waste piece from a countertop sink cutout. Countertop materials are very smooth and flat, and you might be able to pick up a free cutout at your local countertop shop. The one I used in this chapter is made from Corian, a solid-surface countertop material. It's made of a very dense type of plastic, so you can cut it—slowly and carefully—with any carbide-tipped saw blade, like the one on your circular saw and tablesaw.

flatten the back on sandpaper

Start by adhering 220-grit paper to your flat surface, and then lay the chisel or blade on it and rub it forward and back a few times, working to keeping it perfectly flat the whole time. I can't stress enough how important it is to keep the tool flat as you rub it, and how important it is that the sandpaper not have any areas where it isn't stuck soundly to the substrate and has bubbled upward slightly. If you find some of those, peel up the paper, spray the next piece more thoroughly with adhesive, wait a bit longer before sticking it on, and keep rubbing it as the adhesive dries. Bubbles can also happen if the sandpaper gets wet, which is why we aren't lubricating it with water to speed up the process.

Flip the tool over after a few swipes, and the scratch pattern will show you how flat it actually is and how much work you have to do to finish the job. The good news here is that you only need the first $1/2$ in. or so behind the tip to be flat; the rest can just be flat in spots, with a few slight hollows here and there.

If there's a large area to flatten behind the tip, switch to 150-grit paper, plug in your ear buds and get ready for a long flattening session. If the back is mostly or all flat already, you can move up through 320-, 400-, and 600-grit paper relatively quickly, before polishing the back on your three waterstones.

ONE AND DONE. All but the priciest chisels and plane blades need their backs flattened and polished before you proceed to honing the bevel side of the blade, but it's a job you only have to do once in the life of the tool.

Here are a few tips for success. I find it easier to keep tools flat if I rub them back and forth in just one direction, as opposed to rubbing them in circles. You can always reposition your hands and change the direction, but back-and-forth is the ticket. Also, buy a big stack of 150-grit paper and change it often to keep it cutting efficiently.

Once the first ½ in. behind the tip of the tool is showing an even scratch pattern, right up to the edge, you can move on to finer grits. At this point, your heavy material removal is done and all you need to do is replace the deeper scratches from the last abrasive with finer ones. To make sure that's happening, try changing your rubbing direction on the new paper. That will send the scratches in a different direction and let you know when the past ones are gone. Between each new grit of sandpaper, wipe off the tool to remove the little metal filings and the grit from the last paper.

polish the back on waterstones

If you finish up with 600-grit sandpaper, you'll be ready to move onto your 1,000-grit waterstone. But first, you need to know that all three waterstones are dead-flat. So head to the sink and use your diamond plate to flatten them as shown in photo on p. 161. Do this even more frequently to the 1,000-grit stone, which will be relatively soft compared to the others. Also, move the tool around to distribute the wear on each waterstone to keep them as flat as possible for as long as possible.

Aside from that, it's just more rubbing on each stone. Just be careful to keep the blade or chisel flat the whole time and flip the tool occasionally to check your progress. You'll notice the surface going from dull to more polished on each new stone, with the 8,000-grit stone leaving a near-mirror polish on the back of the blade.

STAGE 1: FLATTEN AND POLISH THE BACKS

The key here is keeping the chisel or plane blade perfectly flat on the sandpaper and waterstones at all times, so you don't round the back even slightly. If that happens, you'll need to return to the roughest grit of sandpaper, re-flatten the back, and start the process again.

1 POP OUT THE PLANE BLADE. Lift the lever cap on your block plane and remove the blade. Gather the chisels you want to sharpen also.

2 STICK SANDPAPER ONTO A VERY FLAT SURFACE. Find a safe place to spray the back of the sandpaper with contact cement, give it a minute or two to get sticky, and then press it down into place, making sure there are no bubbles or raised edges. Keep pressing it down for another minute or so, then leave it 10 minutes to dry before using it.

3 START FLATTENING. I usually start flattening on 220-grit paper. The first few swipes will tell you how flat the back is. At that point you can move to a rougher or finer grit as needed. The key here is to focus your pressure at the tip of the tool without tilting it or lifting the back. It's easier to keep it level if you move the tool forward and back only.

4 THE AREA NEAR THE TIP IS CRITICAL. Notice how the 150-grit scratches haven't quite removed the manufacturer's grinding marks at the very tip. That means there's more work to do.

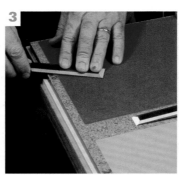

5 CHANGE THE PAPER OFTEN. The initial flattening stage will take a while, but it will go a lot faster if you change the paper when it gets dull. Peel it up, clean off the remaining adhesive with paint thinner, wipe it dry, and stick down a new piece.

6 BRUSH IT OFF FROM TIME TO TIME. A hand broom whisks away the metal powder, helping the paper last longer.

7 **INITIAL FLATTENING IS DONE.** Notice how the entire back doesn't need to be flat, but the area near the tip is essential.

8 **MOVE UP TO THE NEXT GRIT.** Move up through the different grades of sandpaper, from 220 to 320, 400, and 600. To avoid tipping the tool and rounding the surface, move it back and forth in one direction only.

9 **CHECK YOUR PROGRESS.** All you need to see at each stage is that the deeper scratches from the last grit have been erased by the finer ones from the present one.

10 **FLATTEN YOUR WATERSTONES.** Do this over the sink by rubbing the waterstone against your diamond plate. This is an older stone that I've been using for 20 years.

11 **CHECK YOUR PROGRESS.** Fresh, clean abrasive will be lighter colored. Keep flattening until the darker, dished-out areas are gone.

12 **POLISH THE BACK ON WATERSTONES.** Continue the polishing process on the 1,000-grit waterstone. As always, be very careful not to lift or tilt the blade as you rub it forward and back.

13 **TWO STONES TO GO.** Move up through the 4,000- and 8,000-grit waterstones. Each one removes the scratches from the last, polishing the back to a higher shine each time. Look for a near-mirror polish at the end.

11 handy sharpening station handles grinding and honing

After flattening and polishing the backs of your blades, you can move on to the bevel side of the blade, which is where you'll focus your sharpening efforts from here on. This compact sharpening station has everything you need for years of successful sharpening.

The sharpening station has room for a full sheet of sandpaper, where you can grind the bevels of your tools; stable spots for your waterstones, where you'll do your honing; and stops for setting up your honing guide for all of the above.

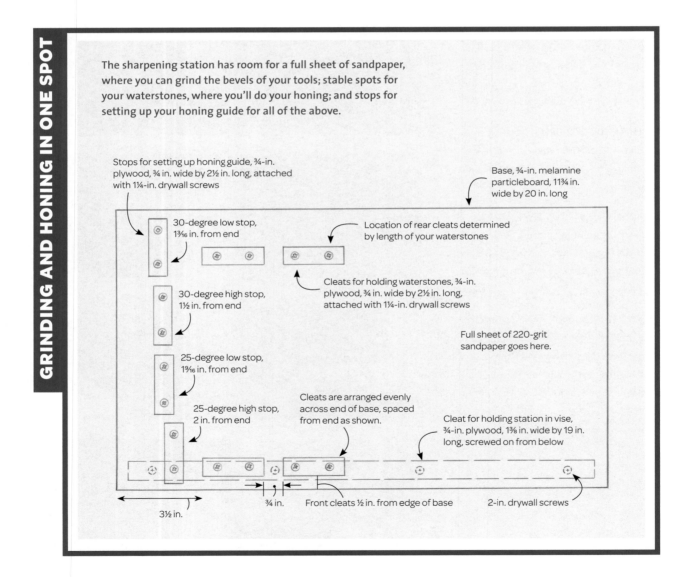

Stops for setting up honing guide, ¾-in. plywood, ¾ in. wide by 2½ in. long, attached with 1¼-in. drywall screws

Base, ¾-in. melamine particleboard, 11¾ in. wide by 20 in. long

30-degree low stop, 1³⁄₁₆ in. from end

Location of rear cleats determined by length of your waterstones

Cleats for holding waterstones, ¾-in. plywood, ¾ in. wide by 2½ in. long, attached with 1¼-in. drywall screws

30-degree high stop, 1½ in. from end

Full sheet of 220-grit sandpaper goes here.

25-degree low stop, 1⁹⁄₁₆ in. from end

25-degree high stop, 2 in. from end

Cleats are arranged evenly across end of base, spaced from end as shown.

Cleat for holding station in vise, ¾-in. plywood, 1⅜ in. wide by 19 in. long, screwed on from below

¾ in.

Front cleats ½ in. from edge of base

2-in. drywall screws

3½ in.

QUICK AND EASY TO BUILD

1 PREP THE BASE. Buy a small piece of melamine particleboard and cut it to size on the tablesaw. Then soften the sharp edges with your sanding block.

2 SCREW ON THE BOTTOM CLEAT. Drill and countersink clearance holes in the cleat, clamp it in place, and then drill smaller pilot holes in the base before driving the 2-in. screws.

3 LAY OUT THE STOP LOCATIONS. Mark the stop locations with a sharp pencil, as precisely as you can.

4 SCREW ON THE STOPS. Drill and countersink them ahead of time, and then clamp them in place before attaching them with 1¼-in. screws.

5 ATTACH THE FRONT CLEATS FOR THE WATERSTONES. Predrill these like the others. Then mark a line ½ in. from the front of the base, clamp down the cleats, and attach them with 1¼-in. screws.

6 USE THE STONES TO POSITION THE REAR CLEATS. Drop each waterstone into place and put a thin piece of cardboard between it and the rear cleat, so the fit isn't too tight. Clamp the cleat snug against the cardboard and screw it down.

7 ATTACH THE SANDPAPER. Use spray adhesive to attach a fresh sheet of 220-grit sandpaper.

8 LABEL THE STOPS AND YOU'RE DONE. There are two stops for each angle. That's because there are two clamping positions in the honing guide.

9 HANDY CLAMPING CLEAT. The cleat under the base is for clamping in your bench vise, which keeps your sharpening station steady and stable.

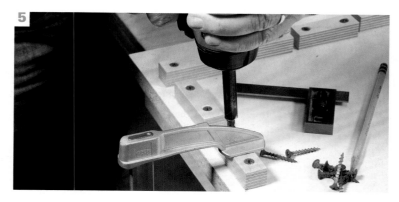

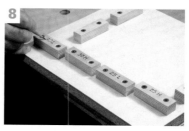

GRINDING ON SANDPAPER

With the back flat and polished, the rest of the sharpening process—from now into the foreseeable future—happens on the bevel side of the tool, at your handy sharpening station (see p. 162). You might be wondering why you don't just do your grinding on the sandpaper-coated lapping plates you set up earlier. That will work just fine, but our sharpening station is plenty flat for grinding bevels, and it's nice to able to put away that heavy lapping plate (or plates) once the backs are prepped and do all future sharpening in one place using the same honing guide.

Others of you will wonder why you can't grind your edges on a bench grinder. You can. If you do use a bench grinder, buy a 60- to 100-grit "friable" wheel (usually white) that will be much less likely to overheat your blades and kill their hardness, and a wheel "dresser" to keep the abrasive clean and fresh. A slow-speed grinder (roughly 1,800 rpm vs. 3,600) is another very good idea. There are also wet grinders that spin even slower, making the process easier to control and preventing edges from overheating.

I went with sandpaper here for grinding because it's cheap, it fits nicely on our sharpening station, and it works with the same honing guide. We're grinding our bevels at 25 degrees. The honing guide has two different clamping positions built into it, placing chisels a little lower than plane blades, so there are two stops on our sharpening station for that 25-degree angle (see "Honing guide basics" on the facing page).

After clamping a tool in the guide, using one of the handy stops on your sharpening station, just push the guide and the tool back and forth on the sandpaper to grind a fresh bevel. Check your progress by inspecting the bevel from time to time and stop when most of the bevel—most importantly the area right at the tip—is freshly ground.

Just as you did when flattening the backs, change out the sandpaper often or you'll be rubbing forever on dull paper. To make the paper last longer, move the honing guide around to distribute the wear over the sheet. As I mentioned earlier, you don't have to grind a fresh bevel every time you sharpen a tool. Instead, you can just rehone the secondary bevel we're about to create next.

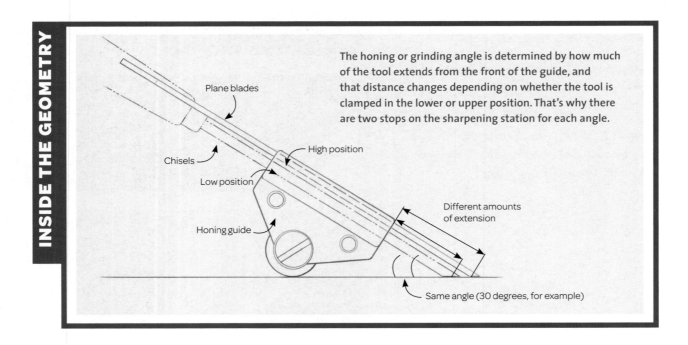

INSIDE THE GEOMETRY

Plane blades

Chisels

High position

Low position

Honing guide

The honing or grinding angle is determined by how much of the tool extends from the front of the guide, and that distance changes depending on whether the tool is clamped in the lower or upper position. That's why there are two stops on the sharpening station for each angle.

Different amounts of extension

Same angle (30 degrees, for example)

HONING GUIDE BASICS

The honing (and grinding) guide has different clamping positions for different tools, and that changes the geometry a little.

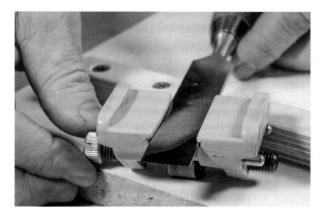

LOW POSITION FOR NARROW TOOLS. Chisels and very narrow handplane blades go in the lower notches in the guide.

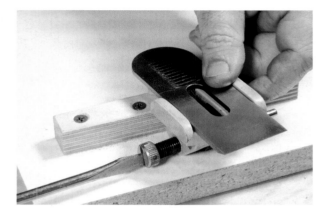

HIGH POSITION FOR WIDE BLADES. Most plane blades go in the upper clamping area. By the way, you can use a screwdriver to tighten the guide, so the tool doesn't move during grinding or honing.

BASIC GUIDES ARE THE SAME HEIGHT. The stops on our sharpening station are based on a standard honing guide, with a wheel that rides 1³/₈ in. below the top of the guide.

ANGLES CONFIRMED. I checked the honing-guide setups with this handy angle block from Veritas.

STAGE 2: GRINDING A FRESH BEVEL

You won't have to do this every time, but you should do it the first time you sharpen a tool and whenever the secondary bevel gets too wide for efficient honing. The grinding angle is 25 degrees.

1 SETUP IS QUICK AND EASY. This plane blade goes in the upper position on the guide, so I'm using the "25-high" block to set it up for grinding. When using the setup blocks, be sure the tool is flat and relatively snug in its clamping position, and also flat on the base of the sharpening station, before tightening the guide.

2 GRIND AWAY. Keep the tool and honing guide stable as you push it back and forth on the sandpaper. Move it around the sheet to distribute the wear and make the sandpaper last longer.

3 CHECK YOUR PROGRESS. Wherever the sandpaper hits first, keep grinding until there's a fresh surface all the way to the tip of the tool. Change the paper when it starts cutting slowly.

FOOLPROOF SHARPENING

HONING ON WATERSTONES

For all the reasons mentioned earlier, waterstones are great for honing hand-tool blades of all kinds. Their softness is both an asset and a drawback, however. On one hand, it makes them easy to flatten and refresh, keeping them cutting quickly and efficiently. On the other, it means they wear away relatively quickly. This is especially true for the 1,000-grit stone, so I always flatten my stones before any big sharpening session. It goes quickly on the diamond plate, and you can see very clearly when the stone is fully flattened because the worn, dished areas will be darker and fresh abrasive is lighter-colored.

To get started honing, you need to change the angle of the tool in the honing guide by using the 30-degree stops on your sharpening station. Once you do that, you can jump from one stone to the other without a pause.

Remember that waterstones are relatively soft, and you've raised the angle of the chisel or blade so only the sharp tip is touching the stone. If you push forward right away, it will dig in and gouge the stone. So make your first four or five strokes on the 1,000-grit stone backward only. After a few strokes, there will be a little flat spot at the tip, and you'll be able to push forward and back with no problems. I do this backward-only move for the first few strokes on the finer stones too, just to be safe.

Only the very tip of the tool needs to be sharp, so you don't need to create much of a secondary bevel. Maybe this is why they call it a micro-bevel. Keep going on the 1,000-grit stone just until there is a distinct bevel across the entire width of the blade, and then stop.

The next two waterstones—4,000 and 8,000 grit—serve only to remove the scratches from the previous stone, bringing that little honed bevel to a higher level of polish. Keep checking your progress as you hone on each stone. When you don't see any deep scratches left over from the last stone, and the level of polish is uniform, you're ready to move on to the next stone.

If you've done your job well, the 8,000-grit stone will leave a mirror polish across the micro-bevel. But sometimes I move too fast through the three stones and then notice some deeper scratches in the mirror polish. The fix is easy: Just return to the 1,000-grit stone and work more methodically up through stones to the finest one.

One quick tip for the combination stone. I always dip mine in the water bath before I flip it, just in case the finer side picked up some rougher grit when it was face-down on the sharpening station.

> Waterstones are great for honing hand-tool blades of all kinds. Their softness is both an asset and a drawback.

finish with a flip

The grinding and honing process will often leave a thin whisker of metal rolled over the back side of the edge. Removing it is easy. Once you're done honing the bevel on the 8,000-grit stone, just flip the tool over and rub the back of the edge on that same stone, keeping it flat as you do, to avoid rounding the back. A few swirls will do the job, leaving your plane blade or chisel incredibly sharp.

STAGE 3: HONING A SECONDARY BEVEL

This honing happens only at the very tip of the tool, so it doesn't take long.

1 RESET THE HONING GUIDE. Honing happens at a higher angle, so reset the tool in the guide.

2 START ON THE 1,000-GRIT STONE. To prevent the sharp tip of the tool from digging into the soft stone, drag it backward for the first few swipes, raising it when pushing it forward. After that, you can hone in both directions.

3 STOP HERE. Once you've formed a continuous honed bevel across the entire blade, you can stop honing on the 1,000-grit stone.

4 MOVE ON TO THE NEXT STONE. I flipped this combination stone to the 4,000-grit side for the next honing pass. Waterstones need a thin puddle of water on top to do their best work, so give them a spritz with a spray bottle from time to time.

5 FINISH AT 8,000 GRIT. Before you switch stones, make sure the deeper scratches from the previous one are gone.

6 A MIRROR POLISH IS THE GOAL. This shiny stripe is the hallmark of a finely honed edge.

7 ONE FINAL STEP. After sharpening any blade, there will be a small sliver of steel hanging off the back of the edge. You'll often be able to feel it with your fingertip. Flip the tool and rub it on the finest waterstone to remove this "wire edge."

8 TIME TO REGRIND. To resharpen the tool, you can keep rehoning the same bevel, working through the same three waterstones, until it gets about this wide. At that point it will take too much time to hone it on your waterstones, so the whole bevel needs to be reground on sandpaper (or with a bench grinder). Then you can form another tiny honed bevel at the tip.

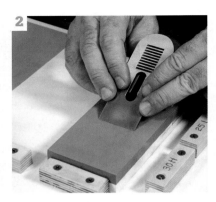

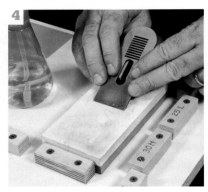

FINISHING TOUCHES

If you've never felt or used a truly sharp tool, you're going to be shocked at how sharp yours now are. There are a couple of popular tests for sharpness. One is to push the blade or chisel across the end of a pine board. Pine is a little spongy and grippy, and only a very sharp blade will shave its end grain cleanly.

My favorite test for sharpness is quicker and doesn't require you to dig up a piece of pine. Just touch the blade to the surface of your fingernail. If it's sharp, it will catch immediately and try to dig in. If it's not, it will skitter across the surface.

After sharpening chisels and plane blades on waterstones, wipe them off with a dry paper towel or cloth and put some sort of rust-prevention fluid on them. The cheapest rust-prevention fluid is good old WD-40, which is available everywhere and goes on nice and thin. Just spray some on a paper towel and rub it all over the blade before putting it away or loading it into your block plane.

Put some on the outside of the block plane too. Your hands have corrosive oils on them, and air can be moist in basement shops and humid regions. This quick dose of rust prevention will protect your lovely new hand tools, and keep them looking and working great. By the way, if your hand tools do pick up some rust, buy one of those abrasive 3M pads and use it with WD-40 to buff away the corrosion.

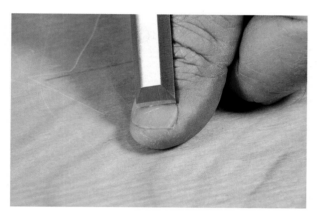

RAZOR SHARP. Touch the sharp edge on the surface of your fingernail and note how it catches immediately. A dull blade will skitter forward without catching.

RUST PREVENTION. Woodworkers use a variety of oils to keep their planes and chisels rust-free, but inexpensive WD-40 does as good a job as any of them. Apply it to the blade and plane body (and your chisels) with a paper towel after every sharpening session.

HANDPLANE CLINIC

With just a few simple steps, you can turn a relatively cheap or beat-up handplane into a very solid performer. And you don't need any special tools beyond the sanding plate we used to flatten the backs of chisels and hand tools, and a basic metal file called a "mill bastard." You want the "single-cut" variety, not the type with cross-hatched teeth that are more aggressive. These skills and know-how will let you make the most of a flea-market find or a less-expensive new tool. The only deal-breakers for a used tool are significant damage (any crack is game-over), extensive rust, or missing parts.

BLOCK PLANE MECHANICS

Once you understand the basic parts of a block plane and the forces at play, you'll understand why it's important there are no gaps between the critical parts.

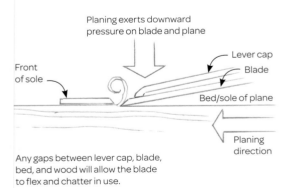

Planing exerts downward pressure on blade and plane

Front of sole

Lever cap

Blade

Bed/sole of plane

Planing direction

Any gaps between lever cap, blade, bed, and wood will allow the blade to flex and chatter in use.

Aside from replacing the blade, which isn't always necessary, and sharpening it properly, which is, the rest of the work happens on the plane itself. To understand the logic behind the steps, it's important to understand the forces at play. Because the blade travels along at an angle to the wood, the cutting force presses down hard on the leading edge. That in turn presses down hard on the bed of the plane, which in turn presses down on the wood below. The cutting action also puts pressure on the "lever cap," the part that holds the blade down on the bed. In a nutshell, if there are any gaps between any of those critical parts, the blade will flex and vibrate in use.

One of the critical zones is the area of the sole that surrounds the blade. This needs to be dead flat and in good contact with the wood or the whole plane will flex downward and chatter as you use the tool. So one of the key steps in most handplane tune-ups is flattening the sole. Don't do that with the plane disassembled. You need the blade in the plane when you do it, clamped in place by the lever cap. This flexes the sole slightly, just as it will when you use the plane.

Work through these steps carefully, and soon a pile of separate parts will feel like one solid unit, and your sharp plane blade will slice through wood like butter.

REHABBING A BLOCK PLANE, STEP-BY-STEP ━━━━━

This is a contractor-grade Stanley block plane, which needs work to perform at a high level. The same tune-up steps will work for a used plane as well.

1 CONSIDER A BLADE CHANGE. I replaced the stock blade with one from Hock Tools that's slightly thicker and made from better steel, which will hold an edge much longer. Whichever blade you go with, the most important thing is that you sharpen it well.

2 FILE THE BED. Use a single-cut mill bastard file to flatten the contact area in the bed of the plane. Try to match the existing angle while making the surface flat.

3 FILE THE THROAT PLATE. The front of the sole is an adjustable plate, designed to let you close the opening around the blade (left). File the sliding surfaces on the back side of that plate and the surfaces it rides on inside the plane (right). This will help the plate stay level with the sole of the plane as you adjust it back and forth.

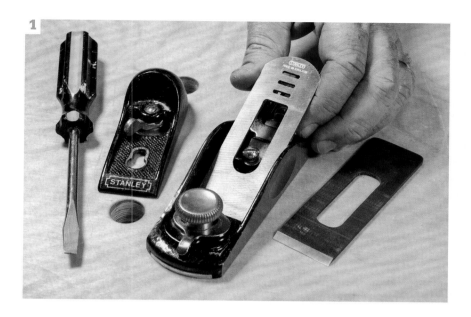

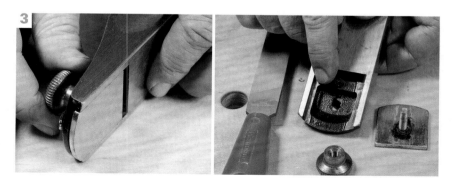

4 RE-ASSEMBLE THE PLANE. Put everything back together, including the blade, and adjust the lever cap to it put firm pressure on the blade.

5 WITHDRAW THE BLADE A LITTLE. Adjust the blade backward so it isn't sticking out from the bottom of the plane.

6 FLATTEN THE SOLE. Go back to the flattening plate you used for the plane blade and chisels, put some fresh 220-grit paper on it, and rub the plane on it to flatten the bottom.

7 CHECK YOUR PROGRESS. Stop when you see an even scratch pattern surrounding the blade opening on all sides. The whole sole doesn't have to be flat, but the areas around the blade do. Don't worry about the visible scratches: Those won't affect performance.

8 FROM ZERO TO HERO. A basic tune-up turned this inexpensive block plane into a top performer.

SETTING UP YOUR BLOCK PLANE

With the blade sharp and ready to go, you can re-assemble your plane and put it to work.

1 INSERT THE BLADE. The blade goes down on the bed, and then the lever cap goes on. All lever caps have a screw for adjusting their tension. Once you get that just right, you'll be able to pop off the cap and remove the blade easily and re-insert it just as quickly.

2 SET THE CUTTING DEPTH. The small thumbscrew at the back pushes the blade forward and back. Advance it until you can just feel it poking out of the bottom of the plane. You can fine-tune the adjustment when you start making shavings.

3 CLOSE UP THE THROAT. A plane will cut more cleanly with just a small opening in front of the blade. Loosen the big thumbscrew that holds the throat plate in place, and then use the little toggle to position it before tightening the screw again. You're looking for a roughly ¹/₁₆-in.-wide opening ahead of the blade. If chips start getting clogged in the throat, you can always open it up bit.

4 MAKE A FEW TEST CUTS. You're looking for a very thin but continuous shaving. Note how an extra hand helps steady the plane.

5 PERFECTION. This WoodRiver block plane needed nothing more than a proper sharpening to make perfect shavings, leaving a glassy surface below.

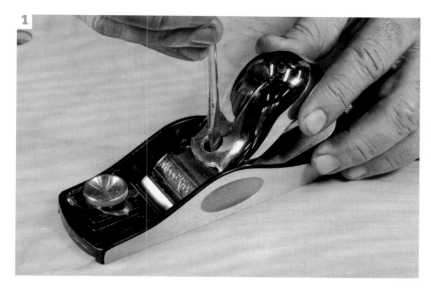

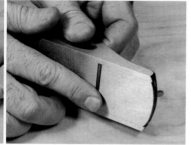

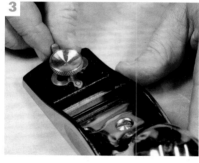
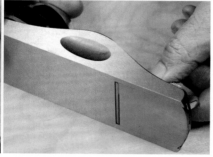

8

versatile shaker bench combines hand and power skills

Now that you've got a set of sharp chisels and a well-tuned block plane in hand, let's put them to work on a great project. This design can be found in Shaker villages going back hundreds of years, and it offers a great opportunity to combine machine and hand skills. While some woodworkers choose to use hand tools almost exclusively, most use hand tools in conjunction with power tools, to take work to a higher level. As a beginner, hand tools also let you do things that would otherwise require more expensive power tools.

This project showcases all of the above. It takes advantage of all of the power-tool woodworking you've learned so far and demonstrates a range of essential hand skills. It also includes your first high-end woodworking joint: the wedged mortise and tenon.

As always, the skills you'll build are even more important than the projects themselves. You'll have a chance here to build knowledge and muscle memory around the four most valuable hand tools: chisels, planes, handsaws, and a marking knife. If you're new to these tools and techniques, or out of practice, don't be too hard on yourself as you build this project. Take this as a chance to learn, not pressure to achieve perfection. Mistakes are the path to woodworking glory, and venturing out of your comfort zone is the fastest way to improve. I'll give you as many tips as I can fit into the following pages, but there are some things you have to learn through experience. Give yourself the chance to do that and embrace your mistakes as valuable lessons.

HANDSOME BENCH. This low bench (facing page) is a Shaker classic and has multiple uses around the home.

STRONG, STYLISH FOOTSTOOL. Scale down the same bench and you have a handy footstool. You can use it to reach a high shelf or leave it under your dog's food and water bowls to raise them to a comfortable height.

EXPOSED JOINERY. You'll learn to cut and fit traditional joints that are both strong and beautiful. These will put your newly sharpened hand tools to good use, as well as the power tools covered earlier in these books.

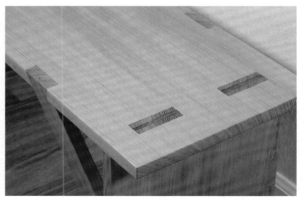

HANDSOME DESIGN WORKS AT ALMOST ANY SIZE

This project is very similar to one we ran in *Fine Woodworking* magazine in 2013, and just as we did in the article, I built the design in two sizes to show off its versatility. The low version is a handy footstool for

Here are full dimensions for the footstool we'll build in this chapter. Alternate dimensions for the bench and sofa-table versions are on the opposite page. Starting with a single, wide board looks best and makes things easier, but only if it's straight and flat. If you can't find one that will work, feel free to glue narrower boards together to produce the parts you need.

Legs attach to top with wedged through-tenons.

Diagonal braces are notched in to add stability.

FOOTSTOOL
All parts ¾ in. thick

Mortise sizes: 2 in. wide by ¾ in. thick (or whatever leg thickness is)

FOOTSTOOL

Top, 9¼ in. wide by 20 in. long

Mortise locations: 1¼ in. from each edge and 1½ in. from ends of top

Braces, 1⅜ in. wide by 8 in. long, with ends mitered at 45 degrees

Notches are 1³⁄₁₆ in. square.

Notches cut at 45 degrees, starting at beginning of miters

Legs, 9¼ in. wide by 9½ in. long

Foot profile, 3¾ in. radius with 1⅜-in.-wide feet

reaching high shelves. When we're not standing on it, it lives under our dog's food and water bowls. Medium and large dogs like it when they don't have to reach down to the floor to chow down.

The medium-sized version is a lovely sitting bench. Mine goes by the front door for putting on shoes, but this bench could live in lots of places in the house. I've also included overall dimensions for an even larger version, to be used as a sofa or entryway table. Whichever variation(s) you choose to build, the tools and techniques are all the same.

On both the footstool and the bench, I went with a classic curve at the bottom of the legs, but there are other nice cutouts to choose from (see "Two foot variations" on p. 198). This clean, practical design is typical of Shaker work. What I love most is the exposed joinery. Some classic woodworking joints are hidden from view, but the joints in this project are all out in the open, making the piece unmistakably handmade. Exposed joinery also exposes mistakes, but I'll show you how to minimize those and fix a few if they happen.

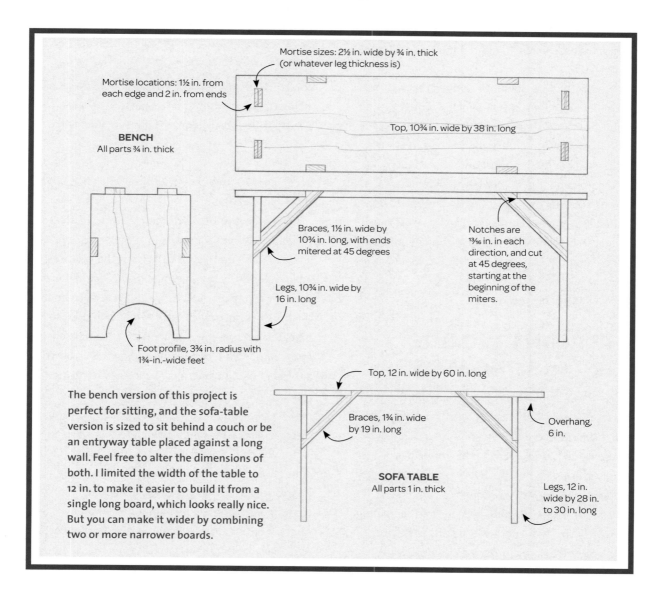

Mortise sizes: 2½ in. wide by ¾ in. thick (or whatever leg thickness is)

Mortise locations: 1½ in. from each edge and 2 in. from ends

BENCH
All parts ¾ in. thick

Top, 10¾ in. wide by 38 in. long

Braces, 1½ in. wide by 10¾ in. long, with ends mitered at 45 degrees

Notches are 1³⁄₁₆ in. in each direction, and cut at 45 degrees, starting at the beginning of the miters.

Legs, 10¾ in. wide by 16 in. long

Foot profile, 3¾ in. radius with 1¾-in.-wide feet

The bench version of this project is perfect for sitting, and the sofa-table version is sized to sit behind a couch or be an entryway table placed against a long wall. Feel free to alter the dimensions of both. I limited the width of the table to 12 in. to make it easier to build it from a single long board, which looks really nice. But you can make it wider by combining two or more narrower boards.

Top, 12 in. wide by 60 in. long

Braces, 1¾ in. wide by 19 in. long

Overhang, 6 in.

SOFA TABLE
All parts 1 in. thick

Legs, 12 in. wide by 28 in. to 30 in. long

In the magazine article, the legendary Christian Becksvoort built his footstool using only hand tools as an exercise in honing a wide range of those skills. He also used slightly more complicated joinery. I'm building it here the way I would do it, using slightly simpler joinery and a blend of power and hand tools. It's also the way I recommend that beginner and intermediate woodworkers do it.

Whether you build this project small or large, it starts as one wide board. After cutting that board into three pieces, you'll join them together by cutting square tabs (called tenons) on the legs and square holes (called mortises) in the top. We'll also add some wedges to those joints, to tighten the tenons in their mortises.

Even with those powerful wedged tenons, the Shakers knew these stools or benches would get wobbly over time, so they added diagonal braces to the sides. These are notched in a clever way, so they can't slip out of position, and fit seamlessly into the legs and top, so your bench or footstool will look amazing and stand up to a lifetime of use. Mechanically interlocking joints like these are much stronger than joints that rely on glue alone, and they are a hallmark of fine furniture. This is the hardest project in the book, but you're ready for it at this point. So dive in and enjoy the journey.

THE RIGHT WOODS FOR THIS PROJECT

Wood choice can make any project unique, but there are a few caveats in this case. There's a lot of hand work involved here, and workability varies widely between woods. So you'll want to choose a tool-friendly species for this project. I would also look for a single board that's wide enough to contain the legs and top. That will look a little better than gluing together two or more narrower boards to get the width you need. On the other hand, wide boards tend

HIGHLY WORKABLE WOOD. The footstool is made from ³/₄-in.-thick basswood, a softwood that cuts beautifully.

to cup (warp across their width), so you'll need one that's nice and flat.

The closer your board is to exactly ³/₄ in. thick, the easier this project will be. That's because we'll be using a ³/₄-in. Forstner bit to drill out the mortises, which need to fit the thickness of the legs. If you have a jointer and planer, you'll already know you can buy thicker stock and mill it flat, straight, and perfectly ³/₄ in. thick. If not, you'll either need to be very choosy at the lumberyard or find one willing to mill down a thicker board to a perfect ³/₄ in. Many hardwood retailers will be willing to do this for a small fee. But no worries. If your board is a little under or over ³/₄ in. thick, you'll still be able to complete this project.

If you can't find material that's wide and flat enough, feel free to glue up separate, narrower boards to make what you need. To do that, I highly recommend using the techniques in chapter 5. Another option for wide, flat material is a "project panel" available at Lowe's and other home centers, made of a number of smaller pieces. These are generally flat and true, and very close to 3/4 in. thick.

As for the wood species itself, the Shakers probably would have used Eastern white pine for these projects, which is very easy to work with hand tools. Whatever wood you choose, be sure it is "clear" and free of knots and other major defects. Unless you are ready for an extremely tough test of your sharpening skills, you don't want to hit any knots.

In the middle of the pandemic, I couldn't find wide Eastern white pine boards at my West Coast lumberyard, so I used two of my other favorite options. For the footstool, I went with basswood, probably the most workable wood of them all. Buttery soft, it slices beautifully. Cedar and poplar are also good choices for workability. For the larger bench, I chose clear, vertical-grain fir, a West Coast classic. It's more brittle and splintery than basswood, so it offered more of a challenge.

You don't need to stick with softwoods to have success with hand tools. Walnut and soft maple are good choices for handwork, and cherry is tool-friendly also. Unless you are a hand-tool whiz, however, I would avoid birch, hard maple, and the oaks. That goes double for tropical hardwoods, as well as any wood with crazy grain or "figure."

BEAUTIFUL BLEND OF POWER AND HAND WORK

Like many woodworkers, I treat hand and power tools equally, using each where it makes the most sense. I like power tools and machines for their power, speed, and repeatability, and hand tools for their amazing control and unique abilities. This project is a great example of how to blend old and new tools to create the straightest possible path to success.

That said, there are lots of ways to go about any project, so feel free to use the tools and techniques you like best. Here is a quick overview of the techniques I used on these projects, and why I used them. The photos and drawings later in the chapter will take you much deeper.

tenons first

In most cases as a woodworker, you'll cut mortises first and then form tenons to fit them. In this case, it's easier to cut the tenons first and use those to mark matching mortises in the top. Since the tenons go all the way through the top, gaps will be very obvious, so it's critical that the tenons come out square and straight. If they are crooked at all, the tips you are marking around won't necessarily represent the full size of each tenon, making it nearly impossible to end up with a tight fit on the top side. So we'll take advantage of the tablesaw to cut our tenons perfectly and uniformly, using the dado blades and crosscut sled I covered earlier in the book (see "Set up for tenoning" on p. 186). Cutting the tenons on the tablesaw also makes them symmetrical across the top of the leg, meaning you'll be able to flip the parts any which way and still have them fit (see "Tenon the legs" on p 187).

then the mortises

After cutting the tenons, we'll trace their outline with a marking knife to lay out matching mortises in the top (see "Transfer the tenon locations to the top" on p. 188). Our simple, effective marking knife is nothing more than a utility knife with a blade that breaks away in sections, exposing a fresh edge when you need one. There are a range of classic marking knives for woodworking, but those require careful sharpening.

Marking with a knife is a little trickier than marking with a pencil, but it's very helpful for precise joinery and well worth the short learning curve. The incised line gives your chisel a positive place to land when you are paring away the last few whiskers of wood, making for very tight-fitting joints. It's a time-tested technique that old-time woodworkers relied on to do incredibly fine work without power tools.

After marking the mortises in the top, we'll cut them with a classic combination of power and hand work. We'll clear out most of the waste with a ³/₄-in. Forstner bit on the drill press (see "Drill out the mortises" on p. 189), and then square the mortises with a sharp chisel (see "Chisel the mortises square" on p. 190). A Forstner bit has the unique ability to drill overlapping holes without wandering, so it's perfect for the job. The straight holes then act as a visual guide for the chisel work.

wedge the tenons

To add some strength and close up any tiny gaps, we'll insert wedges in the tips of the tenons, as artisans have done for centuries (see "Prep the mortises and tenons for wedging" on p. 192). These also add a really nice decorative touch to the exposed joints. There are some decisions to make around the wedging process, but I'll cover those in a separate section below.

add diagonal braces

After forming the mortises and tenons but before gluing and wedging them together, we'll make and fit the diagonal braces (see "Make the side braces" on p. 194). Once again, we'll use a combination of power tools and hand tools. Just as we did with the tenons, we'll form the notched braces first, and then use them to mark matching cutouts in the legs and top. And once more, straight, square cuts on the ends of the braces will be key to fitting them into the legs and top with no visible gaps. So we'll miter their ends on the miter saw, and then cut their little V-notches on the tablesaw.

After that, just as with the tenoned legs, we'll place the braces directly onto the mating parts and mark around them with our knife (see "Transfer the layout of the braces" on p. 195). We'll use the clamping blocks we made in Chapter 3 to hold the legs and top

square to each other as we mark around the braces. It's just one more way everything builds on itself in these books.

notch the legs and top

From there, we'll go back to our dado blades and crosscut sled to cut out most of the mating notches in the legs and top (see "Notch the sides" on p. 196). That will give each notch a nice even bottom, which we'll take advantage of in the next step. The dado blades will leave a little triangle of wood that will need to be cleared out before the braces will drop into place, and we'll use 100% hand tools to remove those last corners. We'll start by sawing inside our knife line and pare and chop out the rest of the wood with a wide chisel. The dado blades leave a square notch with a flat bottom, and we'll rest the chisel on that to pare the rest of the bottom just as flat and even. The last step is wedging and assembly, and that stage deserves a discussion of its own.

THE WEDGE QUESTION(S)

Glued-in wedges are a proven way to strengthen joints, close gaps, and add a decorative touch to all sorts of tenons. Like everything else in woodworking, there are a number of ways to approach wedges and a few important fundamentals that all good approaches have in common.

No matter how you orient your wedges, you'll use a handsaw or bandsaw to create a thin slot (or "kerf") in each tenon before assembly. Then, after applying glue and clamping the parts tightly together, you tap a small wedge into that slot to lock the joint.

Wedges can be placed across the length or width of a tenon. In general, you want the wedging action to go against the grain of the larger surface, not across it, to guard against splitting the board if you pound on the wedges too hard. For this project, that meant

HOW TO CUT WEDGES BY HAND

It's usually best to make wedges from a wood that's harder than the wood you are wedging. This is especially true if your project wood is relatively soft. I used oak wedges in the basswood stool and fir wedges for the fir bench. There are a number of ways to cut clean, accurate wedges. Here's an easy way using the tools covered in this book.

1 SLICE OFF A STRIP. Rip a piece of wood to the width of your mortises, and then turn it on edge (as shown) to rip off a strip equal to the fat end of your desired wedges.

2 MARK THE LENGTH. This line represents the length of the wedge.

3 CLAMP DOWN THE STRIP. Place a piece of sacrificial material under the strip and use your workbench holdfast to clamp it down quickly and securely.

4 SHAVE WITH A CHISEL. Pare away thin slivers until there is a smooth ramp from the layout line to the end of the wedge, with the tip ending in a point.

5 SAW IT OFF. Saw along the layout line and the wedge is done. Use the same strip to make more.

placing a single wedge along the length of the tenon. This orientation allows the wedge to close gaps along the long edges of the joint, where you are most likely to have trouble fitting the tenons perfectly.

The next big choice is whether to leave the mortise square and simply pound in a skinny wedge or slope the sides of the mortise to accommodate a larger wedge (see "To slope or not to slope" on p. 193) and create a dovetail-like locking action. That choice depends on how your mortises turn out.

If the chisel work goes great and you end up with clean, straight edges at the top of the mortises, I'd go with the skinny wedge. It's a quicker and easier approach. But that might not happen, for a couple of different reasons. If your board is a little thinner than ³/₄ in., your mortises will need to be thinner too, and the ³/₄-in. Forstner bit won't fit them perfectly, leaving drilling marks at the edges. If the board is thicker than a standard bit size, you'll have more chisel work to do at the edges.

Whatever the reason, if you end up with visible gaps between your tenons and mortises, you have a second chance at a perfect fit. As I demonstrate in the step-by-step photos, you can then scribe slightly wider mortise sides and use those new knife marks to make a sloped cut down to the bottom of the square mortise. These sloped walls let the tenon split farther outward, making room for a larger wedge, and locking the tenon in place even more powerfully. It sounds tricky to cut the sloped walls but it's not really hard in practice.

Note in the drawing on p. 192 that the bigger wedge is a little fatter at the top than the amount you'll remove from the sloped sides. The extra width is there to make up for the compression of the wood fibers as you hammer in the wedge. With the sloped-wall approach, there's a slight chance your wedges won't expand the tenon enough to close the gaps, but I'll show you how to fill them after the fact with another skinny wedge, leaving no one the wiser.

Straight walls and skinny wedge, or sloped walls

and fat wedge, the choice is up to you, and there is no wrong answer. Just trust your instincts and go for it. Other than that, assembling this project is a breeze. Tenons, mortises, wedges, and braces all work together to hold the parts together square and tight.

BLOCK PLANE SWOOPS IN TO FINISH THE JOB

One of the tricks with exposed joints is intentionally leaving one component sticking out a little when fitting the parts together, knowing that a nicely tuned handplane can trim it flush after assembly. This is much easier than trying to get these parts perfectly level with each other from the start.

Flush-trimming is also one of my favorite uses for the block plane, and a job that no other tool does half as well. Try sanding these parts flush, either with a power sander or sanding block, and you'll end up digging into the surrounding wood. A handplane is much easier to control, taking small slivers in quick succession without cutting into the surrounding wood until the part is just about flush (see "Trim the protruding parts" on p. 200). At that point you just switch to a sanding block to finish the job.

In this case the protruding parts are the tenons and the side braces, both left a little "proud" at first and trimmed flush after the fact. Here are a few tips for planing them successfully. On end grain, which is what the protruding tenons and wedges are, it helps to have a low-angle block plane (like all of the options shown in the last chapter), make sure the blade is freshly sharpened (also covered in the last chapter), and push the plane slowly and deliberately. It also helps to skew the plane sideways, to create more of a shearing cut than a head-on attack, and to put a swipe of furniture wax on the sole of the plane to eliminate friction.

When planing the braces flush, pay close attention to grain direction. Planing and chiseling wood is like petting a dog, with the wood grain being the fur. Push in the right direction and the fur/grain

VERSATILE SHAKER BENCH COMBINES HAND AND POWER SKILLS

lies down and cooperates. Push against sloping wood grain and you'll lift fibers and break them off, creating ugly "tearout" that will require a lot of sanding to remove.

The braces have two surfaces left intentionally proud of the legs and top: their ends and their outside faces. The grain at the ends of the braces is sloped at 45 degrees. Push against that slope with your block plane, and you'll dig in immediately and get nowhere. Push in the same direction, like petting a dog, and the planing will go wonderfully. The grain on the faces could be either straight or sloped, depending on the boards you used. To see how to read the grain direction, see "Plane with the grain" below.

When your handplane can't trim any more off without digging into the surrounding wood, switch to your sanding block, loaded with 120-grit paper. Sand the parts totally flush, and then keep going until any little cuts or dents from the plane are gone, as well as any residual glue stains. Then switch to 150- or 180-grit paper, then 220, and you're done.

You'll use this flush-trimming approach many times in your woodworking career, and you'll enjoy it every time. It looks especially cool on the tenons and wedges, which create dark rectangles on the top of your bench, stool, or table. No one will be able to resist running their fingers across the smooth surfaces.

choose your finish

For a rustic look, you can simply apply a coat or two of any oil finish, following the instructions in the final chapter of the book. I went with another finish from that chapter, wipe-on polyurethane, building up five or six coats for additional protection and a deeper luster. My basswood footstool is pretty white, and I didn't want it getting stained by dirty shoes. As for the fir bench, I knew it would be even prettier with a deep sheen.

After your project is finished, take a moment to appreciate the traditional, hand-fit joints you've managed to create, and don't worry about the little gaps and glitches. No one else will care about them, and they'll only get smaller as you repeat these techniques on future projects.

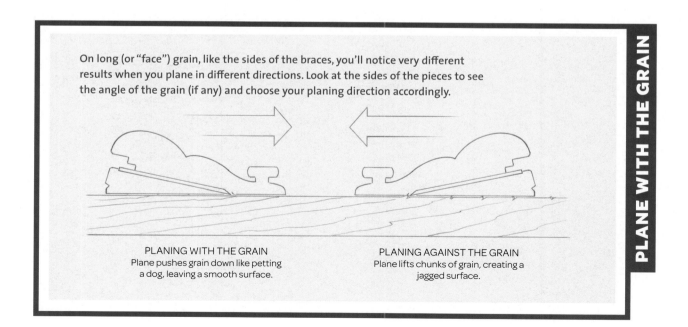

On long (or "face") grain, like the sides of the braces, you'll notice very different results when you plane in different directions. Look at the sides of the pieces to see the angle of the grain (if any) and choose your planing direction accordingly.

PLANING WITH THE GRAIN
Plane pushes grain down like petting a dog, leaving a smooth surface.

PLANING AGAINST THE GRAIN
Plane lifts chunks of grain, creating a jagged surface.

PLANE WITH THE GRAIN

12

shaker footstool/bench

This classic Shaker design can be scaled up or down to suit a variety of purposes. Different woods also make each piece unique. I used basswood for the stool and vertical-grain fir for the bench, but many other woods will work.

VERSATILE SHAKER BENCH COMBINES HAND AND POWER SKILLS

PREP YOUR PARTS

If possible, start with smooth, straight, flat boards, as close to ³⁄₄ in. thick as possible. Use the tablesaw techniques covered earlier in the book to cut them cleanly and squarely to size. I'll be building the footstool in the following photos, but the techniques are the same for the other versions of this project.

1 RIP PARTS TO WIDTH. Make sure the tablesaw blade is set at exactly 90 degrees and cut all the necessary parts to width.

2 REFRESH YOUR SLED. Your tablesaw sled will be altered by the mitering we did earlier, so detach the ¹⁄₄-in. MDF base plates, move them inward over the 90-degree blade slot, and press them down firmly over a few new pieces of double-stick tape. Then add a new layer of ¹⁄₄-in. MDF to the front fence. The first cut will create a new zero-clearance slot that will prevent chipping on the bottom and back edges of workpieces.

3 CROSSCUT THE PARTS TO LENGTH. To cut parts to the same length, start by making a clean cut at one end, and then place that end against a stop block to cut the other end to length.

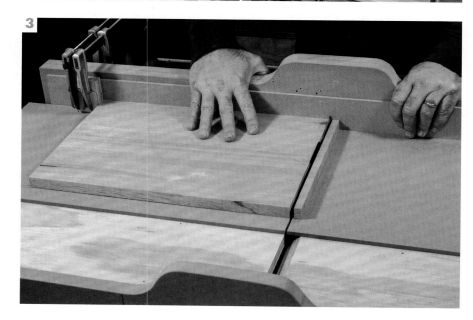

SET UP FOR TENONING

We'll be combining a dado set and your crosscut sled to cut square, accurate tenons on the ends of the legs. The critical setup steps are creating a new zero-clearance slot in the fence and setting the blade height accurately.

1 INSTALL THE DADO SET. Put a stack of blades together that adds up to roughly $1/2$ in. thick. Make sure you put the correct blades on the outside, facing the right way.

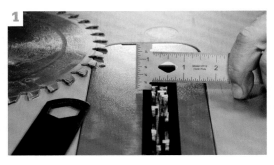

2 MOVE A FEW SCREWS. The dado blades will remove a large notch from the base of the sled. Some of the screws used to attach the fences might be in the way, but they are easy to relocate.

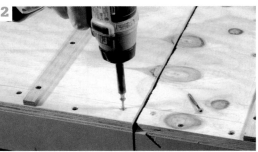

3 MAKE A PASS THROUGH THE SLED. Replace or rotate the $1/4$-in. MDF layer attached to the front fence of the sled. Then set the blade height so it will end up less than $3/4$ in. above the sled base and make a pass.

4 SET THE FINAL HEIGHT. Place one of your workpieces on the sled and raise the dado blades until they are $1/32$ in. to $1/16$ in. above the board.

5 MAKE ANOTHER PASS. This establishes a zero-clearance slot in the base and fence, which will prevent chipping on the back edge of your workpieces.

6 OOPS. I realized that I needed more vertical support for the tall workpieces, so I added this extra piece of $1/4$-in. MDF to the fence.

TENON THE LEGS

This tablesaw approach guarantees clean, square, symmetrical tenons, spaced the same on each leg.

1 LAY OUT ONE BOARD. Mark the tenon locations on just one edge of one leg, using your combination square and a sharp pencil.

2 EDGES FIRST. We'll start by notching out the ends of the leg. Line up one of your layout marks with the outside edge of the slot in the sled and set up a stop block as shown.

3 NIBBLE YOUR WAY ACROSS THE NOTCH. Cut about ¼ in. away with each pass, until the workpiece is up against the stop block.

4 FLIP THE LEGS AND REPEAT. This will form the same notches on both edges of both legs. Note that the workpiece can't go any farther than the stop block, which guarantees uniform tenons. Be sure to notch both legs before changing this setup.

5 SET UP FOR THE CENTER NOTCH. Use the inner layout lines as shown, plus two stop blocks this time, to set the width of the inner notch.

6 NIBBLE YOUR WAY FROM BLOCK TO BLOCK. Take it slow on the first cut, which engages the full width of the dado stack, and then nibble away ¼ in. or so with each successive pass until you're up against the opposite stop block. Cut this same center notch in the other leg and your tenons are done.

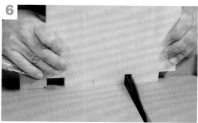

TRANSFER THE TENON LOCATIONS TO THE TOP

We'll use a marking knife to transfer the locations of our clean, square tenons onto the top. The knife is not only very precise, but it also creates an incised line where we will place the tip of the chisel when chopping the mortises clean and square. The upper face of the top is the most important on these exposed joints, so that's where we will do all of our mortise layout and cutting.

1 MARK THE TOP. The top overhangs the legs by a different amount on each design. Mark a sharp pencil line at that dimension, at both ends of the top, on its upper face. This line marks the outside edge of the mortises.

2 CLAMPING BLOCKS STRIKE AGAIN! The clamping blocks we made in Chapter 3 are very helpful here. Start by clamping them to the edges of the legs, with both the blocks and the legs touching the benchtop. Use only the outer clamping hole for this step.

3 CLAMP THE LEG ONTO THE TOP. Line up the outside of the leg with the pencil line and make sure the edges of the leg and top are flush. Then clamp down the other edge of the clamping block, using the inner hole this time.

4 CHOOSE YOUR WEAPON. At right is a classic spear-point marking knife from hocktools.com. There are lots like it on the market, and they require careful sharpening. A utility knife is a simple, effective alternative, with a breakaway blade that needs no sharpening.

5 MARK CAREFULLY. Mark around all four sides of each tenon. It takes a little practice to figure out how to angle the blade so it won't cut into the tenons or wander away from them, so make the first couple of passes very light ones. Once you have a clean, straight path established, right up against the tenon, you can bear down a little and make a deeper line.

6 FOLLOW WITH A SHARP PENCIL. This will darken the fine knife lines, making them easier to see during the next step.

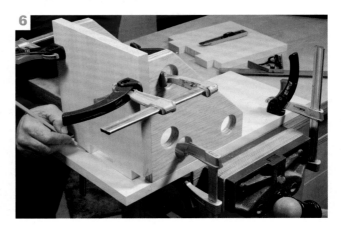

VERSATILE SHAKER BENCH COMBINES HAND AND POWER SKILLS

DRILL OUT THE MORTISES

We'll be using a ³/₄-in. Forstner bit to remove most of the waste in the mortises. You can use it with a cordless drill, but it will help you create more accurate mortises if you use it in a drill press. Also, if your legs (and therefore the tenons) are less than ³/₄ in. thick, you might have to use a smaller Forstner bit.

1 SET UP A FENCE. Place a piece of sacrificial material under the workpiece, to prevent chipping on the back side of the holes, and clamp down a fence to align the bit with your knife lines.

2 SIDE-TO-SIDE ALIGNMENT. You can do this by eye as you drill the outer holes, staying just a hair away from the ends of the mortise.

3 DRILL OVERLAPPING HOLES. Start at the ends and then drill in the middle. The Forstner bit is great at drilling partial holes without wandering.

4 QUICK AND EASY. Note how the fence keeps all of the holes in a perfect line. Drill out the mortises at both ends of the top.

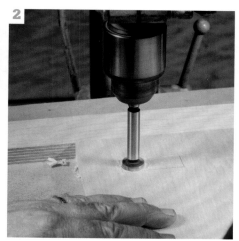

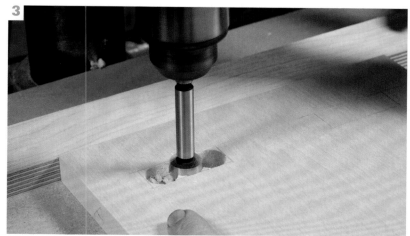

CHISEL THE MORTISES SQUARE

The accurate holes guide the chisel work. There's a logical sequence to squaring a mortise like this, and you'll develop a good feel for your chisel as you work through it. A $1/2$-in. chisel will do most of the work.

1 CLAMP DOWN THE TOP. Your holdfast works great here. Place a sacrificial board below the workpiece to avoid damaging your workbench.

2 START ALONG THE SIDES. The way to use a chisel is to make small paring cuts, working backward one thin slice at a time. If you take too big a cut all at once, the chisel will want to dive backward past your layout lines.

3 FINISH IN THE KNIFE LINE. Once you've pared away most of the waste, sit the tip of the chisel right in your knife line and push straight down.

4 A MALLET CAN HELP. If you can't get the job done with hand pressure alone, tap on the chisel with a wooden mallet or small hammer. As you do so, keep the chisel as perpendicular as you can.

5 ATTACK THE CORNERS IN A SERIES OF STEPS. Start as shown, with a straight chop along the long side of the mortise, a little inboard from the knife line. Do that in all four corners.

6 CLEAR OUT THE ENDS. Place your $1/2$-in. chisel right in the knife line, centered in the end of the mortise, and chop straight down.

7 FINISH OFF THE SIDES. To finish squaring the mortise, place the chisel along the long edge of the corner, right in the knife line, and chop straight down.

8 PERFECT ENOUGH. The part of the mortise that matters most is the top rim since that's what people will see. That's why we did all of our layout, drilling, and chisel work on that side. Note how the drilled holes act as a visual guide for the chisel work. If the mortise narrows at the bottom, use your $1/2$-in. or $3/4$-in. chisel to shave the sides without touching the top rim.

9 TEST THE FIT. Flip the top over and try to insert the tenons from the bottom. This will show you if the mortises need a bit more work.

SHAKER FOOTSTOOL/BENCH

TO SLOPE OR NOT TO SLOPE

If the top edges of your mortises are clean and your test-fit looks decent, you can leave the mortises as is and go with a thinner wedge. If your drilling holes are visible at the edges or your chisel work went awry, don't worry: You can widen the tops of the mortises as shown in the photos and use thicker wedges. The upside will be an even stronger joint, due to the locking effect of the sloped mortise sides.

1 HOW TO SLOPE THE SIDES. Start by scribing knife lines just outside the mortise walls, on the upper face of the top. Keep the offset less than $1/16$ in.

2 START THE CHISEL IN THE KNIFE LINE. If you keep the chisel relatively vertical, it will naturally want to slope inward as you tap it down. Place yourself to the side of the chisel to keep an eye on the angle and pare away a little more of the mortise wall if your first angled cut doesn't meet the bottom edge of the mortise.

3 EXTRA STEP FOR THE SLOPED-WALLS APPROACH. Use a $3/16$-in.-drill bit to drill a hole along the bottom of the blade slot. If it won't reach all the way to the far side of the tenon, go as far as you can or choose a slightly larger bit.

4 LAST LOOK. This is what the tenons and mortises will look like if you slope the walls. These joints are ready for wedging, but don't do that until you've cut and fit the side braces.

Wedge is ⅛ in. thick at fat end and ¾ in. long.

Saw kerf

Material is ¾ in. thick.

Wedge is ³⁄₁₆ in. wide at the top and 1³⁄₁₆ in. long.

Sides are a little less than ¹⁄₁₆ in. thicker at the top, tapering to zero at the bottom.

Saw kerf

³⁄₁₆-in.-dia. hole at bottom helps prevent splitting and makes it easier for tenon to spread outward.

MORTISE WITH STRAIGHT SIDES

MORTISE WITH SLOPED SIDES

SLOT THE TENONS

Whether you decide to slope the mortises or not, each tenon needs a slot cut down the middle to accept its wedge. Here's how to do it with any basic handsaw. And don't forget to prep the wedges now, too, as shown on p. 181.

1 SLOT THE TENONS. Draw a layout line along the center of the tenons and use your handsaw to saw along that line. Start by sawing into one corner as shown, keeping the saw on the line and centered in the side of the tenon (as best you can).

2 LEVEL OUT THE SAW AND FINISH THE JOB. Once you've sawed down one side of the tenon, start leveling out the saw to finish the slot. Stop when you're just above the bottom of the tenon, so you don't damage the wood below.

MAKE THE SIDE BRACES

We'll cut these on the miter saw and tablesaw so each one is accurate and identical, making them easy to fit into matching notches in the legs and top.

1 MITER THE ENDS. Cut the braces to width on the tablesaw and miter their ends on the miter saw, the same way we cut mitered frames in Chapter 6. Check the drawing of the version you're building (see pp. 176–177) for the tip-to-tip distance of these braces and cut a few extras in case you make a mistake cutting their notches.

2 LAY OUT ONE NOTCH. Each leg of these notches is slightly longer than the thickness of the legs and top of the project. Lay out each leg of one notch, and then flip the workpiece to lay out the other side of the same notch.

3 TILT THE SAW BLADE TO 45 DEGREES. A digital angle gauge works great here. Sit it on the saw table and set it to zero, and then stick it on the blade to set it to 45 degrees exactly. For an accurate reading, make sure the gauge is attached squarely on the blade.

4 MAKE THE FIRST CUT. Attach a sacrificial fence to your miter gauge to prevent chipping and use your layout lines to set up the stop block and dial in the blade height.

5 FLIP AND REPEAT. The setup guarantees that the cut at the opposite end will be the same, with no additional layout required.

6 SET UP THE NEXT CUT. Move the miter gauge to the opposite side of the blade for this cut. You'll also need to flip the workpiece to set up the cut, which is why we laid out both sides of the same notch. Use the pencil layout to position the workpiece and stop for this cut. Adjust the blade height if the small waste piece doesn't come free.

7 FLIP AND REPEAT. Once again, the setup guarantees uniform cuts at both ends of the workpiece. If you have the blade height, blade angle, and stop-block position just right, the second cut will create a clean, square notch with a sharp corner.

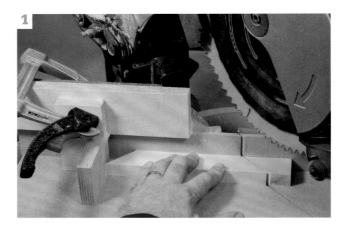

VERSATILE SHAKER BENCH COMBINES HAND AND POWER SKILLS

TRANSFER THE LAYOUT OF THE BRACES

Just as we did with the tenons, we'll use the braces to mark matching cutouts in the legs and top.

1 CLAMP THE PARTS INTO POSITION. To mark the brace locations accurately, you need to get the legs and top into their proper final positions. Clamp the leg to push the tenons all the way into place and then use a clamping block to make sure the parts are square to each other.

2 MARK ALONG THE EDGES. Adjust the brace until its notches are just even with the inside edges of the leg and the slight overhang on each end of the brace is straight and even. As before, start with very light pressure to establish a path and help you find the right angle for your knife. Then press a little harder on subsequent passes.

3 EXTEND THE LINES. After marking the notches for all four braces, disassemble the legs and top and wrap the layout lines around the corners. To do this, place your knife in the line you scribed earlier and tilt it around the corner. That will create a small nick on the face of the board, where you can place your knife to mark the adjacent surface.

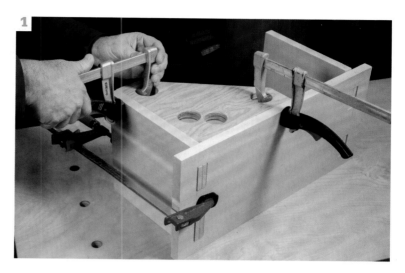

NOTCH THE SIDES

We'll start by cutting a square notch on the tablesaw, using the crosscut sled and dado blades the same way we did for the tenons. This will remove most of the waste and create a flat-bottomed notch, making it easy to saw and chisel out the last little corner of these notches.

1 SET UP THE TABLESAW. The same $\frac{1}{2}$-in. stack of dado blades works well here. Lower the blades until they are just under the thickness of your project material, by $\frac{1}{32}$ in. or so. Then install a new layer of $\frac{1}{4}$-in. MDF on the back fence, so the blades cut a fresh opening there. This is critical for preventing chipout on the back side of the workpieces.

2 CUT ONE NOTCH. Make sure the skinny side of the notch is facing the blade, line up the blades with one of your knife marks, and take it slow with the first full cut. Then nibble your way across to the other mark with successive passes.

3 CHECK THE DEPTH. Use the same piece of project material to check the depth of the notch. The material should be a little taller than the notch, by $\frac{1}{32}$ in. or so. Adjust the blade height if it isn't.

4 NOTCH THE REST OF THE PARTS. Dado the legs and top the same way. Make sure the skinny side of the notch is facing out as you line up and make these cuts, and don't go past your knife lines.

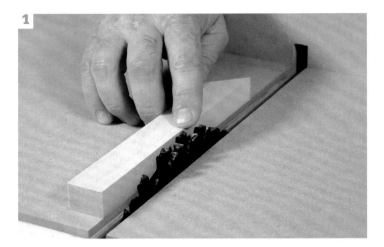

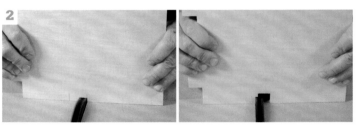

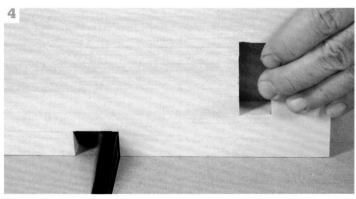

VERSATILE SHAKER BENCH COMBINES HAND AND POWER SKILLS

FINISH THE NOTCHES BY HAND

With the square side cleared out, we'll use a handsaw and a ³/₄-in. chisel to remove the angled corner and complete each notch. It's a great lesson in hand-tool use.

1 SAW INSIDE THE LINE. Use your handsaw to make a cut just inside your knife line, stopping just before the bottom of the notch.

2 CHIP OUT THE WASTE. Use your ³/₄-in. chisel to pop out the waste one sliver at a time, working down to the bottom of the saw cut. Be careful with the very first slice here, or you might push the chisel into the good wood on the other side of the saw cut.

3 CLEAN UP THE BOTTOM OF THE NOTCH. Start by tapping the chisel down along the back wall, and then pare from the front, using the clean, square notch to guide your chisel.

4 THE LAST CUT IS THE MOST IMPORTANT. Sit your chisel in the knife line on the edge of the board, make it as vertical as you can, and tap it straight down with a mallet or hammer. Just trust yourself here and do your best. The goal is to follow the knife lines down to the bottom of the notch. You can always take a few more slivers after the fact, if you don't cut all the way to your lines with the first chopping cut. Pare any bits of waste out of the corner and you're done.

5 TEST THE FIT. Re-assemble the stool and try the braces in their notches. Trim the notches with your chisel if necessary, but be careful not to overcut them.

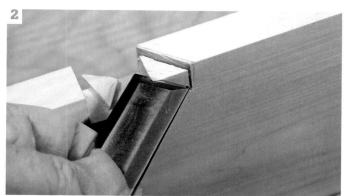

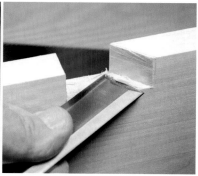

CUT OUT THE FEET

These projects will sit more solidly on four feet than two square legs. I went with simple foot curves in the footstool and bench, but there are other options for these cutouts (see the drawing below).

1 PLACE THE LEGS END TO END TO MARK THEIR CURVES. The center of the curve for these footstool legs lies beyond the end of each leg. If you clamp the two legs end to end, you'll have a level spot to place the point of your compass. Set the compass to the right radius, mark the inside edges of the feet, draw a centerline on the legs, and move the compass point along it to line up the curve with your feet marks.

2 SAW AND SAND THE CURVES. Use a jigsaw, bandsaw, or coping saw to cut close to your pencil lines, and then sand right up to them on the benchtop sander. To produce a smooth, even curve, make light, smooth passes as you near the line.

TWO FOOT VARIATIONS

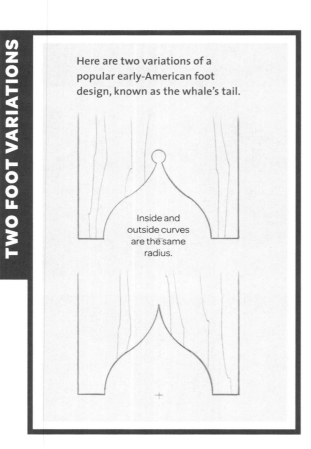

Here are two variations of a popular early-American foot design, known as the whale's tail.

Inside and outside curves are the same radius.

VERSATILE SHAKER BENCH COMBINES HAND AND POWER SKILLS

ASSEMBLE THE STOOL AND WEDGE THE TENONS

The stool goes together in three quick stages. Work through them quickly without stopping. Make sure you have your wedges, clamps, and supplies together before starting.

1 START BY GLUING THE TENONS INTO THEIR MORTISES. Use a small brush to wipe glue onto the mortise walls and the sides of the tenons, and clamp the legs firmly against the top as shown.

2 BRACES GO IN DRY. Install the braces to square up the legs and top, but don't apply glue to them yet.

3 HAMMER IN THE WEDGES. Wedges can be a little fragile, so use a small block to protect their tops as you tap them in with a hammer. Be sure to keep the wedge vertical as you get it started. If you go with skinny wedges and straight mortises, you won't have to tap the wedges down very far. If you went with fat wedges and sloped mortises, you'll likely need to drive the wedges all the way down, as I did here.

4 QUICK FIX. If you can't get your tenons to expand all the way out to meet the sloped sides of the mortises, make a skinny wedge out of the tenon material and tap it into place with glue after the fact. Saw it off after the glue dries, plane the tenon flush, and the fix will be almost impossible to detect.

5 GLUE IN THE BRACES. Now you can take the time to wipe glue onto the notches and braces and clamp the ends of the braces tightly into place.

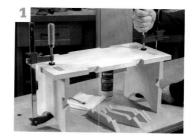

TRIM THE PROTRUDING PARTS

Your newly tuned and sharpened block plane is indispensable here, quickly shaving each brace, tenon, and wedge level with the surrounding surfaces.

1 START ON TOP OF THE STOOL. Set the plane for a light cut, and trim the ends of the braces in the direction shown, to be sure you are planing with the grain. Stop when the plane starts to dig into the surrounding wood.

2 TRIM THE TENONS THE SAME WAY. Saw off the protruding wedges if necessary, and then plane the tenons flush. A few tips: Skew the plane sideways to create a shearing cut; make your cuts slow and deliberate; and come at the tenon from different angles to plane away as much as you can.

3 SANDER DOES THE REST. Break out your random-orbit sander (or sanding block), attach a 120-grit disk, and sand the top evenly until everything is smooth and all of the glue stains and planing marks are gone. Follow with 150- or 180-grit paper, and then 220.

4 SIMPLE SUPPORT FOR PLANING THE ENDS. Clamp a narrow piece of plywood to your workbench as shown, to support the assembly in a comfortable planing position.

5 PLANE THE OTHER ENDS OF THE BRACES. Once again, set the plane for a light cut, skew it sideways to create a shearing cut, and plane with the grain, in this case pushing away from the top.

6 FINISH WITH YOUR SANDING BLOCK. Load it with 120-grit paper and sand until the whole surface is smooth, with no glue stains or planing marks. Continue up through 220 grit and you're done.

7 PLANE THE FACES OF THE BRACES. Clamp the project to your workbench as shown, determine the proper planing direction, and plane and sand these surfaces flush. Use your block plane and/or sanding block to break all of the sharp corners on this project, and then apply a finish of your choice. I went with five coats of Minwax Wipe-On Poly, to add good protection and a deep, beautiful sheen.

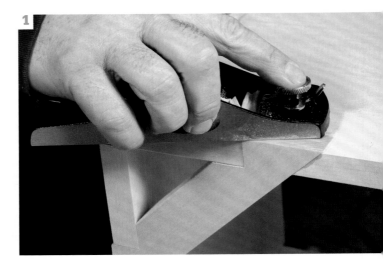

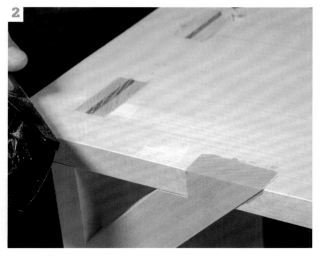

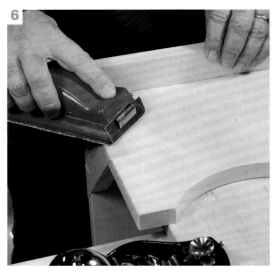

three foolproof finishes

Like everything else in woodworking, a beautiful finish requires concentration and care, but it's so worth it. You've worked hard to make a project just as good as you can, and the last thing you want to do is fast-track the finishing stage and end up not being happy with the final look. Do it right, though, and you'll bring the bare wood to its true potential and do justice to the time and money you've invested.

Finishing strikes fear in some people's hearts, since there's a lot on the line at that stage. But I'm here to tell you it doesn't have to be scary or mysterious. Follow the essential steps outlined below, and you'll be delighted at how lovely your projects will turn out.

GREAT OPTION FOR SMALL PROJECTS. I finished all of the projects in Chapter 6 in about two hours flat, using shellac and wax. Read on for two other great finishing options.

STEP ONE IS BUYING GOOD MATERIALS

One of the reasons people struggle with finishing is that they think it means "staining." Somewhere along the way the two terms became synonymous in popular usage. While some expert finishers do use stains and dyes to add color or highlight grain, staining and dying are best left to the pros.

For factories and hobbyists, stain is often used as an attempt to make cheap wood look expensive. But it's difficult to stain wood in a subtle way and too easy to create a blotchy mess. The good news is that you can avoid stain altogether, and your woodworking will be the better for it.

Once you've seen beautiful wood, sanded carefully, with a clear finish properly applied—adding subtle warmth and letting you peer deeply into the shimmering grain—you'll see the light. Almost any clear finish will do—oil, polyurethane, shellac—if the wood is beautiful to start with. So step one for any great finish is buying good materials. Check out my "Advice on finding the right lumber" on pp. 88–89 in Chapter 5, for more on this fundamental topic.

STEP TWO IS SURFACE PREP

Surface preparation is another key step that's often overlooked. Skimp on this stage and your haste will be highlighted by the finish. Take the time to do it right, and almost any finish will look amazing.

All machines leave marks on the surface of the wood, including the power planers that surface wood for sale. These shallow scallops might be too subtle to see on bare wood, but they will be obvious when you apply a lustrous finish. Job one is removing those machine marks—as well as other stains, dirt, dents, and whatever—from every visible surface of your project. Surface prep also includes lightly rounding or beveling edges, to make them friendlier to the eye and

hand. Do this uniformly and carefully, and your whole project will take on a more-refined look.

There are two main approaches to surface prep: planing and scraping with hand tools, followed by light sanding; and sanding on its own. Sanding is by far the easiest path, though once you get good at using handplanes, you'll find they speed up the process considerably, and save you some money on sandpaper. We've covered basic block-plane use in this book, but using a full-size handplane to prep all of your surfaces is a trickier endeavor, however wonderful to be sure, but best left to a later stage of your journey.

The bottom line: Sandpaper is all you need to prepare surfaces for a fine finish. Like many of the straightforward techniques in this book, sandpaper levels the playing field, letting beginners produce as beautiful a finish as the pros.

how sanding is supposed to work

There are a few keys to sanding success. Ignore them at your own peril. First, you need a basic understanding of how sanding works its magic. In short, you move through a series of successive grits, each one finer than the last, each new set of scratches replacing the slightly deeper ones from the last grit, until you reach a point—usually around 150 to 220 grit on bare wood—when the scratches are so fine they aren't visible to the naked eye, even under a shiny finish.

For each new grit of paper to erase the scratches from the last one, a number of other things need to happen. First, you need to keep the surface flat as you sand it. This prevents hollows you might miss with the next grit, leaving deep scratches that will be obvious later. Flat surfaces also reflect light in a beautiful way, making your whole project prettier in the end. This is why you should use a sanding block (vs. holding the paper in your fingers) when prepping bare wood for finishing. The block keeps the surface relatively level, so each successive grit reaches every part of the surface.

The other key is sanding each part of the surface the same amount, so you don't start developing those hollows again. To do that you need to work your way methodically across the surface with your sanding block. The same principle applies when you use a power sander: You need to move the pad methodically over the surface, maintaining the same pace as you make a series of slightly overlapping passes. I'll provide more tips on power sanding below. As for which grit to start with, that depends on how deep the machine marks, stains, dents, or other marks are that you're trying to remove. Generally, I start with 120-grit paper, but if the surface is rougher, I occasionally start at 80 grit. On plywood, however, which is often smoother than solid wood, you can usually start at 150 grit. The common grit sequence goes 80, 120, 150, 220, 320, 400. You'll need to sand bare wood up to 220 before applying most finishes, and then use the finer grits to smooth the surface between coats.

power-sanding tips

On larger surfaces you can speed up your surface prep with a 5-in. random orbit (RO) sander. There are larger models, but the 5-in. size offers a perfect blend of balance and coverage. I use my RO sander on any surface wide enough to balance it on without rocking and rounding the edges of the workpiece. For a 5-in. sander, that means anything wider than 3 in. or so, and longer than 5 or 6 in.

There's a big misunderstanding about the motion of the pad on a RO sander, which rotates slowly and vibrates at the same time. If you watch DIY shows on TV, you'll see people skittering the sander around the surface, thinking they are helping the process along. But there's no way you can move the sander around faster than it's vibrating, so all you're doing by moving it quickly and randomly is losing track of where you've sanded and how much.

MY FAVORITE SANDING BLOCK. The Preppin' Weapon is my favorite sanding block by far. It fits the hand perfectly, has a soft rubber bottom, and features handy little clamps that stretch a $1/4$-strip of sandpaper across it.

HOMEMADE BLOCK IS ALSO GOOD. This is nothing more than a block of $3/4$-in. MDF, with self-adhesive cork shelf liner on the bottom to even out the sanding pressure. Size your block to fit $1/4$ of a sandpaper sheet, ripped into squares.

The right way to use a random-orbit sander is in slow, slightly overlapping passes, letting it do its thing as you move it uniformly across the surface. This will keep the surface flat and make sure you remove all the scratches from the last disk you used. Try to keep the sander flat and level on the surface as you move it, don't press down hard, and don't overhang edges very much or you'll round them.

The other key to successful power sanding is attaching a shop vacuum to it. Power tools come with little onboard dust bags, but those collect next to nothing. So always replace the bag with a vac hose and active suction. There are little holes in the pad of the sander, which match up with holes in the disks, letting the vacuum remove dust as you create it. This not only keeps your nose, lungs, and workshop cleaner, but it also makes sandpaper last much longer and work better because it doesn't have to fight through a pile of dust to reach the wood.

Other than that, the basic sanding principles are the same for power and hand. See the photos on p. 206 for more surface-prep tips.

sand before assembly, and a little bit after

It's much easier to do the bulk of your surface preparation while parts are still separate. That way, you won't have to work into any tight corners. You'll have some light sanding to do after assembly too—to remove nicks, dents, and glue smudges—but it will be light lifting at that point.

THE FUNDAMENTALS OF A GOOD FINISH

I'll be covering three finishes in this chapter—oil, polyurethane, and shellac—but the basic steps are similar for any successful wood finish. First, you need to sand the bare wood to 150 grit at a minimum, and

HANDY SANDPAPER CUTTER. This simple jig is nothing more than a plywood base and fence, and an old hacksaw blade, screwed on with washers under it to lift it slightly. Position the fence and blade to rip strips that fit your sanding block.

preferably 220 grit, and vacuum away the dust, leaving a clean surface.

No matter how you apply the coats—with a brush or rag—the first one is a sealer coat. This first layer of finish saturates the surface of the bare wood and tends to lift little whiskers that were burnished smooth by sanding. Some people call this step "raising the grain." Those whiskers need to be sanded away with the next finest grit, usually 320, to pave the way for the coats that come next. You can just fold up the paper and hold it in your fingers for this step, as all it takes is a light sanding to smooth the sealed surface and there's no danger of creating hollows in the surface. Sand as lightly and evenly as possible, stopping when the surface feels smooth to your fingers. What you don't want to do is sand all the finish away.

After vacuuming away the sanding dust—always a must to keep dust out of the next coat of finish—you'll build up coats until you get the level of depth and shine you want. Other than drips and runs, the only issues with these coats will be airborne dust settling into the wet surface as it dries. If your chosen finish takes a while to dry, more dust will have a chance to settle in, and you'll feel it on the surface afterward. That's why we're using very thin mixtures

SURFACE PREP IS THE MOST IMPORTANT STEP

All boards have machine marks on them, left by milling machines. You may not see them on the bare wood, but they'll show up under a shiny finish. The finishing process starts with sanding away those marks and leaving a clean, flat, smooth surface in their place.

POWER-SANDING BASICS. On larger surfaces, you can speed up surface preparation with a random-orbit sander. Move the sander slow and straight, in slightly overlapping passes, so you sand the overall surface uniformly with each successive grit. Keep the sander balanced, don't press down hard, and attach a shop vac to remove dust as you go.

HAND SANDING 101. Sanding is easier before assembly, when parts are still separate. Start at the lowest grit you need to produce a clean surface, usually 120 grit, and sand in slightly overlapping passes before moving on to 150-grit and 220-grit paper. The idea is to sand evenly, so each new grit replaces the scratches left but the last one.

A NIMBLE TOOL. Keep the sanding block balanced on narrow surfaces, to avoid rounding them over.

ALWAYS REMOVE SANDING DUST. Any time you sand, either before finishing or between coats, vacuum away the dust.

of finish in this chapter, so they dry fast, leaving dust very little time to settle in and hardly any sanding to do between coats.

After you've built up the sheen and depth you want, anywhere from matte to glossy, you'll need to do one last light sanding, usually with 400 grit, before applying a final coat of finish. After that you just might be done, but I'll also show you how to apply furniture wax with very fine steel wool, to knock down the shine to a soft glow and make the surface feel buttery smooth (see pp. 217–218).

By the way, I always wear disposable gloves when finishing. It's just too much of a pain to clean sticky finish off my hands. Avoid latex gloves, which will let some finishes seep through to your skin. Instead go with vinyl gloves, or even better, nitrile, which are pricier but totally impervious to all finishes and solvents.

ALL YOU NEED. Here are two examples of oil finishes, plus foam brushes to apply them and paper towels to wipe them off.

SHORT GUIDE TO THE BIG THREE

I'm sticking here to finishes you can apply by hand, as opposed to those that are sprayed with a gun, usually by pros. Spraying is super-fast, and can be super-effective as well, but it requires pricey equipment, a specialized enclosure, and a good deal of experience. Hand-applied finishes require none of that and are as beautiful as anything out there.

1 oil finishes are quick and easy

There are three main types of clear, hand-applied finishes that most woodworkers use, and all three are widely available at home centers and hardware stores.

The first is an oil-varnish blend. I think of these as oil finishes, because the amount of resin (varnish) in them is so small that it takes a lot of coats to build up any kind of protective film. But that's just fine. These finishes are for pieces that don't need a deep, flawless sheen and tons of protection. You just apply a couple

FLOOD ON THEN WIPE OFF. Use a foam brush or a cotton rag to apply a liberal coat of oil. Keep applying the first coat until the wood isn't drinking up any more finish. Leave it for a few minutes before wiping off the excess with a clean rag. Sand lightly with 320-grit paper before applying a second coat, and you're done.

of quick coats, which soak in and beautify the wood, adding some protection against water, stains, skin oil, and such—just not quite as much as the other two finishes in this chapter.

These oil finishes include Watco, most teak or tung oil finishes, Minwax Antique Oil, and a few others. I tend to use these as quick-and-easy finishes for shop projects and other things that need a little protection but don't need to look perfect.

What's really great about these finishes is how easy they are to apply. You just flood on the finish with a rag or brush (either foam or bristle), let the oil soak in for 5 or 10 minutes, and then wipe off the excess with paper towels or a cotton rag. Sometimes I add a second coat and sometimes not, depending on the result.

An oil finish was perfect for the workbench and workbench cabinet featured earlier in the book. Workbenches take a lot of abuse, and a really cool thing about oil finishes is how easy they are to refresh. Whereas a severely damaged film finish, like polyurethane or shellac, would need to be sanded off and reapplied, oil finishes can be renewed simply by applying another coat, anytime in the future.

For the same reason, oil finishes are great for food-related items like cutting boards. Those will get scarred by use, but you can always brighten them up with a light sanding and a fresh coat of oil. There's a lot of fuss made over "food-safe" finishes, but all finishes are nontoxic once they fully dry, and all of the oil finishes mentioned above will do just that. One to avoid is mineral oil, which never full dries and just gets gummy over time.

2 oil-based varnishes are the most popular type of finish

The majority of clear wood finishes are some type of oil-based varnish, thinned for wiping on with a rag, or left thicker for brushing. That said, all of these can either be brushed or wiped on. These finishes build up a thin film after just a few coats. Brush or wipe on a few more, and you get a deeper sheen and even more protection. That makes them very versatile. For example, you can apply a few coats to the base of a table, for a subtle sheen, and then build up more on the tabletop, to defend against water, food, and harder use.

The most popular varnish is oil-based polyurethane, and it's popular for a reason. Made with polymers that crosslink and become extremely tough as they cure, polyurethane is the finish of choice for wood flooring, where durability is paramount. Better yet, polyurethane is sold in a variety of blends, designed for either wiping or brushing. I covered the thicker, standard version in Book 1, which I brushed onto a number of projects, but I'm going to focus on my new favorite here: Minwax Wipe-On Poly.

You'll also notice a few water-based poly-urethanes out there. The Minwax version is called

MY FAVORITE WIPING VARNISH. Minwax Wipe-On Poly is thinned perfectly, goes on easily, and won't turn lighter woods yellow. It also dries quickly so very little dust has a chance to settle on the wet surface. I like the satin variety, which dries to a soft glow. It has flattening agents that gunk up at the bottom, so always stir the can well before using the finish.

Polycrylic. While these create less fumes and dry faster than oil-based versions, I can't quite recommend them. They are far less durable in my experience, especially on a dining table, for example. And once they become damaged and gummy, the only solution is sanding them off entirely and refinishing the surface.

3 shellac is a different animal

Harvested in India and Thailand from excretions that the lac bug leaves on trees, shellac has been a favorite wood finish for centuries. Shellac is unique in many ways, most of them great. For one, it is dissolved in alcohol, which helps it dry very quickly, letting a woodworker apply many coats in a single day. It also dries very hard, making it easy to sand, which is why so many woodworkers use it as their first sealer coat. And shellac is odorless after it dries, making it great for the inside of boxes, for example, where an oil-based finish will continue to off-gas and stay smelly for many years.

Shellac is available in various forms, based on when and how it is processed. Purchased in solid form, as flakes or small buttons that vary naturally in color, it can be ground up and dissolved in alcohol to impart a variety of subtle tones to wood. I've done a fair amount of that over the years, to warm up the color of walnut, for example. But using shellac to add a subtle hue isn't really necessary for most projects.

Lucky for all of us, Zinsser sells a couple of types of premixed shellac, which are widely available. The one we'll use here, and by far the most useful blend out there, is Zinsser SealCoat. Sold as a sanding sealer—in other words, to be used as that first sealer coat I mentioned—the product definitely delivers. But I tend to use SealCoat as an entire finish unto itself, taking advantage of its fast drying time and odorless nature. Those qualities were perfect for the small boxes and frames in Chapter 6. SealCoat is a dewaxed shellac, meaning you can put any other finish on top of it and get good adhesion. Many other forms of shellac contain wax, which would resist an oil-based finish, for example.

GO WITH SEALCOAT. Zinsser's SealCoat shellac is premixed and relatively clear, so it will warm up the look of wood without turning lighter species yellow. Use the finish within six months to make sure it is fresh. Beside the can of SealCoat are the other simple supplies you'll need to wipe on a lovely shellac finish and add wax as a final touch, including super-fine steel wool (0000 grade).

THIN IT FOR WIPING. You can brush SealCoat as is, but for wiping it on it's better to thin it 50 percent, by mixing it 1-to-1 with denatured alcohol.

left: **NO CLEAN-UP NECESSARY.** Because shellac is always dissolvable, even when dry, you don't have to clean your brush. Let it dry hard, and then soften it in alcohol before you use it.

bottom left: **SAVE YOUR SHELLAC RAG.** Store the wet rag in a small container and you can use it for multiple coats in a row. Unlike an oily rag, it won't heat up when you leave it bunched up in a container.

WIPE-ON POLY DOES IT ALL

Over the past few years, I've been brushing Minwax Quick-Drying Polyurethane onto most of my projects. It dries quickly and builds up a durable film after just a few coats, making it a great fit for my busy schedule. As an oil-based finish, it also penetrates deep into the wood, bringing out the beauty of the grain. Then I finally tried the wiping version of the same polyurethane, and I think I'm done with brushing.

Here are the many advantages of Minwax Wipe-On Poly. First and foremost, it wipes on with a clean cotton rag or the thick paper towels sold at home centers. That makes it easy to apply a thin, even coat with no drips or runs. I've gotten pretty good at brushing, but it takes some practice and experience to do it well. Wiping doesn't. Second, for some reason related to the wiping formulation, Minwax Wiping Varnish adds less yellow color to lighter woods than the standard version, meaning I can use it for almost everything I build, dark or light.

And last, it goes on very thin and dries in just an hour or two in a warm shop, significantly faster than the standard Minwax polyurethane. That not only lets me apply multiple coats in a day but also leaves a lot less time for dust to settle in the finish, meaning once the first sealer coat is down and sanded, I can build up four or five coats in a single day, without sanding between them. Compare that to brushing on the

The main downside of shellac is its susceptibility to damage from alcohol. That makes it iffy for tabletops. It gets some bad press about water damage as well, but that's overblown. If the shellac is relatively fresh, it will cure hard and be just fine if water spills on it. But I wouldn't leave the spill very long before wiping it up, and I wouldn't use shellac as a finish for a plant stand, for example.

Shellac's unique ability to be dissolved by alcohol, even decades after it was applied, is also a plus. You can dedicate a brush to shellac and simply let it dry between uses. Sit it in some fresh alcohol for an hour before each use, and it will soften up and be ready to roll, with no cleaning necessary.

standard version, which tends to collect dust as it dries and needs to be left overnight before it's hard enough to sand between coats.

Like all wiping varnishes, wipe-on polyurethane can be applied more thinly to the base of a table, for example, and then coats can be added to the top for more protection and a deeper sheen, without making the two parts of the project look obviously different. See the slab-topped coffee table in Chapter 5 for a great example of this versatility. Last, Minwax Wipe-On Poly is affordable and widely available at hardware stores, home centers, and paint stores. Bottom line: I can't think of a more straightforward path to a gorgeous finish.

guaranteed success with wiping poly

This finish goes on in the same basic stages outlined up higher in this chapter. For the full process, check out the photos on pp. 212–213. Here are a few highlights.

For a start, I recommend the satin version of this finish for beginners. More advanced woodworkers sometimes choose the glossy version, and then rub it out with wax and steel wool at the end to replace the sticky shine with a softer glow. But I think the satin version ends up looking very similar without the extra steps. The only downside to satin poly is the flattening agent that settles into a gunky layer at the bottom of the can. Be sure to stir that up with a stick each time you open the can. You'll know it's fully mixed when the stick comes up clean.

Start by sanding the whole piece up to 220 grit, using the tools and techniques mentioned earlier and shown in the photos on p. 206. I like to apply this finish with thick, disposable paper towels, which I hang over the edge of my garbage can to dry before tossing out. NEVER leave oil-soaked rags of any kind wadded up. The oil will heat up as it dries and can cause the wadded-up rags to spontaneously combust. I know a few people who burned down their workshops after

making this innocent mistake. Keep the varnish-soaked rags relatively flat and open until they dry stiff. Then you can discard them with no worries.

I usually just fold up my paper towel and pour some finish into it before wiping it on. But if the surface you're finishing is horizontal, you can pour the finish onto it directly in a small puddle and use the towel to spread it around.

After the first coat dries, sand the surfaces lightly with 220- or 320-grit paper to knock down the whiskers that lifted up from the wood when the wet finish hit them. Now you're ready to build up a bunch of coats in a row. These will dry so quickly that not much dust will settle into the wood, so you don't have to sand between these coats. But leave each one to dry fully for a couple hours before applying the next one. Keep applying coats until the dry surface has an even sheen. If you want an even deeper luster or more protection, feel free to apply more. When you like the look of the surface, you're ready to sand it and apply a final thin coat.

Leave the project overnight for all the base layers to fully cure. Then all it takes is a light sanding with a folded-up piece of 400-grit paper to get ready for the final coat. The idea is to smooth the surface to a smooth, soft feel before applying a very thin coat, which will dry so fast that dust will have very little chance to settle into it. Make sure you stir the can well before the final coat and wipe off all the excess finish this time. After this coat dries, if you can feel a few dust nibs on the surface, you can rub it down with a brown grocery bag to get rid of them.

WIPE-ON POLYURETHANE, STEP BY STEP

This is hands-down my favorite finish for the vast majority of projects. It wipes on easily in thin coats, makes any wood beautiful, and quickly builds up a protective layer and a deep sheen.

1 FLOOD IT ON. The bare wood will drink up a lot of finish so apply it liberally. You can wipe it on it with a cotton rag or paper towels but I like to apply with a disposable foam brush. Give the first coat 5 or 10 minutes to soak in and dry a little before wiping off the excess.

2 WIPE IT OFF. Use thick paper "shop towels" to wipe off most of the excess, leaving a thin, smooth, wet coat. DO NOT leave wet oily rags or paper towels wadded up, or they can spontaneously combust. Instead, hang them over the edge of your waste basket to dry before discarding them.

3 DEAL WITH PROBLEMS NOW. The first coat of finish will show any glue squeeze-out you may have missed earlier. Remove it with a sharp chisel. It will also show hazy areas where glue soaked into the wood. Sand the wet finish with 220-grit paper until the haze goes away, then wipe off the excess finish.

4 SAND THE FIRST COAT. After leaving the first coat to dry for an hour or two, you'll notice it has raised the wood fibers, making the surface a little rough again. Fold up some 220-grit paper and sand lightly by hand, just until the surface feels relatively smooth again.

5 ALWAYS VACUUM THE DUST! I use a brush attachment, which makes the job quicker. Notice that I'm finishing the top and base of this table separately. That's easier than finishing them as one unit.

6 GET WORSE TO GET BETTER. Sanding the first coat makes your project look worse, but the next coat of finish goes on like a dream.

7 BUILD UP COATS UNTIL YOU LIKE THE LOOK. Let each one dry for an hour or two before applying the next one. When the sheen is even and you're happy with the look, do one last light sanding with 400-grit paper and then apply one last thin coat.

8 PAPER-BAG TRICK. To remove any dust nibs in the last coat of finish, leave it overnight to fully dry and then rub the surface with a brown grocery bag to give it a softer feel.

AMAZING RESULTS. The satin polyurethane leaves a soft glow on any wood. This is the floating-top side table in Chapter 5, made from hemlock.

BUILD IT UP AS THICK AS YOU LIKE. I applied extra coats to the top of the walnut coffee table in Chapter 5 and left it thinner on the base. The two parts of the table still look very cohesive.

FINISH AN ENTIRE PIECE IN A SINGLE DAY WITH SHELLAC

If you don't want to take a few days to apply a finish, go with shellac. While it's not quite as tough and durable as polyurethane, it dries even clearer, with a crystalline quality that is distinctive to a trained eye. That's partly because each new coat melts into the last.

That melty quality means you want to thin out your shellac and apply it relatively quickly, before it has a chance to make the surface sticky. With oil-based finishes, you can continue to wipe and refine the surface for a while as you apply it, but with shellac it's lay it down and leave it. And that's just fine, because it does a good job of self-leveling as it fuses with the layers below.

guaranteed success, step by step

Like polyurethane, you can apply shellac with a rag and brush, but the rag is easier. To wipe it on successfully, you'll need to thin it significantly. One of the great things about SealCoat shellac is how thin it is to start, but you should still thin it by 50% (one part SealCoat to one part denatured alcohol) before applying it with a rag.

Do the mixing in a separate container, and then dip your rag into that. That leaves the original finish pure in the can. You generally don't want to dip your rag or brush into a can of clean finish, because every time you do, you're leaving a little bit of dust, fluff, or other debris in the can, which will build up over time.

Speaking of a brush, I still use one from time to time when wiping on shellac, to get into very tight areas where the rag won't reach, like the thin slots in the frame projects in Chapter 6. As for the rag, I use a cotton one for shellac—not paper towels this time. Shellac can get a little sticky as you apply it and even

pull paper into the finish, but a cotton rag is more durable. You can leave your rag in a small container with a screw-on lid and use it indefinitely. The alcohol won't heat up like oil will, so your wet rag is safe in its jar.

The goal here is to apply thin, even coats of shellac, so they dry quickly before dust has a chance to settle. You don't want your rag to be too wet with finish. Just dip it slightly it slightly into your container of diluted finish before wiping. Soon the rag will be fully saturated with finish, and you'll be able to make a number of swipes before needing to dip it.

It helps a lot to set up a light that reflects on the surface or place your work where overhead lights will reflect off it. That will let you see how even your coverage is with each swipe, so you don't have to go back over the surface too much. The thin coats start drying quickly, and you'll start dragging the shellac and leaving ridges once they do.

The first coat will raise the grain, so it needs to be followed with light sanding. Then you can wipe on three or more coats of shellac until you like the sheen you're getting. Sand lightly again and apply a final thin coat. It's really that simple. As opposed to the satin polyurethane, however, the shellac will look a bit glossy for some tastes, so you could consider dulling the sheen to a soft glow with steel wool and wax, which is coming up next.

PERFECT SHELLAC FINISH, STEP BY STEP

The main steps are the same as those for the wiping varnish above, but shellac dries quickly, so you need to apply it in even strokes and leave it. A cotton rag works better than paper towels for applying it.

1 LAY IT DOWN AND LEAVE IT. Dip the rag lightly in the shellac, make even strokes to cover one area, and then move on to a new area. Try not to go back over places you've already wiped, as they will quickly get sticky. I started on the back of this frame, and then flipped it to do the front side.

2 WORK INSIDE-OUT ON BOXES. I applied shellac to the interior of this box before moving on to the sides and bottom.

3 IT BRUSHES GREAT TOO. Use a brush with synthetic bristles to reach into areas where your rag won't go. I only had to brush shellac into these cracks once, to even out the color. I wiped on the rest of the coats with my shellac rag.

4 SAND THE FIRST COAT. As with the wiping varnish above, sand the first coat lightly with 320-grit paper, feeling for rough spots and stopping when it feels smooth all over.

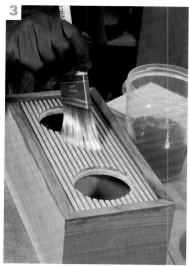

5 **ALWAYS VACUUM!** This is the best way to remove dust after sanding and keep it out of the next few coats of finish.

6 **BUILD UP THE COATS WITHOUT SANDING.** Shellac dries super-fast, so give the project 15 or 20 minutes to dry, apply another coat, wait again, and repeat as needed.

7 **STOP WHEN YOU LIKE THE SHEEN.** When the dried surface has a nice, even sheen, without major areas that look dull or uneven, you're ready for the final step.

8 **SAND ONE LAST TIME.** A light sanding with 400-grit paper will smooth out the earlier coats, including any little drips or puddles.

9 **ONE LAST COAT.** Lay this one on as thinly and evenly as you can. Don't dip too much of your rag in the finish each time you need to wet it, or you might leave puddles behind. If you do end up with obvious imperfections, let the finish dry, re-sand it, and lay down another thin coat.

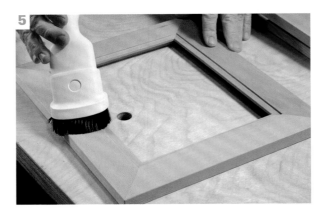

FINISH YOUR FINISH WITH STEEL WOOL AND WAX

One mistake beginners make is not "finishing the finish." In other words, they leave it shiny and sticky looking. Once you see the soft glow of a proper finish, however, you'll want that every time. "Rubbing out" a finish with steel wool and furniture wax is quick, easy, and effective, which is why it made the cut for this book.

Applying wax with steel wool does a few important things at once. It burnishes the glossy surface, gets rid of any little dust nibs in the final coat, and adds a softer feel. The wax lubricates the steel wool for nice, even buffing. The wax will wear away at some point, but the soft glow won't, because the very fine scratches from the steel wool are permanently etched in the surface. Any paste wax designed for wood will do the trick, and the #0000 "super-fine" steel wool is available everywhere. I leave most finishes overnight to fully cure before rubbing out, but with shellac, you have to wait only a couple of hours.

One mistake a lot of people make is applying too much wax, which then dries hard and becomes very hard to buff off evenly. The easiest way to lay down a thin coat is by simply wetting the steel wool a little bit with solvent before dipping it into your can of wax. The solvent in almost all waxes, including the Minwax Paste Finishing Wax I'm using here, is some form of mineral spirits or turpentine, so any standard paint thinner will do. The only exception I know is called Briwax, which has toluene as its solvent.

After wetting the steel wool slightly, you can dip it into the wax, making it moist and thin when you apply it. Buff the surface evenly with the steel wool, and you'll be applying a thin coat of wax in the process. Then just rub the surface dry with a clean cotton cloth. Keep rubbing until the surface is dry and glowing. If the surface looks dull or uneven afterward, you probably didn't apply enough wax. Dip the steel wool back into the jar and apply a little more. The continued buffing with steel wool shouldn't be a problem. In the end, just buff the surface dry again with the cotton cloth.

a few helpful pointers

You don't need to apply wax everywhere, just the areas that are most visible. And don't work it into any details you can't access with your buffing cloth. Also, don't put wax inside boxes and drawers. Just like an oil-based finish, the solvent will continue to off-gas for years and be very obvious each time you access the interior. On the other hand, wax is super helpful on sliding surfaces like the sides and bottoms of drawers. In fact, it's often the only finish woodworkers use in those areas.

If your project has inside corners, for example where a door panel meets a door frame, make sure you work the steel wool all the way into those areas. If you don't, you might leave some glossy finish untouched, which will stand out when you're done. No worries if that happens; just repeat the process to get into the corners you missed.

It takes a little bit of experience to get a feel for these finishes, but not much. Like everything else in this book, don't be afraid to dive in and make a few mistakes. If you're nervous, try finishing a scrap board first before taking a whack at a real project.

STEEL WOOL AND WAX, STEP BY STEP

This isn't as necessary on the satin polyurethane we used earlier, but shellac dries a little glossier and will benefit from a coat of wax, applied with steel wool to dull the shine at the same time. Any paste wax designed for wood will work.

1 THE SOLVENT TRICK. To avoid applying a thick coat of wax that will be difficult to buff off after it dries, wet the steel wool with a little bit of paint thinner or mineral spirits first.

2 THE SOLVENT THINS THE WAX. When you dip the steel wool in your can of wax, the solvent thins whatever you pick up.

3 RUB IT ON WET. The wax will go on wet at first, but most of that moisture is solvent, with a little wax mixed in. Rub the surface evenly with the steel wool to dull the shine of the finish below.

4 BUFF THE SURFACE AND YOU'RE DONE. Rub the surface dry with a clean cotton cloth and it will glow beautifully.

CLOSING THOUGHTS

There is so much woodworking info out there, and so many beautiful projects on social media, that it's easy to get intimidated into thinking everything you make needs to be perfect or built in some perfect way. Instead of watching yet another YouTube video, buy some materials and build something. As painful as mistakes are in the moment, trust me when I say that they are the path to glory. The head-smacking moments are the ones that stay with you, imprinting their important lessons into your memory.

Looking back at my first projects, I have to laugh at some of the dumb moves I made. But I'm proud of the fact that I used the limited tools and experience I had and did the best I could, taking my tough lessons in stride. Working with what you have will tell you a lot about which tools you actually want and need. So start where you are, and go from there. Your taste and eye will evolve also, and soon you'll be surprised at what you're able to make.

I've given away my earliest attempts to friends and family, and they think they're just fine. That cleared out space in my house for the next wave of projects I built. Moving helps too, as each new apartment or house is another chance for remodeling and filling your new space with handmade work. Kids are another great reason to build projects. I made toys and fun furniture for my kids as they grew up, and now I make them finer furniture they can keep forever.

Taking classes at your local woodworking club or community college is a good way to dive in and learn. You'll have an expert by your side when you hit a snag, and the support of your classmates too.

Last, don't let anyone tell you what you should or shouldn't make, what type of workbench you should have, or which tools you should be using. Like power tools? Go for it. Love the calm, quiet world of hand tools? Dive in. Happier building a deck than a dining table? It's all good. Build whatever you want, and you'll be glad you did.

—A.C.

METRIC EQUIVALENTS

INCHES	CENTIMETERS	MILLIMETERS	INCHES	CENTIMETERS	MILLIMETERS
1/8	0.3	3	13	33.0	330
1/4	0.6	6	14	35.6	356
3/8	1.0	10	15	38.1	381
1/2	1.3	13	16	40.6	406
5/8	1.6	16	17	43.2	432
3/4	1.9	19	18	45.7	457
7/8	2.2	22	19	48.3	483
1	2.5	25	20	50.8	508
1 1/4	3.2	32	21	53.3	533
1 1/2	3.8	38	22	55.9	559
1 3/4	4.4	44	23	58.4	584
2	5.1	51	24	61	610
2 1/2	6.4	64	25	63.5	635
3	7.6	76	26	66.0	660
3 1/2	8.9	89	27	68.6	686
4	10.2	102	28	71.7	717
4 1/2	11.4	114	29	73.7	737
5	12.7	127	30	76.2	762
6	15.2	152	31	78.7	787
7	17.8	178	32	81.3	813
8	20.3	203	33	83.8	838
9	22.9	229	34	86.4	864
10	25.4	254	35	88.9	889
11	27.9	279	36	91.4	914
12	30.5	305			